# Black Planner

## Daily History for Daily Planning

### Customizable for Any Year

Name

Phone

Email

Address

**Logo:** The mythical bird in the logo symbolizes Sankofa (SAHN-koh-fah), the Twi word of the Akan people of Ghana. The term, from an Akan proverb, translates loosely as *"Go back and get it."* Sankofa is a quest for knowledge via critical examination of the past, which may have been forgotten. The meaning is clear: *learn from the past to inform the future.* In the logo, the bird's feet are planted forward while its head turns back to reach for an egg, which symbolizes the seed of knowledge.

# The Planner. Reinvented.

Conventional planners are task-oriented. They tie you to the clock and lack any semblance of vision. To learn anything new, you have to turn elsewhere.

You are holding a new type of planner. With it, you can still do all the conventional things: schedule appointments, list to-dos, jot notes, set goals, etc. But we've given it a wealth of new capabilities. First, we put daily doses of Black history at your fingertips. They're easy to consume, and every calendar day presents something fresh and intriguing. On top of this, we've added scannable codes. They're the key to unlocking the fascinating sights, sounds, and stories of the past and present. Scan any QR code with your mobile device, and Black history will spring to life.

You can use this planner to read Black classics, hear music, view art masterpieces, listen to speeches and poetry, tour historic buildings, see the nation's premiere Black museum, view movie trailers, watch the world's top athletes compete, see "fights of the century," make restaurant reservations, and worship in live services in the nation's oldest Black church.

While ordinary planners are paper-centric, this one harnesses the power of the internet so Black history will leap off the page and into your life. We hope it will make your day and year enjoyable and meaningful.

## How to Use This Planner

This planner is customizable. You can use it in any year, including leap years. Refer to the calendar on the next page, and fill in the dates in the blank spaces of the following calendars. Be sure to align each date with the correct corresponding weekday. Date the weekly and monthly planner sections as the year progresses. That's it. Enjoy the daily doses of Black history, scan the QR codes at your leisure, and reflect on the past as you shape the future.

**Front cover:** Model Pat Evans photographed by Anthony Barboza
**Back cover:** Frederick Douglass engraved by J.C. Buttre from a daguerreotype, 1855

# 2025

## JANUARY
| SU | MO | TU | WE | TH | FR | SA |
|----|----|----|----|----|----|----|
|    |    |    | 1  | 2  | 3  | 4  |
| 5  | 6  | 7  | 8  | 9  | 10 | 11 |
| 12 | 13 | 14 | 15 | 16 | 17 | 18 |
| 19 | 20 | 21 | 22 | 23 | 24 | 25 |
| 26 | 27 | 28 | 29 | 30 | 31 |    |

## FEBRUARY
| SU | MO | TU | WE | TH | FR | SA |
|----|----|----|----|----|----|----|
|    |    |    |    |    |    | 1  |
| 2  | 3  | 4  | 5  | 6  | 7  | 8  |
| 9  | 10 | 11 | 12 | 13 | 14 | 15 |
| 16 | 17 | 18 | 19 | 20 | 21 | 22 |
| 23 | 24 | 25 | 26 | 27 | 28 |    |

## MARCH
| SU | MO | TU | WE | TH | FR | SA |
|----|----|----|----|----|----|----|
|    |    |    |    |    |    | 1  |
| 2  | 3  | 4  | 5  | 6  | 7  | 8  |
| 9  | 10 | 11 | 12 | 13 | 14 | 15 |
| 16 | 17 | 18 | 19 | 20 | 21 | 22 |
| 23 | 24 | 25 | 26 | 27 | 28 | 29 |
| 30 | 31 |    |    |    |    |    |

## APRIL
| SU | MO | TU | WE | TH | FR | SA |
|----|----|----|----|----|----|----|
|    |    | 1  | 2  | 3  | 4  | 5  |
| 6  | 7  | 8  | 9  | 10 | 11 | 12 |
| 13 | 14 | 15 | 16 | 17 | 18 | 19 |
| 20 | 21 | 22 | 23 | 24 | 25 | 26 |
| 27 | 28 | 29 | 30 |    |    |    |

## MAY
| SU | MO | TU | WE | TH | FR | SA |
|----|----|----|----|----|----|----|
|    |    |    |    | 1  | 2  | 3  |
| 4  | 5  | 6  | 7  | 8  | 9  | 10 |
| 11 | 12 | 13 | 14 | 15 | 16 | 17 |
| 18 | 19 | 20 | 21 | 22 | 23 | 24 |
| 25 | 26 | 27 | 28 | 29 | 30 | 31 |

## JUNE
| SU | MO | TU | WE | TH | FR | SA |
|----|----|----|----|----|----|----|
| 1  | 2  | 3  | 4  | 5  | 6  | 7  |
| 8  | 9  | 10 | 11 | 12 | 13 | 14 |
| 15 | 16 | 17 | 18 | 19 | 20 | 21 |
| 22 | 23 | 24 | 25 | 26 | 27 | 28 |
| 29 | 30 |    |    |    |    |    |

## JULY
| SU | MO | TU | WE | TH | FR | SA |
|----|----|----|----|----|----|----|
|    |    | 1  | 2  | 3  | 4  | 5  |
| 6  | 7  | 8  | 9  | 10 | 11 | 12 |
| 13 | 14 | 15 | 16 | 17 | 18 | 19 |
| 20 | 21 | 22 | 23 | 24 | 25 | 26 |
| 27 | 28 | 29 | 30 | 31 |    |    |

## AUGUST
| SU | MO | TU | WE | TH | FR | SA |
|----|----|----|----|----|----|----|
|    |    |    |    |    | 1  | 2  |
| 3  | 4  | 5  | 6  | 7  | 8  | 9  |
| 10 | 11 | 12 | 13 | 14 | 15 | 16 |
| 17 | 18 | 19 | 20 | 21 | 22 | 23 |
| 24 | 25 | 26 | 27 | 28 | 29 | 30 |
| 31 |    |    |    |    |    |    |

## SEPTEMBER
| SU | MO | TU | WE | TH | FR | SA |
|----|----|----|----|----|----|----|
|    | 1  | 2  | 3  | 4  | 5  | 6  |
| 7  | 8  | 9  | 10 | 11 | 12 | 13 |
| 14 | 15 | 16 | 17 | 18 | 19 | 20 |
| 21 | 22 | 23 | 24 | 25 | 26 | 27 |
| 28 | 29 | 30 |    |    |    |    |

## OCTOBER
| SU | MO | TU | WE | TH | FR | SA |
|----|----|----|----|----|----|----|
|    |    |    | 1  | 2  | 3  | 4  |
| 5  | 6  | 7  | 8  | 9  | 10 | 11 |
| 12 | 13 | 14 | 15 | 16 | 17 | 18 |
| 19 | 20 | 21 | 22 | 23 | 24 | 25 |
| 26 | 27 | 28 | 29 | 30 | 31 |    |

## NOVEMBER
| SU | MO | TU | WE | TH | FR | SA |
|----|----|----|----|----|----|----|
|    |    |    |    |    |    | 1  |
| 2  | 3  | 4  | 5  | 6  | 7  | 8  |
| 9  | 10 | 11 | 12 | 13 | 14 | 15 |
| 16 | 17 | 18 | 19 | 20 | 21 | 22 |
| 23 | 24 | 25 | 26 | 27 | 28 | 29 |
| 30 |    |    |    |    |    |    |

## DECEMBER
| SU | MO | TU | WE | TH | FR | SA |
|----|----|----|----|----|----|----|
|    | 1  | 2  | 3  | 4  | 5  | 6  |
| 7  | 8  | 9  | 10 | 11 | 12 | 13 |
| 14 | 15 | 16 | 17 | 18 | 19 | 20 |
| 21 | 22 | 23 | 24 | 25 | 26 | 27 |
| 28 | 29 | 30 | 31 |    |    |    |

# 2026

## JANUARY
| SU | MO | TU | WE | TH | FR | SA |
|----|----|----|----|----|----|----|
|    |    |    |    | 1  | 2  | 3  |
| 4  | 5  | 6  | 7  | 8  | 9  | 10 |
| 11 | 12 | 13 | 14 | 15 | 16 | 17 |
| 18 | 19 | 20 | 21 | 22 | 23 | 24 |
| 25 | 26 | 27 | 28 | 29 | 30 | 31 |

## FEBRUARY
| SU | MO | TU | WE | TH | FR | SA |
|----|----|----|----|----|----|----|
| 1  | 2  | 3  | 4  | 5  | 6  | 7  |
| 8  | 9  | 10 | 11 | 12 | 13 | 14 |
| 15 | 16 | 17 | 18 | 19 | 20 | 21 |
| 22 | 23 | 24 | 25 | 26 | 27 | 28 |

## MARCH
| SU | MO | TU | WE | TH | FR | SA |
|----|----|----|----|----|----|----|
| 1  | 2  | 3  | 4  | 5  | 6  | 7  |
| 8  | 9  | 10 | 11 | 12 | 13 | 14 |
| 15 | 16 | 17 | 18 | 19 | 20 | 21 |
| 22 | 23 | 24 | 25 | 26 | 27 | 28 |
| 29 | 30 | 31 |    |    |    |    |

## APRIL
| SU | MO | TU | WE | TH | FR | SA |
|----|----|----|----|----|----|----|
|    |    |    | 1  | 2  | 3  | 4  |
| 5  | 6  | 7  | 8  | 9  | 10 | 11 |
| 12 | 13 | 14 | 15 | 16 | 17 | 18 |
| 19 | 20 | 21 | 22 | 23 | 24 | 25 |
| 26 | 27 | 28 | 29 | 30 |    |    |

## MAY
| SU | MO | TU | WE | TH | FR | SA |
|----|----|----|----|----|----|----|
|    |    |    |    |    | 1  | 2  |
| 3  | 4  | 5  | 6  | 7  | 8  | 9  |
| 10 | 11 | 12 | 13 | 14 | 15 | 16 |
| 17 | 18 | 19 | 20 | 21 | 22 | 23 |
| 24 | 25 | 26 | 27 | 28 | 29 | 30 |
| 31 |    |    |    |    |    |    |

## JUNE
| SU | MO | TU | WE | TH | FR | SA |
|----|----|----|----|----|----|----|
|    | 1  | 2  | 3  | 4  | 5  | 6  |
| 7  | 8  | 9  | 10 | 11 | 12 | 13 |
| 14 | 15 | 16 | 17 | 18 | 19 | 20 |
| 21 | 22 | 23 | 24 | 25 | 26 | 27 |
| 28 | 29 | 30 |    |    |    |    |

## JULY
| SU | MO | TU | WE | TH | FR | SA |
|----|----|----|----|----|----|----|
|    |    |    | 1  | 2  | 3  | 4  |
| 5  | 6  | 7  | 8  | 9  | 10 | 11 |
| 12 | 13 | 14 | 15 | 16 | 17 | 18 |
| 19 | 20 | 21 | 22 | 23 | 24 | 25 |
| 26 | 27 | 28 | 29 | 30 | 31 |    |

## AUGUST
| SU | MO | TU | WE | TH | FR | SA |
|----|----|----|----|----|----|----|
|    |    |    |    |    |    | 1  |
| 2  | 3  | 4  | 5  | 6  | 7  | 8  |
| 9  | 10 | 11 | 12 | 13 | 14 | 15 |
| 16 | 17 | 18 | 19 | 20 | 21 | 22 |
| 23 | 24 | 25 | 26 | 27 | 28 | 29 |
| 30 | 31 |    |    |    |    |    |

## SEPTEMBER
| SU | MO | TU | WE | TH | FR | SA |
|----|----|----|----|----|----|----|
|    |    | 1  | 2  | 3  | 4  | 5  |
| 6  | 7  | 8  | 9  | 10 | 11 | 12 |
| 13 | 14 | 15 | 16 | 17 | 18 | 19 |
| 20 | 21 | 22 | 23 | 24 | 25 | 26 |
| 27 | 28 | 29 | 30 |    |    |    |

## OCTOBER
| SU | MO | TU | WE | TH | FR | SA |
|----|----|----|----|----|----|----|
|    |    |    |    | 1  | 2  | 3  |
| 4  | 5  | 6  | 7  | 8  | 9  | 10 |
| 11 | 12 | 13 | 14 | 15 | 16 | 17 |
| 18 | 19 | 20 | 21 | 22 | 23 | 24 |
| 25 | 26 | 27 | 28 | 29 | 30 | 31 |

## NOVEMBER
| SU | MO | TU | WE | TH | FR | SA |
|----|----|----|----|----|----|----|
| 1  | 2  | 3  | 4  | 5  | 6  | 7  |
| 8  | 9  | 10 | 11 | 12 | 13 | 14 |
| 15 | 16 | 17 | 18 | 19 | 20 | 21 |
| 22 | 23 | 24 | 25 | 26 | 27 | 28 |
| 29 | 30 |    |    |    |    |    |

## DECEMBER
| SU | MO | TU | WE | TH | FR | SA |
|----|----|----|----|----|----|----|
|    |    | 1  | 2  | 3  | 4  | 5  |
| 6  | 7  | 8  | 9  | 10 | 11 | 12 |
| 13 | 14 | 15 | 16 | 17 | 18 | 19 |
| 20 | 21 | 22 | 23 | 24 | 25 | 26 |
| 27 | 28 | 29 | 30 | 31 |    |    |

# Holidays & Observances

| Name | 2025 | 2026 |
|---|---|---|
| **New Year's Day** | Jan 1 (Wed) | Jan 1 (Thu) |
| **Martin Luther King Jr. Day** | Jan 20 (Mon) | Jan 19 (Mon) |
| **Civil Rights Day** AZ, NH | Jan 20 (Mon) | Jan 19 (Mon) |
| **Black History Month** First Day | Feb 1 (Sat) | Feb 1 (Sun) |
| **Rosa Parks Day** NY, CA, MO | Feb 4 (Tues) | Feb 4 (Wed) |
| **Valentine's Day** | Feb 14 (Fri) | Feb 14 (Sat) |
| **Presidents' Day** | Feb 17 (Mon) | Feb 16 (Mon) |
| **African American Scientist and Inventor Day** VA | Feb 25 (Tues) | Feb 25 (Wed) |
| **Women's History Month** First Day | Mar 1 (Sat) | Mar 1 (Sun) |
| **Easter Sunday** | Apr 20 (Sun) | Apr 5 (Sun) |
| **Mother's Day** | May 11 (Sun) | May 10 (Sun) |
| **Memorial Day** | May 26 (Mon) | May 25 (Mon) |
| **Father's Day** | Jun 15 (Sun) | Jun 21 (Sun) |
| **Juneteenth** | Jun 19 (Thu) | Jun 19 (Fri) |
| **Independence Day** | Jul 4 (Fri) | Jul 4 (Sat) |
| **Barack Obama Day** IL | Aug 4 (Mon) | Aug 4 (Tues) |
| **Labor Day** | Sep 1 (Mon) | Sep 7 (Mon) |
| **Columbus Day Indigenous People's Day** | Oct 13 (Mon) | Oct 12 (Mon) |
| **Halloween** | Oct 31 (Fri) | Oct 31 (Sat) |
| **Barack Obama Day** AL | Nov 10 (Mon) | Nov 9 (Mon) |
| **Veterans Day** | Nov 11 (Tues) | Nov 11 (Wed) |
| **Thanksgiving Day** | Nov 27 (Thu) | Nov 26 (Thu) |
| **Rosa Parks Day** AL, OH | Dec 1 (Mon) | Dec 1 (Tues) |
| **Christmas Day** | Dec 25 (Thu) | Dec 25 (Fri) |
| **Kwanzaa** (First Day) | Dec 26 (Fri) | Dec 26 (Sat) |
| **New Year's Eve** | Dec 31 (Wed) | Dec 31 (Thu) |

# January

| SUN | MON | TUE | WED | THU | FRI | SAT |
|-----|-----|-----|-----|-----|-----|-----|
|     |     |     |     |     |     |     |
|     |     |     |     |     |     |     |
|     |     |     |     |     |     |     |
|     |     |     |     |     |     |     |
|     |     |     |     |     |     |     |

Martin Luther King Jr.

# January

**WEEK 1**

_____
_____
_____
_____

**WEEK 2**

_____
_____
_____
_____

**WEEK 3**

_____
_____
_____
_____

**WEEK 4**

_____
_____
_____
_____

**WEEK 5**

_____
_____
_____
_____

**NEVER BE LIMITED BY OTHER PEOPLE'S LIMITED IMAGINATIONS.**
        DR. MAE JEMISON

**MAJOR**

**MINOR**

**HABIT TRACKER**     S  M  T  W  T  F  S

_____
_____
_____
_____

**MISC**

# To-Do List

Date:

# NOTES

# Weekly Planner

WEEK OF _____

**SUNDAY**

**MONDAY**

**TUESDAY**

**WEDNESDAY**

**THURSDAY**

**FRIDAY**

**SATURDAY**

1808: An act of **Congress bans the international slave trade** in the U.S.

1823: **Alexander Twilight graduates from Middlebury College,** becoming the first African American to receive a college degree. Eventually, a building on the Middlebury campus will bear his name, Twilight Hall. His father, Ichabod, had earned his freedom after serving as a soldier in the Continental Army during the American Revolution. Alexander will become the first African American elected as a state legislator, serving in the Vermont House of Representatives.

1863: The **Emancipation Proclamation, which officially frees enslaved people in Confederate states, takes effect at the stroke of midnight.** President Abraham Lincoln signed a preliminary decree on September 22, 1862. The Emancipation Proclamation will mark a turning point in the Civil War and the war for freedom and racial equality for African Americans.

**The First Black Supermodel**

1965: Donyale Luna, at 6'2", becomes the first Black woman to appear on the cover of a major fashion magazine, Harper's Bazaar, in a sketch. A photo of her will appear on the cover of British Vogue in March 1966. The New York Times will call her "a stunning Negro model whose face had the hauteur and feline grace of Nefertiti." A Time magazine article on April 1, 1966, entitled "The Luna Year," will describe her as "a new heavenly body who, because of her striking singularity, promises to remain on high for many a season" and say she is, at age 20, "unquestionably the hottest model in Europe at the moment."

1955: **Willie Cole is born** in Somerville, NJ. He will be a sculptor, printer, and conceptual and visual artist. He will be best known for assembling and transforming ordinary domestic and used objects (including irons, ironing boards, hair dryers, high-heeled shoes, bicycle parts, lawn jockeys, and discarded appliances) into imaginative works of art.

1969: **Shirley Chisholm, elected to represent New York's 12th Congressional District, begins her initial term, becoming the first Black woman to serve in the U.S. House of Representatives.** She will be a founding member of the Congressional Black Caucus in 1971 and become the first Black presidential candidate and woman of any race to run for the Democratic Party's nominee (see January 25). She will place seventh during the primary season in votes won among Democratic contenders and be the first woman in a U.S. presidential debate. President Barack Obama will posthumously award her the Presidential Medal of Freedom in 2015.

## Rosewood Massacre

January 1-7, 1923: **The small, primarily Black town of Rosewood, a whistle-stop on a railway line through Florida, becomes the scene of a massacre** after a Black resident, accused of assaulting a white woman, is lynched and a white mob hunts Black people and burns down the town. Survivors hide in nearby swamps until they can escape by train or car. No one will be arrested for the massacre. Officially, 6 Blacks and 2 whites are killed; unofficially, the death toll is 27-150.

## Tubman Coins

2024: The **U.S. Mint announces the release of three coins commemorating Harriet Tubman** for purchase: a gold $5 coin, $1 coin (center), and one-half dollar coin (right).

Courtesy The Library Con

1807: **Ohio's congress becomes the nation's first legislative body to enact Black Laws restricting free Blacks' rights.** The new measures force Blacks and mulattos to obtain certificates of freedom from a U.S. court before settling in Ohio. Also, anyone employing a Black person who cannot present a certificate of freedom will have committed a punishable offense, and anyone who harbors or helps a fugitive slave will be fined $1,000. Informers will receive half of the fine. Ohio will toughen these laws before the month is out, and other states will adopt similar measures. The Black Laws will remain in effect until 1849.

George Washington Carver, a Tuskegee Institute faculty member, greeted President Franklin D. Roosevelt when the latter arrived at Tuskegee, AL, on March 30, 1939.

1943: **George Washington Carver Recognition Day** is celebrated as a national holiday by the Franklin D. Roosevelt administration. Carver's achievements are credited as instrumental in feeding the U.S. during World War II and for saving Southern agriculture.

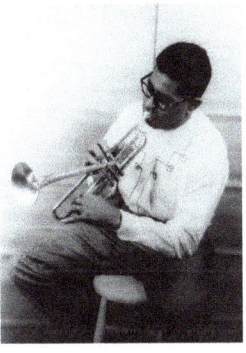

Dizzy Gillespie

## Bending Sound

1953: **Dizzy Gillespie throws a birthday party for his wife Lorraine at Snookie's, a Manhattan club, and dance duo Stump and Stumpy falls on Dizzy's trumpet, bending the bell upward** at a 45-degree angle. Dizzy blows the horn and likes its new tone. The next day, when he straightens the trumpet, he discovers that he likes the tone of the disfigured horn better. "I can hear my mistakes quicker," he says. So he orders a specially manufactured bent-up trumpet from Martin Committee. It will become his trademark, recognized globally. In 1995, his battered Martin trumpet will sell at auction for $63,000.

# Weekly Planner

_____**WEEK OF**_____

**SUNDAY**

_____

**MONDAY**

_____

**TUESDAY**

_____

**WEDNESDAY**

_____

**THURSDAY**

_____

**FRIDAY**

_____

**SATURDAY**

_____

Scan for book preview

1891: **Zora Neale Hurston is born** in Notasulga, AL.

1927: **The Harlem Globetrotters, an exhibition team of Black basketball players, plays its first game, in Hinckley, IL.** (Previously known as the Savoy Big Five, it played exhibitions to attract patrons to dance halls such as the Savoy Ballroom on Chicago's South Side.) The team will be unbeatable, and its players will clown on the court partly to make it easier for white audiences to watch the Globetrotters pummel white teams. The Globetrotters will win the World Professional Basketball Tournament in 1940 and go on a 102-game winning streak before facing—and beating—the nation's best white team, the Minneapolis Lakers at Chicago Stadium in 1948. Tens of thousands of basketball fans will show up to watch the Lakers take on an all-Black team for the first time—and lose. The Globetrotters will attract the best Black players in the country until the 1950s, when the NBA lifts its color barrier and recruits Black ballplayers. The Globetrotters will play over 26,000 exhibition games in 124 countries and territories.

**1811 Slave Revolt**
One of the largest slave revolts in U.S. history begins in the Territory of Orleans at Woodland Plantation (now the 1811 Kid Ory Historic House). Some 200-500 slaves rise up against cruel treatment on Louisiana sugar plantations. The revolt has been called America's "first freedom march."

**Bus Tour: All Stops, The Truth**
2023: Marvin Dunn, a retired public school principal and university professor, launches the Teach the Truth Bus Tour, which takes high school students, parents, and teachers to Florida sites where racial violence occurred. The tour stops in Rosewood 100 years after its residents were massacred, wiping out the Black town. It also stops in Newberry, where a white mob lynched a pregnant woman, a Black preacher, and four others (the Newberry Six) accused of stealing a hog in 1916. "While the stories aren't pretty, they are a part of our history and need to be told, unadulterated, to everyone," a Miami Herald opinion column reads.

**Fisk University Is Founded**
1866: Fisk University, named for Union General Clinton B. Fisk, is founded in Nashville, TN. It holds its first classes for students aged 7 to 70 in former Union Army barracks. Its future faculty will include W.E.B. DuBois, Booker T. Washington, Ida B. Wells-Barnett, Aaron Douglas, Sterling A. Brown, James Weldon Johnson, and Saint Elmo Brady.

Fisk Jubilee Singers 1870-1880

Founders and charter members of Phi Beta Sigma in 1914

**Phi Beta Sigma Is Founded**
1914: Three young Black men found Phi Beta Sigma Fraternity at Howard University in Washington, D.C.—A. Langston Taylor, Leonard F. Morse, and Charles I. Brown. The Greek letter fraternity is intended to exemplify the ideals of brotherhood, scholarship, and service.

## The Book on Segregation

1950: Pauli Murray, a practicing attorney, writes the introduction to her illuminating book, "States' Laws on Race and Color," a compilation of state laws and local ordinances on race intended to guide readers, including lawyers, through the patchwork of laws on racial segregation and other restrictions from state to state, in effect at the time of publication. The hard-to-find, 776-page tome was conceived to determine the extent to which the nation's racial practices are governed by law. It includes segregation and anti-miscegenation statutes, laws on public accommodations, civil rights laws, Supreme Court rulings, federal government executive orders, anti-lynching statutes, and laws related to Ku Klux Klan activities.

Scan to read book preview

Ice Cube as a senior in high school, 1987

## A Jheri Curl World

1979-1980: Comer Cottrell, CEO of Pro-Line, a company he recently started with just $600 and a broken typewriter, launches the Curly Kit Home Permanent, a do-it-yourself hair product priced at $8. He and business partner James, Comer's brother, will become almost instant millionaires as the kit is whisked off store shelves, bringing the hairdo known as the Jheri Curl, or jerry curl, to the masses. Cottrell sells $1.4 million of product on launch day alone and $11 million within 10 months. Instead of spending hundreds of dollars at a salon, customers could buy a do-it-yourself kit for $8 and have glossy, loosely curled hair like the stars, including the Jacksons, Easy-E, Ice Cube, Lionel Richie, and Rick James.

Yale: The Science of Well-Being (Scan for Free Course)

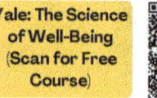

1959: **Birth of Motown** - Berry Gordy uses an $800 family loan to start the empire that will become Motown Records. He wants to apply the assembly line principles he learned in a Ford auto plant to record production and music creation. He will purchase a two-story brick house in a residential section of Detroit and convert it into a recording studio, office, and living quarters. He will eventually buy the house next door, connect the two, and name them Hitsville, U.S.A. The Motown Sound will combine call-and-response gospel, street-corner harmonizing, tambourines, and throbbing bass lines set off by homemade sound effects. Competitors "couldn't get our sound because our echo chamber was the bathroom upstairs," Gordy will explain.

2018: **Laurie Santos** begins teaching Psyc 157, Psychology and the Good Life, at Yale University to about 300 students. Within six days, 1,200 students, nearly a quarter of Yale's undergraduates, will enroll. Santos's Happiness course will become the most popular course in Yale's 316-year history. She will develop an online version (it's free and open to anyone). Her **"Happiness Lab" podcast** will be downloaded more than 90 million times. So binge on it, and get happy.

Happiness Lab

# Weekly Planner

**WEEK OF**

**SUNDAY**

**MONDAY**

**TUESDAY**

**WEDNESDAY**

 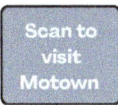

**THURSDAY**

**FRIDAY**

**SATURDAY**

Delta Sigma Theta Sorority, Alpha Chapter, 1914

1913: **Delta Sigma Theta Sorority is founded** by 22 women at Howard University in Washington, D.C. The sorority will distinguish itself as a public service organization by confronting challenges faced by African Americans and thus all Americans. For their initial act of public service, the founders will participate in the Women's Suffrage March in Washington on March 3, 1913. The sorority will go on to provide an array of public initiatives in five areas: economic development, educational development, international awareness and involvement, political awareness and involvement, and physical and mental health. It will become one of the largest sororities founded in the U.S., with over 350,000 initiated, college-educated members and more than one thousand chapters.

**"Black Angels" Helped Cure Tuberculosis**

1929: When White nurses quit their jobs to find work that will not kill them, Black nurses replace them at Sea View Hospital in Staten Island, NY, a sprawling city-run facility that will become a kind of ground zero for tuberculosis victims. The patients will call these Black nurses, the sole caregivers, their "angels." They will attend to the needs of nearly 2,000 patients, double the hospital's intended capacity, in the pre-antibiotic days, when TB is claiming one in seven patients and killing nurses too. Desperate for nurses, NYC health officials recruit Black nurses from the Jim Crow South, where segregation has been ending careers before they've begun. Before long, Sea View's entire nursing staff of 300 is Black, except for a few supervisors, who refuse to care for patients. During the first half of the 20th century, TB, known as the "white plague," will kill 5.6 million people in the U.S. Each Black nurse will care for 20 patients at an average daily care rate of 180 minutes per patient. In the 1950s, the "angels" will work on the frontlines of TB treatment, helping to administer clinical trials, monitor patients, and refine the use of a "wonder drug"—Isoniazid medication—the first successful direct treatment for TB, developed by a Sea View doctor, Edward Robitzek.

1929: **Martin Luther King Jr. is born** in Atlanta, GA.

**Streets Named for MLK Challenge America to Live Up to His Dream**

Eleven state capitals do not have a street or freeway named for Martin Luther King Jr., in some cases because business owners objected, saying an MLK street would be bad for business. One study notes that the areas surrounding MLK streets are predominantly African American with few white residents and that MLK neighborhoods undergo a process of "racialization" in which government resources are unequally distributed among racial groups. As a result, MLK neighborhoods are "all too often susceptible to a policy of benign (or not-so-benign) neglect, property devaluation, and industrial pollution." For more information, see The Root's YouTube video and check out the study (scan QR codes).

**1865: Union General William T. Sherman signs field orders** confiscating a strip of coastline in South Carolina, Georgia, and Florida and **granting 400,000 acres to newly freed slaves in 40-acre parcels.**

Green–Meldrim House (exterior above, and library (below) in Savannah, GA, which Gen. William T. Sherman used as his headquarters during the last year of the Civil War. He and Secretary of War Edwin Stanton met with 20 Black ministers at the house on January 12, 1865, in what will be called the "Savannah Colloquy." The discussion will lead to today's Special Field Order No. 15 issued by Sherman, promising 40 acres and a mule to newly freed slaves.

**1941: The U.S. War Department announces** the formation of the 99th Pursuit Squadron, a group of African American military pilots who will become known as the **Tuskegee Airmen**.

**1759: Paul Cuffe** is born free on Cuttyhunk Island, MA. He will become a merchant, sea captain, and Pan-Africanist. His father, Kofi, is an Ashanti captured in Africa and sold into slavery in Newport, RI, around 1720. Cuffe will sign up for whaling voyages, use a small boat to slip through British blockades to deliver goods to Nantucket during the Revolutionary War, build a shipping business to move goods up and down the Atlantic Coast and beyond, launch the first Back-to-Africa movement, build the largest fortune of any African American in his day, found a racially integrated school, and become one of the first African Americans greeted at the White House by a President, James Madison. Many of his descendants live within 10 minutes of Cuffe's former 116-acre farm in Westport, MA.

**1964: Michelle Obama is born** in Chicago, IL. She will become an attorney, bestselling author, the first African American First Lady of the United States (2009-2017), and one of the most admired women in the world.

Museum of the Bible

One of only three Slave Bibles known to exist

### Slave Bible Inspires Servitude

**1807: The Slave Bible,** as it will become known, is published in London by a missionary organization, the Society for the Conversion of Negro Slaves. It **will be used in Britain's Caribbean colonies to teach enslaved Blacks how to read, inspire obedience, and introduce them to Christianity.** But unlike other Bibles, **the Slave Bible has been stripped of passages that might inspire liberation.** All Bible passages dealing with freedom or God's deliverance have been redacted, including the Old Testament stories about freeing the Israelites from Egyptian captivity. Ninety percent of the Old Testament and half of the New Testament have been deleted. But over time, Black leaders, many of them ministers, will rediscover the missing passages and apply these biblical lessons to freedom movements and struggles.

# Weekly Planner

WEEK OF

**SUNDAY**

**MONDAY**

**TUESDAY**

**WEDNESDAY**

**THURSDAY**

**FRIDAY**

**SATURDAY**

**1788: Thomas Fuller, a 70-year-old African who was kidnapped in Africa and shipped into American slavery at age 14, answers mathematical problems posed by white visitors who have heard about, and are mystified by, his abilities.** Tom could crunch numbers in his head better and faster than anyone with pen and paper—likely while tilling soil. Three Quakers test him on a Virginia plantation. He answers each question within 2 minutes. **Problem #1:** How many seconds are there in a year and a half? **Problem #2:** How many seconds has a man lived who is 70 years, 17 days, and 12 hours old? **Tom's answers:** 47,304,000 and 2,210,500,800, respectively. Tom learned to "figure" as a child and sharpened his wits by counting the hairs in a cow's tail and the grains in bushels of wheat. He could "give the number of poles, yards, feet, inches, and barley-corn in any distance, say the diameter of the earth's orbit," reportedly. And Tom isn't an African rarity. According to a 1732 account of people on the coast where Tom was likely born: "The Fidasians are so expert in keeping accounts, that they easily reckon as exact, and as quick by memory, as we can do with pen and ink …" Abolitionists will publicize Tom's genius as if to prove Blacks are not inferior to whites. But this will only increase his value in his enslavers' eyes. They put his brainpower to work on their 232-acre plantation, asking: How many shingles do we need for a new roof? How many poles and rails do we need to enclose the meadow? How much corn do we need to seed the field?

2009: **Barack Obama** is sworn in as the 44th President of the United States, becoming the first African American to hold the office.

2021: **Kamala Harris** takes the oath of office as the first female Vice President of the United States.

She is also the first African American and first Asian American Vice President and the highest-ranking female official in U.S. history. Harris served as a U.S. senator representing California from 2017 to 2021 and as the California Attorney General. She will become the Democratic nominee for President in 2024.

**Warning to All Black Residents: Leave Town**

1831: Citizens of Portsmouth, OH, today read a notice in their new weekly newspaper, The Courier, just a few publications old. The article carries a message of hatred for Black residents: Get out! Now! "The citizens of Portsmouth are adopting measures to free the town of its colored population," the warning reads. Two years ago, Cincinnati authorities enforced Ohio's Black Laws, codes restricting Blacks' freedoms. The result was the destruction of Blacks' homes and a mass exodus. Half of Cincinnati's Black population left, some going to Canada. The Portsmouth notice sounds the same alarm: What happened in Cincinnati is about to happen here. And so, the "colored people" of Portsmouth, about 80 Ohioans, will likely leave before sundown. They will settle 80 miles north of town, in a community called Huston Hollow, where they will establish a critical link in the Underground Railroad, helping runaway slaves reach Canada and other communities in the north.

## 22

Defense Secretary Lloyd J. Austin III, 2021

**2021: Lloyd J. Austin III, retired U.S. Army four-star general, assumes office as the 28th U.S. Secretary of Defense,** becoming the first African American to hold the position.

Lisa Ferdinando / DoD

Washington Headquarters Services Director Thomas Muir swears in Lloyd J. Austin III as Secretary of Defense.

## 23

Home of Thomas Cadmus in Essex County, NJ, dating from 1793. The loft of the smaller building housed slave quarters.

1866: **New Jersey becomes the last northern state to legally end slavery** when Marcus L. Ward, in his first act as governor, signs a state constitutional amendment to abolish slavery. Slaves in New Jersey found out they'd been cheated out of their freedom about seven months after slaves in Texas learned they'd been freed by President Lincoln's Emancipation Proclamation, which freed slaves in mostly Southern "rebellious states," not in Northern states. However, because profits from slaveholding organizations had been used to build New Jersey's regional centers, including Newark, most legislators refused to condemn slavery and ratify the 13th Amendment. About 16 African Americans in New Jersey were freed three years after President Lincoln signed his executive decree.

1977: **"Roots,"** a miniseries based on the 1976 novel by Alex Haley, premieres on ABC. The series, which will be broadcast on eight consecutive nights, will become one of the most-watched television events in American history and significantly impact attitudes toward race and slavery. It will win numerous awards and inspire African Americans to name their babies after "Roots" characters, including Kizzy and Kunta.

## 24

Arturo Schomburg

**The Negro Digs Up His Past**

1874: **Arturo Schomburg is born** in Santurce, Puerto Rico. He will become an Afro-Puerto Rican scholar, Harlem Renaissance intellectual, author, and archivist whose collection —of literary works, art, photographs, letters, slave narratives, and Black artifacts—will form the basis of the Schomburg Center for Research in Black Culture, the Harlem branch of the New York Public Library. The collection will include the rarest, most useful African American artifacts of any public library in the U.S.

**Scan for Digital Schomburg**

# Weekly Planner

WEEK OF _____

**SUNDAY**
_____

**MONDAY**
_____

**TUESDAY**
_____

Scan to watch mini series

**WEDNESDAY**
_____

**THURSDAY**
_____

**FRIDAY**
_____

**SATURDAY**
_____

# January

## 25

Sojourner Truth seated with photograph of her grandson, James Caldwell of Co. H, 54th Massachusetts Infantry Regiment, on her lap

c. 1797: **Sojourner Truth is born** into slavery as Isabella Bomefree (or "Baumfree") in Swartekill, NY. She will escape slavery in 1826 and eventually become one of the best-known African Americans of the 1800s. She will win a court case to recover her son in 1828, the first such case won by a Black woman. She will speak only Dutch until she is nine. In 1843, she will take on the name Sojourner Truth because she is convinced God has called on her to testify to the hope she bears inside. Her autobiography, "The Narrative of Sojourner Truth: A Northern Slave," will be published in 1850. She will extemporaneously deliver her most famous speech at the Ohio Women's Rights Convention in Akron in 1851. It will become known as "Ain't I a Woman?" (See May 29.) In her speech, she will repeat the question in the title four times and demand equal rights for all women. She will speak out against slavery and for women's suffrage, and during the Civil War, she will help recruit troops for the Union Army and meet President Abraham Lincoln in the White House.

## 26

### Raise the 54th

1863: **U.S. Secretary of War Edwin M. Stanton authorizes Massachusetts Governor John Andrew to raise a regiment of Black soldiers to fight in the Civil War.** Frederick Douglass will help recruit Black soldiers. (His sons Charles and Lewis will enlist.) By May, 1,000-plus African American men will sign up for the 54th Regiment of Massachusetts Volunteer Infantry.

1934: The 125th Street **Apollo Theater opens in Harlem** as a venue for Black performers and patrons. Its first show is "Jazz a la Carte," headlined by Benny Carter and His Orchestra.

Library of Congress

An 1867 Harper's Weekly engraving that tells the story of Margaret Garner.

## 27

### Margaret Garner Tragedy

*Margaret Garner's horrific story will inspire Toni Morrison to write her novel "Beloved" (1987).*

1856: Margaret Garner, born enslaved, flees her master's plantation in Boone County, KY, with her husband Robert, their children, and her husband's parents via a horse-drawn sleigh over the frozen Ohio River. They spend the night in the Ohio safe house of Margaret's cousin. When U.S. Marshals storm the barricaded cabin, the marshals discover a horrid scene: Margaret slit the throat of her two-year-old daughter Mary and has slightly wounded each of her other children, who are fighting for their lives. Margaret, wielding a butcher knife and a coal shovel, is subdued. She is determined to kill her children and then herself rather than return them to the violence and cruelty of slavery. Her mulatto children were fathered by her enslaver, Archibald K. Gaines, the sole adult white male at the Boone County plantation. U.S. Marshals take the Garners into custody, and hundreds gather at the cabin while sheriffs and a coroner collect evidence for a murder trial. The trial will not occur immediately. Meanwhile, Margaret and her family will be returned to Kentucky. Her enslaver will hide her in different cities to prevent extradition to Ohio for trial. She will be sold in 1857 to Judge Dewitt Clinton Bonham for plantation labor in Mississippi and die of typhoid fever in 1858.

### Birth of "Black Is Beautiful"

1962: Photographer Kwame Brathwaite stages a fashion show in a small Harlem nightclub called the Purple Manor: "Naturally '62." Billed as "the original African coiffure and fashion extravaganza," the landmark show features Black models in clothing and jewelry that celebrate African heritage, natural hair, and Black beauty. Until now, these styles were virtually taboo. In the 60s, Black magazines feature mainly light-skinned models wearing European fashions created by white designers. A bold statement of pride in African American style, Afrocentricity, and Black identity, "Naturally '62" will kickstart a global movement, give rise to the cry "Black Is Beautiful," and leave a legacy in fashion and politics.

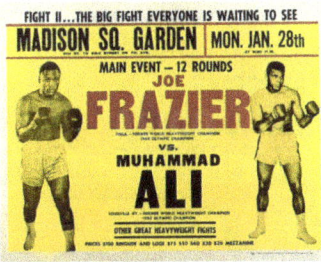

1974: **Joe Frazier and Muhammad Ali meet for the second of three bouts** for the heavyweight boxing title at Madison Square Garden in NYC. Ali, favored to win, defeats Frazier in a unanimous decision after 12 rounds.

Using hand tools, slaves planted Boone Hall Plantation's Avenue of Oaks, the allée leading to the plantation house, in the 1700s. The southern live oaks' root systems are interwoven underground, so the trees live and work as an integral unit to survive even hurricane-force winds.

### Building Charleston Brick-by-Brick

Early 1800s: Boone Hall Plantation, near Charleston, SC, once owned by the ancestors of two founding fathers, is among the most picturesque settings in the South —a 4,300-acre plantation with a house situated at the end of an avenue of oak trees that are older than the nation. But behind the beauty lies a legacy of chattel slavery. Most of Boone Hall's 300-odd slaves pick cotton. Boys as young as eight mass-produce bricks. Every three minutes, each child molds another brick by hand. And every year, Boone Hall slaves produce 4 million bricks, enough to build a city. A year's worth of Boone Hall bricks will go into building Fort Sumter, which lies at the mouth of Charleston Harbor, a few miles away. The fort will stand 50 feet above the water with five sides, three tiers, and five-foot-thick walls. And then it will be shelled.

Boone's slaves leave a lasting impression: fingerprints in the bricks.

 Boone Hall slaves' bricks go into the making of Charleston, including the waterfront estates of some of the nation's wealthiest families.

1956: **One month after the start of the Montgomery Bus Boycott, a man plants a stick of dynamite on the porch of Martin Luther King Jr.'s home in Mobile, AL, just after 9 p.m. It explodes as MLK's wife, Coretta, and a friend run to a bedroom** where newborn Yolanda King is asleep. No one is injured. The following day, from his bomb-damaged porch, MLK speaks to a crowd, saying: "I want it to be known the length and breadth of this land that if I am stopped, this movement will not stop. If I am stopped, our work will not stop. For what we are doing is right. What we are doing is just. And God is with us."

**Ted Corbitt:
The Father of American Long
Distance Running**

1919: **Ted Corbitt, who will
be called the father of
long distance running, is
born** in Dunbarton, SC, the
grandson of slaves. He will
be the first African
American to compete in the
Olympic marathon. He will
run 22 Boston Marathons,
win four Philadelphia
Marathons, and become
the U.S. National Marathon
Champion. He will complete
223 marathons and
ultramarathons, win 30 of
them, and run more than
200,000 miles in his
lifetime. He will co-found
New York Road Runners,
serve as its first president,
and plan the New York City
Marathon course.

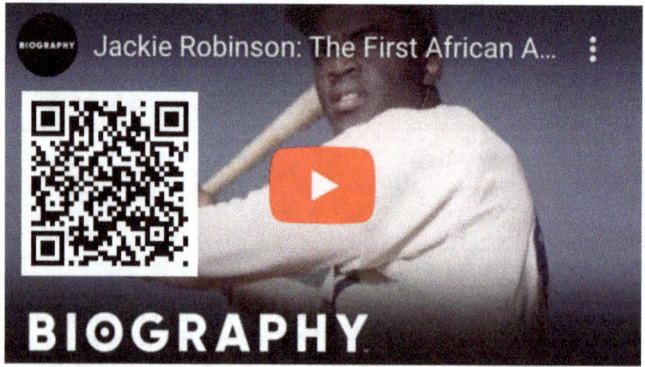

Jackie Robinson: The First African A...

**BIOGRAPHY**

1919: **Jackie Robinson**, future Baseball Hall of Famer, **is born** in
Cairo, GA.

# February

| SUN | MON | TUE | WED | THU | FRI | SAT |
|-----|-----|-----|-----|-----|-----|-----|
|     |     |     |     |     |     |     |
|     |     |     |     |     |     |     |
|     |     |     |     |     |     |     |
|     |     |     |     |     |     |     |
|     |     |     |     |     |     |     |

Constance Baker Motley

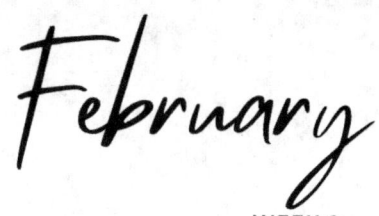

# February

**WEEK 1**

_____
_____
_____
_____

**WEEK 2**

_____
_____
_____
_____

**WEEK 3**

_____
_____
_____
_____

**WEEK 4**

_____
_____
_____
_____

**WEEK 5**

_____
_____
_____
_____

**THE THING ABOUT BLACK HISTORY IS THAT THE TRUTH IS SO MUCH MORE COMPLEX THAN ANYTHING YOU COULD MAKE UP.**
    **HENRY LOUIS GATES JR.**

**MAJOR**

**MINOR**

**HABIT TRACKER**          S  M  T  W  T  F  S

_____
_____
_____
_____

**MISC**

# To-Do List

Date:

# NOTES

# Weekly Planner

WEEK OF _____

**SUNDAY**

**MONDAY**

**TUESDAY**

**WEDNESDAY**

**THURSDAY**

**FRIDAY**

**SATURDAY**

"Almost instantaneously, after sitting down on a simple, dumb stool, I felt so relieved. I felt so clean, and I felt as though I had gained a little bit of my manhood by that simple act."

*Franklin McCain, one of the Greensboro Four*

"There were students behind me saying: 'Let's kill her! Let's kill her!'"

*Autherine Lucy, who integrated the University of Alabama*

# February

## 1

**1901: Langston Hughes is born** into a distinguished family in Joplin, MO.

**1960:** The **Greensboro Four**—Joseph McNeil, Franklin McCain, Ezell Blair Jr. (now Jibreel Khazan), and David Richmond, freshmen at North Carolina Agricultural and Technical State University—**buy items at Woolworth's and then stage a sit-in protest at its racially segregated lunch counter in downtown Greensboro, NC,** proving they were customers by showing their store receipts. It isn't the first such sit-in. Seven African Americans had staged a sit-in three years earlier at the segregated Royal Ice Cream Parlor in Durham, NC. But unlike that 1957 sit-in, **the Greensboro Four's sit-in will spark similar protests across the South.** "We started growing," Joseph McNeil will recall years later. "The first day, four. The second day probably 16 or 20. It was organic. Mind of its own."

## 2

**1935: Raven Wilkinson is born in Harlem. She will be the first African American woman to dance for a major classical ballet company.** In 1956, she will become a soloist with Ballet Russe de Monte Carlo, performing across the U.S., including the segregated South. Her repertoire will include the waltz solo in Les Sylphides and roles in Ballet Imperial (choreographed by George Balanchine), Le Beau Danube, and Swan Lake, among others. In the mid-1960s, she will become a second soloist with the Dutch National Ballet in the Netherlands. Upon returning to New York in 1974, the New York City Opera will seek her out, and she will perform with the opera as a character dancer and actor until 2011.

## 3

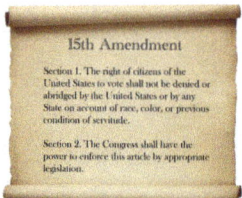

**1870:** The **15th Amendment to the U.S. Constitution is ratified** as the last of three Reconstruction Amendments, adopted between 1865 and 1870, the five years following the Civil War. The 15th Amendment grants African American men the right to vote.

**1956: Autherine Lucy becomes the first African American to attend the University of Alabama,** seeking to earn a second bachelor's degree. Three days later, riots will break out on campus, and a mob of 1,000 will pelt the car she is riding in. **White rioters will trap her in her dorm for hours. Police will rescue her, and the university will suspend her "for defamation" and to ensure campus peace.** A federal court will reinstate her, but the university will expel her. It will annul the expulsion in 1988, finally allowing her to earn a master's degree. In 1992, she will cross the commencement stage to a standing ovation. The university will endow a fellowship in her honor and hang a portrait of her in the student union. Lucy's grandniece, Nikema Williams, will also make history, becoming the first woman to represent Georgia's 5th Congressional District, replacing John Lewis after his death in 2020.

Rosa Parks with Martin Luther King Jr. in the background

Beyoncé on the Renaissance World Tour at Tottenham Hotspur Stadium in London in 2023

**1913: Rosa Parks (Rosa Louise McCauley) is born** in Tuskegee, AL. She will refuse to give up her bus seat to a white passenger, inspire a year-long boycott aimed at desegregating Montgomery buses, and be honored as the "first lady of civil rights" by the U.S. Congress. Raised on her grandparents' farm in Pine Level, AL, she will recall her grandfather standing guard with a loaded shotgun at the front door while watching the Ku Klux Klan parade by. She will marry barber Raymond Parks, serve as secretary of the NAACP's Montgomery chapter, and finally register to vote after being turned away three times. On December 1, 1955, at 6 p.m., after a day's work at a local department store, Rosa Parks, tired and eager to get home, will board the Cleveland Avenue bus and sit in the first row of the "colored" section. Many whites board, prompting driver James F. Blake to order Blacks to stand so whites could sit. Three Black men stand, but Parks scoots into the window seat. Blake summons the police, and Parks is arrested for civil disobedience. After a half-hour trial, she is declared guilty, fined $14, gets fired from her job, and receives death threats. Her willingness to demand fair and equal treatment in a segregated bus system will move Blacks in Montgomery, who comprise three-quarters of riders, to boycott buses. The boycott will last 381 days and deplete public bus companies' coffers. Finally, on November 13, 1956, the U.S. Supreme Court will rule Alabama bus segregation unconstitutional.

**2023: Beyoncé wins her 32nd Grammy,** for best dance / electronic music album, **breaking the record for most wins** at the 65th annual Grammy Awards. **In 2025, she will finally win album of the year, reaching 35 Grammy wins** and 99 nominations.

Daniel Alvarado Silvera

**1905:** Merze Tate is born in Blanchard, MI. She will forge a career as a specialist in diplomatic history and in armaments and their limitations. She will be the first African American woman to attend the University of Oxford and the first to earn a Ph.D. in government and international relations at Harvard University (then Radcliffe College). She will become the Black first woman in Howard University's history department, where she will teach for three decades. There, she will help develop the Howard school of thought in international relations, which emphasizes race and empire. Along with other Howard scholars, Tate will critique theories that undergird international relations, articulating how they are used to establish a racial hierarchy in which European countries, Japan, and South Africa carve out and colonize swaths of Africa and Asia, enact legislation that forbids native rituals, welcome Christian missionaries, and extract natural resources.

**1945: Bob Marley** (Robert Nesta Marley) **is born** in Nine Mile, Saint Ann Parish, Jamaica. He will be a pioneer in reggae and a global pop culture icon.

# Weekly Planner

**WEEK OF**

**SUNDAY**

**MONDAY**

**TUESDAY**

**WEDNESDAY**

**THURSDAY**

**FRIDAY**

**SATURDAY**

# February

## 7

**1926: Carter G. Woodson, the son of former slaves and the first child of slaves to earn a doctorate in history, launches the first Negro History Week celebration,** designated as the second week in February. It will serve as the precursor to Black History Month. Of Negro History Week, he wrote: "It is not so much a Negro History Week as it is a History Week. We should emphasize not Negro History, but the Negro in History. What we need is not a history of selected races or nations, but the history of the world void of national bias, race hatred and religious prejudice."

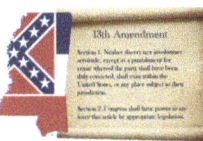

**2013: Mississippi finally certifies the 13th Amendment, becoming the 50th state to abolish slavery legally.** In 1994, 129 years after the Civil War, a clerk in the Texas legislature discovered Mississippi didn't officially ratify the amendment in 1865, so he notified the Mississippi legislature, which on March 16, 1995, voted to ratify the amendment, making Mississippi the last state to do so. However, the secretary of state failed to file the paperwork with the federal registrar. In 2013, two academics discovered the snafu and notified the Mississippi secretary of state, who sent the paperwork to the registrar—148 years late.

## 8

Illustration by Thomas Nast for Harper's Weekly

**1894: Congress repeals portions of the Enforcement Act of 1870 and the Force Act of 1871, eliminating measures that criminalized attempts to deny Black Southerners the right to vote, have their vote counted, and hold office.** Provisions of these acts, known as the Ku Klux Klan Acts, were designed to protect rights guaranteed by the 13th, 14th, and 15th Amendments. The Repeal Act of 1894 will make it easier for states to disenfranchise Black voters, particularly in the states of the former Confederacy. Decades later, the Civil Rights Acts of 1960 and 1964 and the Voting Rights Act of 1965 will recodify election control methods first passed in the Enforcement Act. On August 1, 2023, the U.S. Justice Department will charge former President Donald Trump under the Enforcement Act of 1870, accusing him of a "conspiracy against the right to vote and to have one's vote counted" in an attempt to subvert the 2020 presidential election.

**1986: Debi Thomas wins the senior women's title at the U.S. Figure Skating Championships, becoming the first Black woman to win a non-novice national figure skating title.** She will become the 1986 World Champion and will win a bronze medal in the 1988 Winter Olympics in Calgary, Canada, becoming the first African American to win a medal in any sport at the Winter Olympics. She will go on to become an orthopedic surgeon.

## 9

Virginia DeBolt

**1944: Alice Walker is born** in Eatonton, GA.. In 1983, she will become the first African American to win the Pulitzer Prize for Fiction, awarded for her novel "The Color Purple."

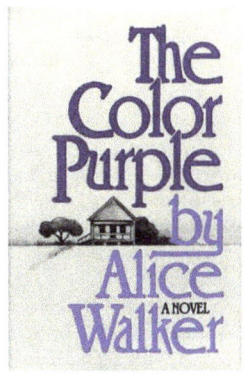

**Scan for Book Preview**

## 10

Madam Walker and several friends in her automobile, 1911

**1910: Madam C.J. Walker arrives in Indianapolis, where she will open a salon in her home, host sales agents, and grow her customer base.** Within six months, she will have thousands of clients in her salon. She will incorporate her company, the Madam C.J. Walker Manufacturing Co., whose mission is to "sell a hair-growing, beautifying, and scalp disease-curing preparation and clean scalps the same." Madam C.J. Walker will open 200 beauty schools, employ 20,000 sales agents, send hair stylists door-to-door, write Illinois's first cosmetology laws, found a sorority and national association of Black beauticians, and become the first self-made millionairess in the U.S.

## 11

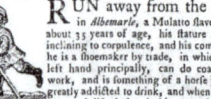

RUN away from the subscriber in *Albemarle*, a Mulatto slave called *Sandy*, about 35 years of age, his stature is rather low, inclining to corpulence, and his complexion light; he is a shoemaker by trade, in which he uses his left hand principally, can do coarse carpenters work, and is something of a horse jockey; he is greatly addicted to drink, and when drunk is insolent and disorderly, in his conversation he swears much, and in his behaviour is artful and knavish. He took with him a white horse, much scarred with traces, of which it is expected he will endeavour to dispose; he also carried his shoemakers tools, and will probably endeavour to get employment that way. Whoever conveys the said slave to me, in *Albemarle*, shall have 40 s. reward, if taken up within the county, 4 l. if elsewhere within the colony, and 10 l. if in any other colony. from
THOMAS JEFFERSON.

Thomas Jefferson's advertisement for the capture and return of Sandy, a runaway slave, in the Virginia Gazette (Purdie & Dixon) 1769

**1788: Ambassador to France Thomas Jefferson, who will own more than 600 slaves in his lifetime, including his children, describes his objection to slavery in a letter but says it is "decent for me to avoid too public a demonstration" of his wish to see it abolished** due to his responsibilities as a public servant.

To Brissot de Warville
Paris Feb. 11. 1788.
Sir

I am very sensible of the honour you propose to me of becoming a member of the society for the abolition of the slave trade. You know that nobody wishes more ardently to see an abolition not only of the trade but of the condition of slavery: and certainly nobody will be more willing to encounter every sacrifice for that object. But the influence and information of the friends to this proposition in France will be far above the need of my association. I am here as a public servant; and those whom I serve having never yet been able to give their voice against this practice, it is decent for me to avoid too public a demonstration of my wishes to see it abolished. Without serving the cause here, it might render me less able to serve it beyond the water. I trust you will be sensible of the prudence of those motives therefore which govern my conduct on this occasion, and be assured of my wishes for the success of your undertaking and the sentiments of esteem and respect with which I have the honour to be Sir

your most obedt. humble servt.
Th: Jefferson

P.S. I send you the journals of Congress of 1787.

Reproduction of Thomas Jefferson's letter

## 12

**1793: Congress passes the first Fugitive Slave Act.** It will be signed by President George Washington, authorizing the arrest or seizure of fugitives and empowering "any magistrate of a county, city or town" to rule on the matter. A similar law will be issued in 1850.

**1909: National Association for the Advancement of Colored People (NAACP) is formed.** It will be the nation's largest and best-known civil rights organization. Its founders include W.E.B. Du Bois, Mary White Ovington, Moorfield Storey, and Ida B. Wells. Its mission is "to ensure the political, educational, social, and economic equality of rights of all persons and to eliminate race-based discrimination."

1900: To commemorate Abraham Lincoln's birthday, James Weldon Johnson, principal in a then-segregated school in Jacksonville, FL, has 500 students recite his newly written poem for school visitor Booker T. Washington: **"Lift Every Voice and Sing."** Johnson's brother, J. Rosamond Johnson, will later set the poem to music, and by 1917, it will be promoted as the Negro national anthem. There are as many versions as there are singers. Listen to some via the QR codes on the next page.

# Weekly Planner

WEEK OF _____

**SUNDAY**

**MONDAY**

Renditions of
"Lift Every
Voice and Sing"

A Cappella

**TUESDAY**

U.S. Navy Band

**WEDNESDAY**

Aretha Franklin

**THURSDAY**

Kirk Franklin

**FRIDAY**

3 Young Kings

**SATURDAY**

# February

## 13

1920: **The Negro National League, the first professional Black baseball league, is formed** in Kansas City, MO, when team owners convene at a YMCA.

1923: The **New York Renaissance, the nation's first all-Black professional basketball team, is founded** by Robert L. Douglas after he strikes an agreement with William Roach, the Harlem real-estate developer who owns the New York Renaissance Ballroom and Casino. The "Rens" will tour the country and win its first game by beating the all-white Collegiate Five, 28-22. Nine seasons later, it will win 88 consecutive games. In 1939, it will win the World Professional Basketball tournament.

## 14

### First Black U.S. Military Unit

Unable to recruit enough white men to fill recruitment quotas set by the Continental Congress, Rhode Island state legislators promise to free all black, Indian, and mulatto slaves who enlist in the 1st Rhode Island Regiment and compensate slave owners up to $400 in colonial dollars for each enlistee. Though George Washington, both a slave owner and commander-in-chief of the Continental Army, fears Black men-at-arms could foment slave rebellion, he reluctantly agrees to accept Blacks due to a severe troop shortage. More than 140 Black men enlist in what will be the nation's first Black military unit, the army's sole segregated regiment, led by white officers. However, Black soldiers have been fighting alongside white counterparts in the Continental Army since 1775, when the first shots were fired at Lexington and Concord. Blacks comprise 10-15 percent of all American troops, serving in almost every unit and every battle.

1867: **Morehouse College is founded** as Augusta Institute at Springfield Baptist Church in Augusta, GA. The Institute will move to Atlanta in 1879 and be renamed Morehouse College in 1913.

1967: **Aretha Franklin records "Respect."**

## 15

Henry Lewis with baton, ca. 1960

1968: **Henry Lewis becomes the first African American to lead a major symphony orchestra in the U.S.** As conductor and musical director of the New Jersey Symphony Orchestra in Newark, NJ, he will transform a small ensemble of part-time musicians into a nationally recognized orchestra. He will increase the number of its concerts from 22 per year to 100-plus per season, attracting internationally known soloists, including Itzhak Perlman. Lewis will diversify his orchestra's audience by scheduling performances in riot-torn and blue-collar neighborhoods, lowering the Symphony Hall admission fee to $1, and bringing world-class musicians to high school auditoriums and concert-in-the-park venues. In 1972, Lewis will become the first African American to conduct at the Metropolitan Opera in New York City. He will guest conduct the symphonies of nearly every major city worldwide. In 2015, he will be inducted into the American Classical Music Hall of Fame.

**1847:** The **Missouri state legislature bans "Negroes and mulattoes" from learning to read and write or assembling for worship.** It also prohibits all free Blacks from emigrating to the state "under any pretext." Violators will be fined up to $5,000 (equivalent to $187,210 in 2023) and/or jailed for up to six months. This new law strengthens restrictions imposed by an 1825 Missouri law that prohibits free Blacks from carrying weapons without a special permit or settling in Missouri without a state citizenship certificate or citizenship papers of another state. Violators could be arrested, ordered to leave Missouri and receive 10 lashes as punishment. A Black person is defined as anyone with at least one Black grandparent.

**1936:** **Jim Brown is born** in St. Simons Island, GA. He will rank as one of the greatest running backs and among the greatest players in National Football League history. He will also be considered one of the greatest lacrosse players ever. He will play fullback for the Cleveland Browns from 1957 to 1965. He will carry the ball 2,359 times, setting records for rushing yards (12,312) and touchdowns (106). He will average 104.3 rushing yards per game, becoming the only player in NFL history to average more than 100 yards per game for his entire career. He will make the Pro Football Hall of Fame in 1971. The Browns will retire his No. 32 jersey. He will become Hollywood's first Black action hero and play many leading roles in the 1970s.

**1963:** **Michael Jordan is born** in Brooklyn, NY. Many will consider him the greatest basketball player in NBA history. He will win six championships with the Chicago Bulls in 15 seasons.

Michael Jordan Tribute | From 6 to 53 Ye...

**1894:** **Future "architect to the stars" Paul R. Williams is born** in Los Angeles, CA. He will design homes for Frank Sinatra, Lucille Ball and Desi Arnaz, Lon Chaney, and Barbara Stanwyck, as well as many public and private buildings.

**1903:** **The landmark musical comedy "In Dahomey" opens on Broadway**, the first all-African American show on Broadway.

**1965:** **James Baldwin and William F. Buckley Jr. square off in a fierce and unforgettable debate on the racial divide in America at the University of Cambridge.** Baldwin argues that the evils of slavery have hardly been exorcised and that "It comes as a great shock around the age of 5, or 6, or 7, to discover that the flag to which you have pledged allegiance, along with everybody else, has not pledged allegiance to you." Scan the QR code below to watch the debate.

Baldwin-Buckley race debate still resonat...

# Weekly Planner

_____ **WEEK OF** _____

**SUNDAY**

_____

**MONDAY**

_____

**TUESDAY**

_____

**WEDNESDAY**

_____

**THURSDAY**

_____

**FRIDAY**

_____

**SATURDAY**

_____

The Audubon Ballroom stage after Malcolm X
was shot. Bullet holes are circled.

Image from 'Crisis, A Record of the Darker Races', (Vol. 18, No. 1, May 1919)

A session of the Pan-African Congress, Paris, February 19-22, 1919.

**1919: The Pan-African Congress, the first in a series of eight meetings, opens in Paris, France.** Organized by W.E.B. Du Bois, Ida Gibbs Hunt, Edmund Fredericks, and Blaise Diagne, it is attended by delegates from Africa, Europe, the West Indies, and North America. Its goal is to unite the global Black diaspora and secure a place for peoples of African descent in the post-World War I new world order. The Congress will become a peacemaker for decolonization in Africa and the West Indies, demand human rights and an end to racial discrimination, and open pathways to equality in economic opportunity. Future Congresses will take place in 1921 (Brussels, London, and Paris), 1923 (Lisbon and London), 1927 (NYC), 1945 (Manchester), 1974 (Dar es Salaam), 1994 (Kampala), and 2014 (Johannesburg).

**1965: Malcolm X tells photographer Gordon Parks that the Nation of Islam was out to kill him.** When Parks asks him if it's true that he is a marked man, he responds: "It's as true as we are standing here. They've tried it twice in the last two weeks." He will be assassinated within 48 hours.

National Park Service

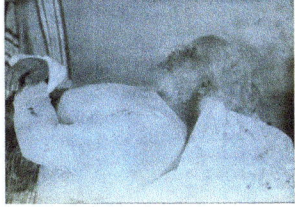

Deathbed portait

**Frederick Douglass Dies**

1895: Frederick Douglass, a leading Black spokesman for nearly a half-century, dies at Cedar Hill, his home for the last 17 years of his life, in the Anacostia neighborhood of Washington, D.C. Cedar Hill will become part of the National Park system in 1962 and designated a National Historic Site in 1988.

Cedar Hill

A rarely photographed smile. Perhaps the last photograph of Frederick Douglass, New Bedford, MA, October 1894.

**1933: Nina Simone** (Eunice Kathleen Waymon) **is born** in Tryon, NC. The sixth of eight children, she will be a singer, songwriter, pianist, composer, arranger—and civil rights activist. She will record more than 40 albums.

Nina Simone performs "Mississippi Goddam" in 1965.

**1940: John Lewis is born to sharecropper parents near Troy, AL,** the third of 10 children. In five years, he will preach to a "congregation" of chickens. In 15 years, he will preach his first public sermon and hear Martin Luther King Jr. on the radio. He will leave an indelible mark on America by creating a heap of "good trouble." He will organize sit-ins at segregated lunch counters, become one of the 13 original Freedom Riders in 1961, become the chairman of the Student Nonviolent Coordinating Committee in 1963, help organize the March on Washington that year, represent Georgia in the U.S. Congress in 1986, be reelected 18 times, introduce a bill to establish a national African American museum (it will open in 2016), and recommend that President Biden pick a woman of color as his running mate. Biden will take his advice.

**1965: Malcolm X is assassinated** in the Washington Heights neighborhood of Manhattan, NY.

Archival Photos & Film Stills

# February

## 22

### First Conductor on the Underground Railroad

**1801: Thomas Smallwood, who will coin the term "underground railroad," is born enslaved in Prince George's County, MD.** Smallwood will buy his freedom in 1831 and run a shoemaking business just steps from the U.S. Capitol. He will also write regular dispatches under the pen name Sam Weller for an abolitionist newspaper, teasing enslavers who are bewildered about their slaves' means of escape, saying they use a mythical transport system, an "underground railroad," and that Smallwood himself is the "general agent" of all branches nationwide.

## 23

**1868: William Edward Burghardt Du Bois is born** in Great Barrington, MA.

W.E.B. Du Bois as an infant with his mother, Sylvina Burghardt Du Bois

## 24

Old Exchange and Provost Dungeon in downtown Charleston, site of the largest slave auction in US history

**1983: The largest slave auction in U.S. history takes place between a downtown Charleston intersection and the harbor where some 40 percent of enslaved Africans entered the U.S.** Six hundred slaves, including drivers, carpenters, coopers, and boatmen, are put up for sale outside the Old Exchange and Provost Dungeon. Families will be torn apart for the highest bids. The slaves are part of the estate auction for John Ball Jr., deceased head of a slave-owning dynasty. Five of his plantations, spanning some 7,000 acres near the Cooper River, are listed for sale along with those enslaved. The estate of Ball Jr.'s father had sold 367 slaves a generation earlier.

*Estate Sale of valuable Personal Property.*
**BY JERVEY, WARING & WHITE.**
THIS DAY, the 24th instant, and the day following, at the North side of the Custom-House, at 11 o'clock, will be sold,
*A very valuable GANG OF NEGROES*
Accustomed to the culture of rice; consisting of
SIX HUNDRED
Among them are Drivers, Carpenters, Coopers, and Boatmen.
Conditions—One third cash; for the balance, a credit of one, two and three years, secured by bond, mortgage, and approved personal security; interest from day of sale, payable annually.
Purchasers to pay for all necessary papers.
Feb. 24

# Weekly Planner

_____**WEEK OF**_____

**SUNDAY**

**MONDAY**

**TUESDAY**

**WEDNESDAY**

**THURSDAY**

**FRIDAY**

**SATURDAY**

# February

## 25

1870: **Hiram Revels of Mississippi, who organized two Black Union regiments and served as an army chaplain during the Civil War, becomes the first African American U.S. Senator.** Everyone in the Senate stands to watch Revels's historic oath.

Martin Luther King Jr., age 19

1948: **Martin Luther King Jr. is ordained into the ministry** at Ebenezer Baptist Church in Atlanta, GA.

1964: **Cassius Clay (who will change his name to Muhammad Ali) TKOs Sonny Liston** after six rounds at Convention Hall in Miami, FL, **and becomes the world heavyweight boxing champion.**

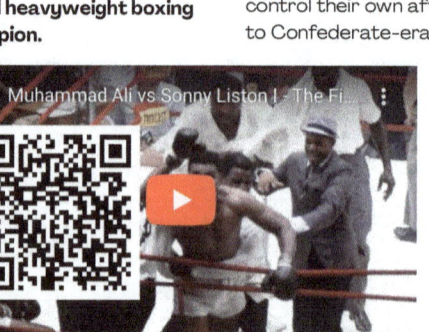

## 26

Wormley Hotel, a five-story hotel at 1500 H Street, NW, Washington, DC

**Who Will Be the Next President—Hayes or Tilden? A Deal Is Struck in Secret at a Black-Owned Hotel**

1877: With the hotly contested presidential election of 1876 and a months-long stalemate that threatens to move the nation toward violence and

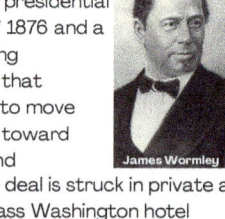

James Wormley

anarchy, a deal is struck in private at a world-class Washington hotel that's a favorite of DC politicos: the Wormley Hotel, owned and managed by a Black man, James Wormley. Emissaries of the presidential contestants hold meetings at the Wormley, where Southern Democrats from Samuel J. Tilden's camp agree to accept Republican Rutherford B. Hayes as President in exchange for Republicans' commitment to withdraw the last federal troops from the former Confederacy, a move that will effectively end Reconstruction along with its guarantees of Black political participation. The secret agreement will give the South back the right "to control their own affairs" and return to Confederate-era politics.

## 27

Swann Galleries/Library of Congress and National Museum of African American History and Culture collections

The only known photograph of John Willis Menard

1869: **Although John Willis Menard had won 64 percent of the vote in a special election in Louisiana to become the first Black man to win a seat in the U.S. House of Representatives, Congress refuses to seat him.** On this day, he requests permission from the Speaker "to make an argument before this House" on the merits of his case. Granted permission, he becomes the first Black man to deliver a speech on the floor of the House while Congress is in session. But James A. Garfield, member of Congress and future president, says it is "too early to admit a Negro to the U.S. Congress" and makes a motion "that the seat be declared vacant, and the salary of $5,000 [saved]." The seat is left vacant for the rest of the 40th Congress.

**1899: It takes an act of Congress and a Presidential signature for Harriet Tubman, who is living in poverty, to receive a monthly pension for risking her life as a Union Army nurse, scout, and spy during the Civil War.** Thirty-four years after the war, Congress passes and President William McKinley signs H.R. 4982 granting Tubman $12 per month for wartime services, including her leadership in the Combahee Ferry Raid, which freed 750 slaves in South Carolina. The $12 monthly pension will be added to the $8 monthly pension she has been receiving since 1890 as the widow of Union veteran Nelson Davis, who was a private in Company G, Eighth U.S. Colored Infantry.

**1940: Hattie McDaniel becomes the first African American to win an Academy Award.** She wins Best Supporting Actress at the 12th Oscars for her role as Mammy in "Gone with the Wind" (1939) but is barred from sharing a table with her costars at the segregated Ambassador Hotel, host of the awards ceremony, so she sits at a small, back table. She was also barred from the film's Atlanta premiere.

The premiere of "Gone with the Wind" on December 15, 1939. Atlanta Mayor William Hartsfield barred Black actors from the segregated theater, but a Black children's choir performed, including 10-year-old Martin Luther King Jr. Confederate War vets attend; 300,000 people line the streets to see the film's stars.

> **"I'd rather make $700 a week playing a maid than earn $7 a day being a maid."**
>
> *Hattie McDaniel*

# March

| SUN | MON | TUE | WED | THU | FRI | SAT |
| --- | --- | --- | --- | --- | --- | --- |
|     |     |     |     |     |     |     |
|     |     |     |     |     |     |     |
|     |     |     |     |     |     |     |
|     |     |     |     |     |     |     |
|     |     |     |     |     |     |     |

Benjamin O. Davis Jr.

# March

**WEEK 1**

_____

_____

_____

_____

**WEEK 2**

_____

_____

_____

_____

**WEEK 3**

_____

_____

_____

_____

**WEEK 4**

_____

_____

_____

_____

**WEEK 5**

_____

_____

_____

_____

**IF YOU HAVE NO CRITICS YOU'LL LIKELY HAVE NO SUCCESS.**
**MALCOLM X**

**MAJOR**

**MINOR**

**HABIT TRACKER**　　　S　M　T　W　T　F　S

_____

_____

_____

_____

**MISC**

# To-Do List

# NOTES

# Weekly Planner

Act of 1788
PLAN OF LOWER DECK WITH THE STOWAGE OF 292 SLAVES
130 OF THESE BEING STOWED UNDER THE SHELVES AS SHEWN IN
PLAN SHEWING THE STOWAGE OF 130 ADDITIONAL SLAVES ROUND THE WINGS OR SIDES OF THE LOWER DECK BY MEANS OF PLATFORMS OR SHELVES IN THE MANNER OF GALLERIES IN A CHURCH. THE SLAVES STOWED ON THE SHELVES AND BELOW THEM HAVE ONLY A HEIGHT OF 2 FEET 7 INCHES BETWEEN THE BEAMS AND FAR LESS UNDER THE BEAMS.


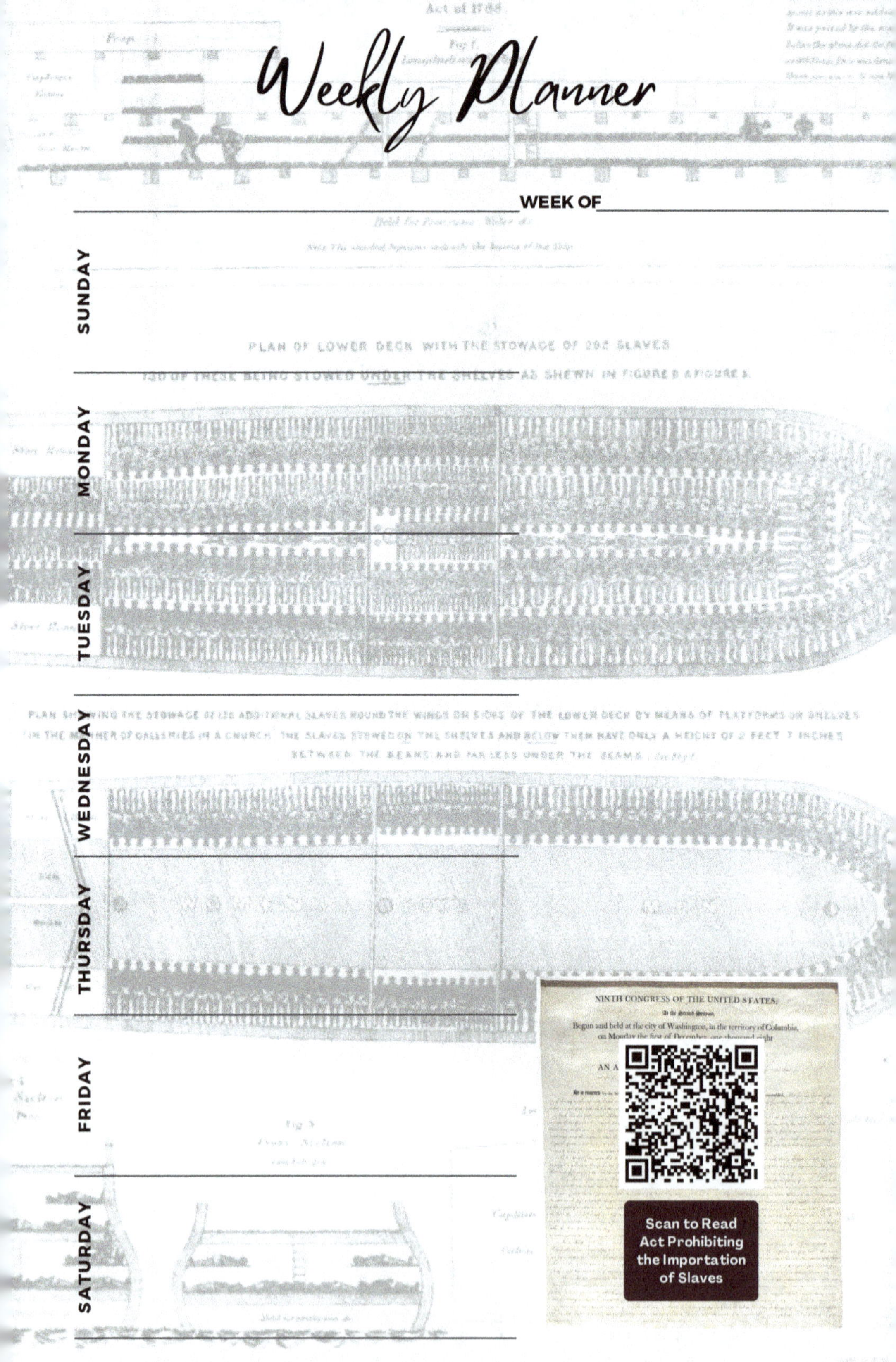

WEEK OF ____________________

**SUNDAY**

**MONDAY**

**TUESDAY**

**WEDNESDAY**

**THURSDAY**

**FRIDAY**

**SATURDAY**


NINTH CONGRESS OF THE UNITED STATES:
Begun and held at the city of Washington, in the territory of Columbia,


Scan to Read Act Prohibiting the Importation of Slaves

# March

## 1

1864: **Rebecca Lee Crumpler becomes the first African American woman to earn a medical degree** in a time when men believe that women are either too delicate or not wise enough to practice medicine. She graduates from New England Female Medical College with a "Doctress of Medicine" degree. After the Civil War, she will work in Richmond, VA, caring for formerly enslaved people. The dire needs of her patients, who faced intense discrimination, will persuade others to pursue medical degrees.

1927: **Harry Belafonte** (Harold George Bellanfanti Jr.) **is born** in Harlem. He will become a titanic figure in show business and play a major role as a Civil Rights activist. He will bring Caribbean music to mainstream audiences, become the first Black man to win a Tony and an Emmy, be the first artist to take an album gold, and co-star in Hollywood movies. But his main focus from the late 1950s onward will be civil rights. He will be a lifelong friend and adviser of Martin Luther King Jr., provide seed money for the Student Nonviolent Coordinating Committee and Dr. King's Southern Christian Leadership Conference, and use his celebrity to raise funds. He will march with Dr. King, participate in the 1963 March on Washington, bail Dr. King and other civil rights protesters out of jail, and donate money to ensure that Dr. King's family is financially secure after his assassination in 1968.

Harry Belafonte | 60 Minutes Archive

## 2

1807: **President Thomas Jefferson signs**. into law an act prohibiting the importation of slaves into the U.S. It will take effect on January 1, 1808.

1867: The **Reconstruction Act of 1867 is enacted** after Congress overrides a veto by President Andrew Johnson. Each of the former Confederate states will be readmitted to the Union after they write a new constitution, which must be approved by a majority of voters in that state, including African Americans, and by the U.S. Congress—and after they ratify the 13th and 14th Amendments to the U.S. Constitution. Several more Reconstruction acts will follow (two in 1867 and one in 1868).

1867: **Howard University is founded** by General Oliver O. Howard on 236 acres of land across the District of Columbia and Maryland. It is open to people of all sexes and races, and within five years, it will educate over 150,000 freed slaves.

1962: **Wilt Chamberlain,** 7-foot 1-inch, 260-pound center for the Philadelphia Warriors, **sets the NBA scoring record for a single game, scoring 100 points** against the New York Knicks, winning 169-147 at Hershey Sports Arena in Hershey, PA.

## 3

Thomas L. Jennings

1821: Inventor **Thomas L. Jennings is granted a U.S. patent** (signed by John Quincy Adams) **for a process called "dry scouring," the precursor to dry cleaning.** He will use the wealth from his patent royalties to buy his wife's freedom (she was an indentured servant) and to fight for abolition. In 1827, he will fund Freedom's Journal, the first African American newspaper, and the Abyssinian Baptist Church in NYC.

1865: **Congress passes the Freedmen's Bureau Act to help newly freed slaves transition to economic freedom.** Within hours, President Abraham Lincoln signs the bill, which creates the Freedmen's Bureau, providing food, shelter, clothing, medical services, and land to displaced Southerners, including 4 million former slaves. But within a month, Lincoln will be assassinated. Vice President Andrew Johnson will assume the presidency and begin to block efforts to grant 40 acres of abandoned and confiscated land in the South to freed people as promised in Gen. William T. Sherman's Special Field Orders No. 15. Johnson's Amnesty Proclamation on May 29, 1865, will return land to ex-Confederates who pledge loyalty to the Union. Many will hold public office and enact Black Codes that limit Blacks' freedoms.

**1877: Garrett A. Morgan is born** in Paris, KY. He will invent a "safety hood" gas mask (see July 25) and a three-position traffic signal (see November 20). Both inventions will save countless lives. In 1905, he will accidentally discover a liquid that straightens hair. He will test it on his neighbor's dog and then straighten his own hair. After transforming the liquid into a refining cream, he will create a chemical hair-processing and straightening solution and a line of hair-care products, including "hair-growing" cream.

"I have tried them all, but there's nothing that does the work quite so well as G.A. Morgan's Hair Refining Cream for straightening the hair."

*Duke Ellington*

Carol M. Highsmith

Crispus Attucks depiction by Herschel Levit, located in the Recorder of Deeds building, built in 1943. 515 D St., NW, Washington, D.C

**1770: Crispus Attucks dies** after British soldiers fire two musket balls into his chest. **He is the first casualty in the Boston Massacre, which will help ignite the American Revolution.**

**1964: Malcolm X publicly announces his break from the Nation of Islam led by Elijah Muhammad** and based in Chicago since the early 1930s.

**1857: The U.S. Supreme Court hands down its decision in the landmark case of Dred Scott v. Sandford, declaring that Black Americans, whether enslaved or free, could not be U.S. citizens and are not entitled to sue in court.** The Supreme Court rules against Dred Scott, a slave, who is someone's property and is thus ineligible to sue his owner to win his freedom. In his majority opinion, **Chief Justice Roger B. Taney writes that Scott as an African American "had no rights which the white man was bound to respect."** The decision, widely considered the worst in Supreme Court history, will polarize the nation and precipitate the Civil War.

Dred Scott

Spider Martin

### Bloody Sunday

1965: On the day that will be remembered as Bloody Sunday, police use billy clubs, whips, and tear gas to beat and suffocate 600 Civil Rights activists at the start of a 54-mile protest march from Selma, AL, to the state capitol in Montgomery to take their cause directly to Gov. George Wallace. The marchers are protesting the denial of voting rights for African Americans and the killing of Jimmie Lee Jackson, a 26-year-old demonstrator who was shot on Feb. 18 as he tried to protect his mother from being beaten by police in Marion, AL, Coretta Scott King's hometown. The marchers—led by then-25-year-old John Lewis, chairman of the Student Nonviolent Coordinating Committee, and Rev. Hosea Williams of the Southern Christian Leadership Conference—cross the Edmund Pettus Bridge and stand face to face with a phalanx of helmeted officers slapping billy clubs in their hands. The bridge memorializes a decorated Confederate General and Ku Klux Klan leader who imprisoned African Americans after the Civil War.

When the marchers do not immediately obey an order to disperse, police on horseback chase them down and beat them as they flee while white spectators wave Confederate flags. Men, women, and children are injured and hospitalized. The assault, which is broadcast on television, shocks the nation and galvanizes the fight for voting rights. Activists organize another march, and two days later, Martin Luther King Jr. joins them along with supporters from across the country. President Lyndon Johnson will sign the Voting Rights Act into law in August.

Spider Martin

"Two Minute Warning" photograph shows marchers facing a line of state troopers in Selma moments before police beat the protesters, giving Bloody Sunday its name.

**"You cannot be afraid to speak up and speak out for what you believe. You have to have courage, raw courage."**

*John Lewis*

1825: **Alexander Augusta is born** in Norfolk, VA. He will become a surgeon and offer his services to the U.S. Army. In 1863, he will be commissioned as a major and serve as the Army's first African American physician and the highest-ranking Black officer. Augusta will become the first African American faculty member of Howard University and the first Black professor appointed to any medical college in the U.S.

1971: **Joe Frazier and Muhammad Ali meet in the ring for the first time,** with the heavyweight boxing championship on the line. Frazier is the WBA, WBC, and The Ring heavyweight champion; Ali is the former undisputed world heavyweight champion. (Ali had been stripped of his title by boxing authorities for refusing to be drafted for the Vietnam War; Frazier supports the war.) The fight is among the most anticipated—and heavily publicized—boxing events in history and the first time undefeated heavyweight champions battle for the world championship. Frazier wins in 15 rounds in a unanimous decision, giving Ali his first professional loss. The two will meet in the ring two more times.

Selma 50 years later: Rem...

Muhammad Ali vs. Joe Frazier I

# Weekly Planner

_____ **WEEK OF**_____

**SUNDAY**

_____

**MONDAY**

_____

**TUESDAY**

_____

**WEDNESDAY**

_____

**THURSDAY**

_____

**FRIDAY**

_____

**SATURDAY**

_____

CONSTITUTION

CONFEDERATE STATES OF AMERICA.

**Scan to read the Confederate Constitution**

1841: The U.S. Supreme Court rules that the **Africans who had taken control of the Spanish schooner La Amistad** ("Friendship") were free men who had been kidnapped and illegally enslaved. In January 1842, the surviving Africans (from the Mende ethnic group) returned to Sierra Leone.

Scan to read about the Supreme Court decision in United States v. the Amistad

### Setting a National Black Political Agenda

March 10-12, 1972: The **National Black Political Convention in Gary, IN, brings together leaders from across the country to create a cohesive political strategy that will advance the Black Civil Rights Movement,** which has stalled since the assassinations of Martin Luther King Jr. and Malcolm X in the 1960s. It is the largest independent Black political gathering in U.S. history, with 10,000 attendees, including state delegates, Socialists, Black Panthers, Republicans, Democrats, and Nationalists.

National Museum of African American History and Culture

1975: Using $25,000 invested by singers Marvin Gaye and Helen Reddy, **Wally Amos opens a cookie store on Sunset Blvd. in Hollywood: Famous Amos.** He will sell $300,000 worth of cookies in his first year and reach $1 million in sales in his second. Within six years, revenues will skyrocket to $12 million, and supermarkets will carry his brand, paving the way for other brands to follow the same path, including Baskin-Robbins and Starbucks. Amos will eventually sell his company and create another brand, "Chip and Cookie."

Thomas Kelly 1897

Jefferson Davis, president of the Confederate States of America, and his cabinet with General Robert E. Lee

### Confederate Constitution

1861: Confederate states approve the Confederate Constitution. For a time, it will rule the lives of more than 9 million people, including 3 million slaves, who live in the states and territories seceding from the Union; 22 million people live outside of these areas. There are seven Southern secessionists; eventually, 11 states will secede and join the Confederacy, which member states regard as a federation of sovereign states. The constitution calls for a president who will serve a single six-year term, an effort to preserve the total autonomy and authority of state governments by forcing presidents out of office before they become too powerful. One article of the constitution bans any Confederate state from making slavery illegal; another ensures that slave owners can travel with their slaves from state to state. The constitution also stipulates that any new territory added to the Confederacy must allow slavery. The constitution will take effect on February 22, 1862.

# Weekly Planner

WEEK OF

**SUNDAY**

**MONDAY**

**TUESDAY**

The Savoy Ballroom

**WEDNESDAY**

**THURSDAY**

**FRIDAY**

**SATURDAY**

## Home of Happy Feet

1926: The Savoy Ballroom opens in Harlem at 596 Lenox Av., occupying the city block between 140th and 141st Streets. So many will show up tonight that 2,000 will be turned away. This joint will jump every night of the week, earning its name as the "Home of Happy Feet." The spring-loaded mahogany and maple floor (scrubbed, polished, and inspected every morning) will be replaced every three years due to the stompin' it takes. The Savoy is a high-class joint with a spacious lobby, a basement check-in, a cut-glass chandelier, a marble staircase, bouncers in tuxedos, a second-floor ballroom the size of several basketball courts, mirrored walls, and a double bandstand (so the music never stops). On the left is "Cat's Corner," where the world's best dancers can do their thing. They will create the Lindy Hop, the Flying Charleston, Rhumboogie, and more. Some will dance professionally on stage and in movies. Admission will be affordable. Tickets: 30-85 cents, depending on the time of arrival. Still, the Savoy will generate a quarter million dollars in profits and welcome 700,000 patrons (or 1.4 million "happy feet") per year, including people of every racial "persuasion," from white Hollywood stars to Black folks who live on Lenox Av.

Bucktown General Store

c.1830: **At age eight, Harriet Tubman, then named Minty, sustains a severe head injury that will change her life.** At the general store in Bucktown, MD, an overseer who is chasing a male slave throws a two-pound iron weight at him but hits Minty instead. The weight breaks her skull and drives a piece of her shawl into it. Slaves carry Minty to her family's slave cabin, where she lay unconscious for two days. She wakes to discover she is disfigured and disabled for life. It will not be unusual for her to fall silent mid-sentence, hang her head, lose consciousness for several minutes, awaken, and continue the conversation without losing a beat. She will suffer from headaches and seizures, see indescribable visions, hear disembodied voices, and fall into trances. Shortly after marriage, Minty will rename herself Harriet to honor her mother. She will learn to trust her visions and use them to make decisions. Her visions will never fail her. She will always evade capture and lead 70+ slaves to freedom. She will carry a pistol in the folds of her dress, and her advice to stragglers will be blunt: "Move—or die." They will move, and every fugitive she leads will make it north to freedom.

## Simone Biles: The G.O.A.T.

1997: **Simone Biles is born** in Columbus, OH. She will accumulate more honors than any other gymnast—11 Olympic medals (7 gold), 30 World Championship medals (23 gold), and 9 US all-around titles, a Presidential Medal of Freedom Award, among many others. The most decorated gymnast in the history of the Gymnastics World Championships, she will be widely regarded as the greatest gymnast of all time. Five virtually impossible-to-do skills in the international gymnastic code will bear her name: two on vault, one on balance beam, and two on floor exercise.

### The Golden Thirteen

1944: Thirteen servicemen break the U.S. Navy's color barrier, becoming the first group of African Americans to complete naval officer training. The new officers will eventually be known as the "Golden Thirteen" in honor of their success. Before their commissioning, Blacks in the Navy were limited to menial jobs, such as cooking and cleaning. But relegating tens of thousands of Blacks to menial duties was an inefficient use of manpower, so the secretary of the navy opened officer training to 16 Black candidates. The Navy put them on a fast track, reducing their training to 8 weeks from the usual 16 weeks for white candidates. Realizing that Navy brass expected them to fail, the Black cadets ignored "lights out" at 10:30 p.m., studied by flashlight, and tested one another repeatedly. When they passed their exams with flying colors, the chain of command still doubted the all-Black class had achieved higher scores than their all-white counterparts, so the Black cadets were ordered to retake the exams. They got even higher scores the second time, with a cumulative average of 3.89 out of 4.0. Although all 16 cadets passed the course, only 13 will receive commissions—12 as ensigns and 1 as warrant officer. No reason is given for rejecting the others, but refusing to commission them, in effect, gives the Black class the same failure rate as white cadets.

1827: **Freedom's Journal, the first African American-owned, -operated, and -edited newspaper, is published in New York City.** It will open a wave of other Black newspapers. By the Civil War, there will be more than 40. A one-year subscription to the weekly costs $3 ($92 in 2023). The objectives of co-editors Samuel Cornish and John Brown Russwurm are to encourage and fortify the common identity of African Americans and oppose slavery and racial injustice. New York City, at this time, has the largest population of Blacks in any Northern city, an estimated 15,000 people, or 10 percent of the 150,000 free Blacks living in the North. The free Black population of the US is about 300,000. The newspaper is circulated in 11 states, the District of Columbia, Haiti, Europe, and Canada.

1912: **Bayard Rustin is born** in West Chester, PA. He will become a leader and activist for many causes: civil rights, nonviolence, socialism, and gay rights. As early as 1941, Rustin, A. Philip Randolph, president of the Brotherhood of Sleeping Car Porters, and socialist A.J. Muste will propose a march on Washington to protest segregation in the U.S. military and racial discrimination in employment. President Roosevelt will respond by banning discrimination in the U.S. defense industry, so the march will be canceled, thus offering Rustin a valuable lesson: planning or creating a major inconvenience can win results. Rustin will work to desegregate interstate busing in 1942, be arrested for sitting in the second row of a bus, and be beaten by police but released uncharged. In 1947, he will organize the first Freedom Rides in 1947. (After a ride, he will end up on a chain gang in North Carolina.) A year later, he will travel to India to study nonviolent civil resistance in the Gandhian movement. He will advise Martin Luther King Jr. on nonviolent tactics during the Montgomery bus boycott in 1956, convince King to form the Southern Christian Leadership Conference, and help plan the March on Washington for Jobs and Freedom in 1963. Rustin will serve on humanitarian missions and work for gay rights in the 1980s, draw criticism for being gay, and work behind the scenes to advise civil rights leaders. President Barack Obama will posthumously award him the Presidential Medal of Freedom in 2013 and, with Michelle Obama, will produce the 2023 film "Rustin."

# Weekly Planner

WEEK OF_____

**SUNDAY**

**MONDAY**

**TUESDAY**

The Golden 13: The Story of The First Afr...
THE GOLDEN 13 THE STORY OF THE FIRST AFRICAN AMERICAN NAVAL OFFICERS

**WEDNESDAY**

Civil Rights pioneer Bayard Rustin honored

**THURSDAY**

**FRIDAY**

**SATURDAY**

## 18

**1976: Well over a century late, the State of Kentucky officially ratifies the 13th, 14th, and 15th Amendments to the U.S. Constitution, abolishing slavery, granting citizenship to former slaves, and giving Black men the right to vote, respectively.** On January 31, 1865, the U.S. Congress passed the 13th Amendment, which then went through the ratification process. This meant 27 of 36 states at the time had to ratify the amendment before it could be added to the U.S. Constitution. The Emancipation Proclamation, issued on January 1, 1863, freed slaves in the Confederacy but left slavery intact in states that did not secede from the Union, including Kentucky. On February 24, 1865, the Kentucky General Assembly refused to ratify the 13th Amendment. But in December of that year, federal law forced Kentucky enslavers to free their slaves. Kentucky did not ratify the 13th, 14th, and 15th Amendments for another 111 years.

Scan to read how two teens have once again proved an ancient math rule

St. Mary's Academy New Orleans

Ne'Kiya Jackson, left, and Calcea Johnson

### Teens Present the "Impossible": Pythagorean Proof

2023: Calcea Johnson and Ne'Kiya Jackson—high school students at St. Mary's Academy in New Orleans—announce a groundbreaking mathematical discovery that has evaded mathematicians for 2,000 years: how to prove the Pythagorean theorem using trigonometry. Their achievement, presented at a regional conference of the American Mathematical Society, contradicts an assumption taught by math educators, including Elisha Loomis, whose widely used 1927 textbook, "The Pythagorean Proposition," maintains that using trigonometry to prove the Pythagorean theorem is impossible. The 17-year-olds have done the seemingly impossible: prove this pivotal and pervasive theorem, which connects algebra and geometry and is used in many fields, including architecture, physics, geology, engineering, astronomy, navigation, and computer science. The Pythagorean theorem is required to calculate building height, wall length, and the paths of rockets and satellites. In 2024, the young mathematicians will publish 10 more trigonometric proofs.

## 19

1894: **Moms Mabley** (Loretta Mary Aiken) **is born** in Brevard, NC. She will become a stand-up comedian and actress, beginning her career in the 1920s and performing in the Chitlin' Circuit (named for the soul food dish chitterlings)—venues that are segregation-era safe spaces for Black musicians and entertainers.

### The Game that Changed Basketball

1966: In a first for an NCAA championship game, Texas Western College (now the University of Texas at El Paso), the first basketball team to start five Black players, defeats the top-ranked, all-white University of Kentucky Wildcats 72-65 in a stadium full of whites, some waving Confederate flags. The Texas Western Miners win the NCAA crown, finishing the season with a 28-1 record and changing college basketball forever. After this championship game, college teams throughout the South will aggressively recruit Black athletes.

**Texas Western Beats Kentucky in 1966 NCAA Tournament Final**

**"I really didn't think about starting five Black guys. I just wanted to put my five best guys on the court. I just wanted to win that game."**
*Texas Western Coach Dan "the Bear" Haskins*

1852: Harriet Beecher Stowe's anti-slavery novel **"Uncle Tom's Cabin" is published**, inspiring opposition to slavery and helping to lay the groundwork for the Civil War. It becomes an instant bestseller—the first printing of 5,000 copies will sell out in two days. Within a year, 300,000 copies will be sold. Within five, it will be translated into 20 languages.

1883: **Jan Matzeliger,** a 25-year-old from Dutch Guiana, receives U.S. patent No. 274,207 for his automatic shoe-lasting machine. It **will revolutionize an entire industry: shoemaking.** At the time, no machine could connect a shoe's upper to its sole. This was done by well-paid shoemakers who pulled, pleated, tucked, tacked, and stitched leather on a foot-shaped mold called a last. Matzeliger designed a contraption and tinkered for years, living on a nickel's worth of food daily until he produced a machine that mechanized the process. Finally, he gathered a few investors to see it. The machine's mechanically operated tools punched holes into an upper, stretched it over a shoe mold and onto a sole at the toe and heel, and stitched it. The machine fed nails into a drive that hammered them into place. A pair of shoes was finished in a minute. Matzeliger went on to make 75 pairs that day. With modifications, his machine will turn out 700 pairs a day—a hand laster could only make 50.

1927: **Josephine Baker dances** in only pearls, wrist cuffs, and a skirt of 16 rubber bananas, in the Folies Bergère production "Un Vent de Folie," setting fire to Parisians' imaginations.

1965: Two weeks after Bloody Sunday, **civil rights demonstrators march across the Edmund Pettus Bridge over the Alabama River in Selma on their way to Montgomery,** the capital of Alabama. The demonstrators will walk 7-17 miles daily and camp in yards along the way at night. They will be entertained by celebrities such as Harry Belafonte and Lena Horne. The number of marchers will swell to 25,000 as they near Montgomery. The march will be credited for attracting national attention and building political momentum for the passage of the Voting Rights Act of 1965. In a speech to Congress, President Lyndon B. Johnson will introduce the bill and use the language of civil rights singers, "We shall overcome."

**Revving Up the Renaissance**

1924: **Seeking to marry talent to opportunity, Alain Locke and Charles S. Johnson host an interracial dinner party** in the Civic Club (the only upper-crust New York club that ignores the color line). The soirée is intended to draw a carefully curated guest list of artistic luminaries and up-and-comers. One hundred attendees, including W.E.B. DuBois, rub shoulders at the Civic Club, discuss the state of the arts and the racial state of the nation, and talk turkey about publishing. Within a decade, 40-plus major works of fiction, nonfiction, and poetry will be published, and scores of writers and artists will settle in Harlem. (Zora Neale Hurston will arrive in January 1925 with $1.50 in her purse and a ton of hope.) **The soirée will be credited for launching the Harlem Renaissance.**

Congress of Racial Equality conducts march in memory of Black children killed in Birmingham bombings.

March 1942: The **Congress of Racial Equality (CORE) is founded** by an interracial group of students at the University of Chicago—28 men and 22 women. With strict devotion to interracial principles, CORE will pioneer nonviolent tactics, including sit-ins and other forms of civil disobedience, to challenge segregation. It will inspire sit-ins at segregated lunch counters in the South, organize Freedom Rides in the spring of 1961 to test two desegregation rulings by the US Supreme Court (see May 4), and conduct a 1964 Freedom Summer voter registration drive during which Chaney, Goodman, and Schwerner will be murdered (see June 21). CORE will work with Martin Luther King Jr. from the late 1950s to the mid-1960s, when it will shift its philosophy, and promote Black power. By 1966 it will adopt a platform based on Black power and limit white involvement in the organization.

# Weekly Planner

WEEK OF _____

**SUNDAY**

**MONDAY**

Henry Box Brown's welcome committee, left to right: William Still, Passmore Williamson (while imprisoned in Philadelphia in 1855 for assisting runaway slaves), and James Miller McKim.

**TUESDAY**

### Cheap postage has an "immense moral bearing."

*Frederick Douglass*
*upon learning of*
*Henry Brown's deliverance*

**WEDNESDAY**

**THURSDAY**

**FRIDAY**

**SATURDAY**

# March

## 23

## 24

## 25

### Henry Brown: Boxed & Shipped to Freedom

1849: Henry Brown, enslaved in Virginia, climbs into a 3' x 2' x 2.5' wooden box marked "Dry Goods" and labeled "This Side Up" ... "Handle with Care," and folds himself as best he can into the box. White friends nail the lid and ship the box via Adams Express Co. from Richmond to Philadelphia—and freedom. The box is handled roughly, sometimes placed upside-down during transport by wagon, railroad, steamboat, ferry, and delivery wagon. It arrives 27 hours later at the Philadelphia Anti-Slavery Society, where the shipment is accepted. Passmore Williamson, William Still, and other Society members are present as James Miller McKim pries off the lid, and Brown stands and says, "How do you do, gentlemen?" Brown's arrival will be celebrated as a "modern postal miracle." He will be known as Henry "Box" Brown.

Second edition, The British Library

### Coming to America

1789: "The Interesting Narrative of the Life of Olaudah Equiano" is published in London. In it, he gives a firsthand account of the transatlantic slave trade, including his abduction from the Igbo village of Essaka in what is now southern Nigeria at age 11, his voyage to the West Indies, enslavement in Virginia, emancipation in 1766, and his life as an abolitionist and lecturer in England. Equiano's autobiography will become the first popular slave narrative.

2002: **Halle Berry becomes the first African American woman to win the Academy Award for Best Actress.** She wins for her role in "Monster's Ball" (2001), at the 74th Oscars.

Eight of the nine Scottsboro Boys with NAACP representatives Juanita Jackson Mitchell, Laura Kellum, and Dr. Ernest W. Taggart in a photo taken inside the prison where the Scottsboro Boys are being held.

### The Scottsboro Boys: A Travesty of Justice

1931: Police arrest nine Black teenagers who were riding on a Southern Railroad freight train through Jackson County, AL. They are charged with raping two white women. The case against the "Scottsboro Boys" will turn into one of the most notorious cases of racial injustice in U.S. history, with a lynch mob forming outside the local jail, the Alabama National Guard called in, a series of trials and retrials, repeated convictions and death sentences, the retraction of false accusations, accusers defending the accused, landmark U.S. Supreme Court decisions, more than a century of collective prison time served, a prison escape, paroles, posthumous pardons—and a bestselling book loosely based on the case and considered among the best novels in U.S history (Harper Lee's "To Kill a Mockingbird," the tale of a Black man accused of raping a white woman and defended in court by a white lawyer despite threats from the white community).

## 26

The Philadelphia Museum of Art

### The Architect Behind Philly's "Rocky" Steps, Harvard's Widener, Duke's Campus & More

1928: The Philadelphia Museum of Art opens the doors of its new building, primarily designed by Julian Abele, the first Black graduate of the University of Pennsylvania's Department of Architecture. Among his designs are the east entrance stairs (72 stone steps), which will become known as the Rocky Steps for its role in the "Rocky" films. These famous steps will become the venue of the international Live 8 Concert (crowd size: up to 1 million) and the Philadelphia Freedom Concert (1 million). Julian Abele will design Harvard University's Widener Memorial Library, the centerpiece of Harvard's library system; many of Newport, Rhode Island's Gilded Age mansions; most of Duke University's campus, including its chapel (though he will never see it in person due to Jim Crow laws), and the white-marble Manhattan mansion of James Buchanan Duke, described as the costliest home on Fifth Avenue in the early 1900s.

1964: **Martin Luther King Jr. and Malcolm X meet** briefly and shake hands while waiting for a Capitol Hill press conference. Both had come to hear the Senate debate on the Civil Rights Act of 1964.

## 27

1924: **Sarah Vaughan is born** in Newark, NJ. In 1942, she will win the Apollo Theater Amateur Night singing contest—a $10 prize and a weeklong engagement at the theater. She will open at the Apollo for Ella Fitzgerald, then tour with most of the era's leading jazz bands, sing with symphonies, make hit recordings, and star in her own radio program, "Songs by Sarah Vaughan," a 15-minute show broadcast four nights per week. Sarah Vaughan will perform at the White House and earn two nicknames: "Sassy" and "the Divine One."

2005: **Shonda Rhimes's television series "Grey's Anatomy" debuts** on ABC. The medical drama features the surgical staff of the fictional Seattle Grace Hospital (which will be renamed Grey Sloan Memorial Hospital). Rhimes, the former intern and mentee of film producer Debra Martin Chase (see August 3), will found the production company Shondaland and become showrunner (creator, head writer, and executive producer) of the series "Scandal" (2012-18) and executive producer of the Netflix series "Bridgerton" (2020-present) and its spin-off "Queen Charlotte: A Bridgerton Story" (2023), among other shows. Rhimes will bring over $2 billion in revenue to ABC's parent company, Disney, and become one of America's wealthiest entertainers, with an estimated net worth of $250 million.

## 28

Lew Alcindor (Kareem Abdul-Jabbar) playing for the UCLA Bruins with the reverse two-handed dunk to score a basket during a game against the Stanford Cardinal, circa 1967.

### The Alcindor Rule

1967: The National Basketball Committee bans dunking in college basketball three days after the 7-foot-2-inch sophomore Kareem Abdul-Jabbar, then named Lew Alcindor, led his UCLA team to win the NCAA championship, the first of its seven consecutive national titles. The ban forces him to develop his "skyhook," which will make the future NBA all-star virtually unstoppable. The college ban will be rescinded in 1976.

March 1960: **Ray Charles, who was born in Albany, GA, records "Georgia on My Mind" in a New York City studio** in just four takes compared to his usual 10-12 takes for songs. It will soar to the top of the charts and earn two Grammys for Charles, whose driver suggested he record the song. **It will become the state's official song in 1979** (see April 24) and in 2003, Rolling Stone magazine will name it the 44th greatest song of all time.

1971: The **Congressional Black Caucus is founded** at the start of the 92nd Congress (1971-1973). Among its 13 founding members are Shirley A. Chisholm (D-NY), John Conyers Jr. (D-MI), Ronald V. Dellums (D-CA), Charles B. Rangel (D-NY), and Louis Stokes (D-OH). The CBC will be called the "Conscience of the Congress" because it is often the first to speak out on issues that Congress must address.

1870: **Thomas Mundy Peterson of Perth Amboy, NJ, becomes the first African American to vote under the just-enacted provisions of the 15th Amendment to the U.S. Constitution.** The Amendment was ratified on February 3 but was not officially certified by U.S. Secretary of State Hamilton Fish until March 30. Peterson's mother had been a slave. In New Jersey, March 31 will be celebrated as Thomas Mundy Peterson Day in recognition of his historic vote. However, Peterson is not the first African American to vote in an election. Towns in New England and northern states had allowed free men of color to vote since colonial days. New Jersey allowed Black men to vote until 1807, provided they met property and resident requirements. States of the former Confederacy had allowed Blacks to vote during the Reconstruction era. An estimated 700,000 African Americans cast votes before Peterson.

1878: **Jack Johnson is born** in Galveston, TX. He will become world heavyweight boxing champion.

# April

| SUN | MON | TUE | WED | THU | FRI | SAT |
|-----|-----|-----|-----|-----|-----|-----|
|     |     |     |     |     |     |     |
|     |     |     |     |     |     |     |
|     |     |     |     |     |     |     |
|     |     |     |     |     |     |     |
|     |     |     |     |     |     |     |

Coretta Scott King and daughter Bernice

# April

**WEEK 1**

**WEEK 2**

**WEEK 3**

**WEEK 4**

**WEEK 5**

THOSE WHO SAY IT
CAN'T BE DONE ARE
USUALLY INTERRUPTED
BY OTHERS DOING IT.
JAMES BALDWIN

MAJOR

MINOR

HABIT TRACKER          S    M    T    W    T    F    S

MISC

# To-Do List

Date:

# NOTES

# Weekly Planner

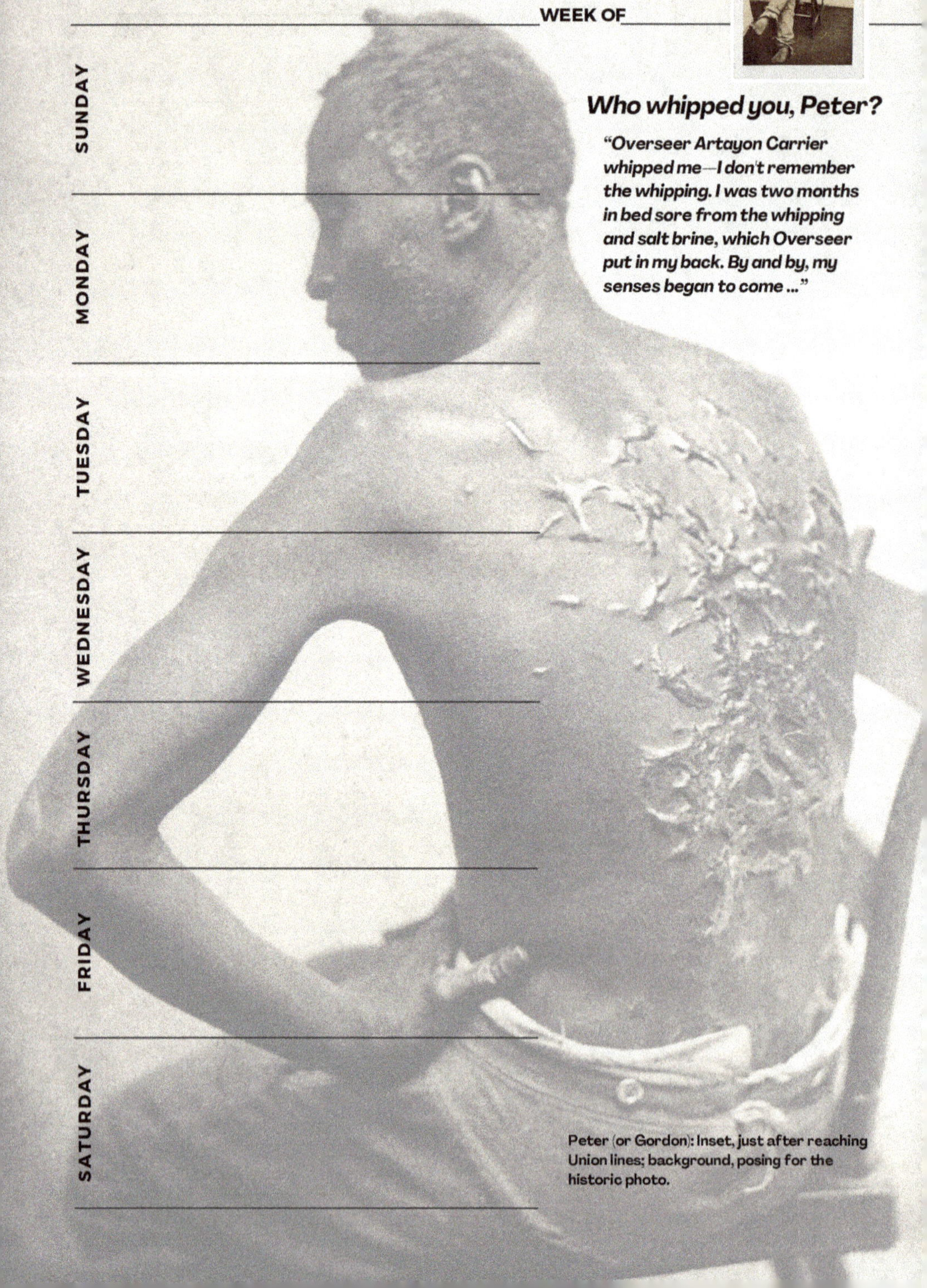

_____ WEEK OF _____

SUNDAY

_____

MONDAY

_____

TUESDAY

_____

WEDNESDAY

_____

THURSDAY

_____

FRIDAY

_____

SATURDAY

_____

## Who whipped you, Peter?

*"Overseer Artayon Carrier whipped me—I don't remember the whipping. I was two months in bed sore from the whipping and salt brine, which Overseer put in my back. By and by, my senses began to come ..."*

Peter (or Gordon): Inset, just after reaching Union lines; background, posing for the historic photo.

1807: **Ohio's "testimony law"** goes into effect. It **prohibits Blacks from testifying against whites** who commit crimes against them. This law, one in a series of laws restricting the freedom and movement of Blacks in Ohio, allows whites to file and win baseless civil suits against Blacks, who are prohibited from testifying in their own defense. Other Black Laws deny Blacks the right to public education, require Blacks to register with authorities and provide proof of freedom upon demand, and bar Blacks from competing against whites for commercial gain.

## Slavery by Another Name

During 1846: **Convict leasing begins in Alabama**—a highly lucrative system of forced labor in which the state fills labor shortages by contracting out prisoners to work in sugar and cotton plantations, turpentine farms, sawmills, coal mines, phosphate beds, and brickyards. Armies of free men convicted of a crime work without compensation sometimes for years, half-clothed and sore. If they die on the job due to inhumane treatment and torture, they will simply be replaced. After the collapse of Reconstruction in 1874, African Americans will make up 88% of the leased population; by 1898, convict leasing will supply 73% of Alabama's annual state revenue. President Franklin D. Roosevelt will abolish the system on December 12, 1941. One historian will estimate that at least 30,000 convicts died in the South's convict leasing system over 55 years. Mass graves will be discovered in towns.

## Whipped Peter (or Gordon)

1863: Peter (or Gordon), a runaway slave in tattered clothes, is interviewed by Union military officers in Baton Rouge, LA, and asks to join a Black regiment to fight the Confederacy. Peter was whipped horribly by the overseer on a Louisiana plantation and then escaped slavery on March 24, 1863, at midnight, reportedly traveling 40 miles at night with three other runaways. At the Union camp, Gordon strips off his shirt, shows the officers his lacerated back, and adopts a dignified pose for his historic portrait, which will launch a new type of slave narrative—photos showing injured bodies accompanied by the words of those who were tortured. A Gordon photo (he posed for three shots on different days) will appear in Harper's Weekly, the most popular magazine in the nation, along with reports of combat by Black troops. It will also become one of the most widely circulated and best-known photos of the century. Gordon will join a Black regiment and meet Confederates in combat. Union surgeons will see other lacerated backs like Gordon's.

2002: **"The Bondswoman's Narrative," one of the first novels by an African American woman and the only known novel by a fugitive slave, is published.** Written in the 1850s by Hannah Crafts (likely a pseudonym), **it will become a New York Times best-seller.** Harvard University professor Henry Louis Gates Jr. discovered the manuscript, described as an unpublished fictionalized autobiography, and purchased it at auction for $8,000 in 2001. He verified its historical authenticity, researched the author, drew on scholars' expertise (including evaluations of the paper, ink, and writing style), then edited the manuscript and arranged for its publication in 2002 with a first printing of 200,000 copies. Eleven years later, a scholar will document the author as Hannah Bonds, who escaped from a Murfreesboro, NC, plantation around 1857, settled in New Jersey, and became a teacher.

Scan to read book preview

The John Wheeler House in Murfreesboro, NC, where Hannah Crafts was enslaved in the 1850s.

**1865:** The **Union army enters and takes the Confederate capital** of Richmond, VA, at 8:15 a.m., after 10 months of attacks. President Jefferson Davis and his Confederate government abandoned the capital on April 2.

**1964: Malcolm X delivers his speech "The Ballot or the Bullet"** at the Cory Methodist Church in Cleveland, OH. He will deliver it again in Detroit on April 12th.

Scan to hear speech

**1968: Martin Luther King Jr. delivers his last speech, "I've Been to the Mountaintop,"** at the Mason Temple in Memphis, TN.

**1968:** Martin Luther King Jr. on the balcony of the Lorraine Motel in Memphis, TN, stands in the spot where he will be assassinated the following day. (Scan below to watch AP documentary.)

**1913: Muddy Waters** (McKinley Morganfield) **is born** in Issaquena County, MS. He will grow up on a plantation, sing in church, purchase a guitar at 17, play in local joints, and move to Chicago, where he will eventually find commercial success and be considered the "father of modern Chicago blues," playing his guitar in a style described as "raining down Delta beatitude." He will also be involved in a legendary rivalry with blues singer and guitarist Howlin' Wolf. Waters will influence many musicians and musical genres, including rock and roll and rock. Rolling Stones members will name their band after Waters's 1950 song "Rollin' Stone," and the founder of Rolling Stone magazine will do likewise. Jimi Hendrix will fear Waters's music before understanding his genius. "I first heard him as a little boy, and it scared me to death," Hendrix will say.

**1968: Martin Luther King Jr. is assassinated** at 6:05 p.m. on the balcony outside his second-floor room at the Lorraine Motel in Memphis, TN. It will trigger riots in more than 100 cities. Within a week, 57,500 National Guard troops will be dispatched to cities across the nation, turning more than a half-dozen into fortresses watched over or occupied by soldiers.

Booker T. Washington 1911

**1856: Booker T. Washington is born** in Hale's Ford, VA.

# Weekly Planner

**SUNDAY**

**MONDAY**

**TUESDAY**

**WEDNESDAY**

**THURSDAY**

**FRIDAY**

**SATURDAY**

# April

## 6

Matthew Henson in Greenland 1901

**1909: Matthew Henson,** who has spent 18 years on expeditions with explorer Robert Peary, **arrives at the geographic North Pole,** making him the **first man to stand on top of the world.** Peary is ill and has frozen toes. Because he can no longer continue on foot, he rides in a dogsled and sends Henson ahead as a scout. Henson plants the American flag at the North Pole. Henson reports later: "I was in the lead that had overshot the mark a couple of miles. We went back then and I could see that my footprints were the first at the spot." Henson plants the American flag at the North Pole. (He is believed to be the great-great-granduncle of actress Taraji P. Henson.)

## 7

Billie Holiday, at the time named Eleanora Fagan

**1915: Billie Holiday is born** in Philadelphia, PA.

William P. Gottlieb

Billie Holiday and her dog, Mister Dog, in the backstage dressing room, probably at the Downbeat, NYC

## 8

**1974: Hank Aaron of the Atlanta Braves hits his 715th home run,** breaking Babe Ruth's career home run record.

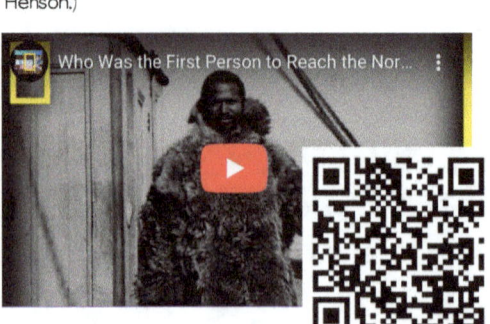

# April

## 9

**1865: General Robert E. Lee and the Confederate Army of Northern Virginia surrender to Union General Ulysses S. Grant at Appomattox.** By the war's end, Black soldiers make up 10 percent of the Union army.

Left: Abyssinian Baptist Church. Right: Congressman Adam Clayton Powell Jr. during a press conference in 1956

**1922: Groundbreaking begins for the Abyssinian Baptist Church** on West 138th Street between Lenox and Seventh Avenues in Manhattan. Thousands show up: men wearing top hats and white gloves, women in bonnets, boys in knickers, and girls in lace. The pastor, Adam Clayton Powell Sr., and his family arrive, including his 14-year-old son, Adam Clayton Powell Jr., who will ascend to the pulpit in 1937 as minister to a congregation of 10,000+. He will be elected the city's first Black Congressman in 1944. Thirteen months from now, an imposing Tudor and Gothic Revival structure of blue stone will stand tall in Harlem. The Abyssinian will become the largest Black church in New York City, with the largest Baptist congregation in the nation.

Scan to hear Martin Luther King Jr. deliver his own eulogy

Moneta Sleet Jr.

Coretta Scott King at the funeral of Martin Luther King at Ebenezer Baptist Church, comforting their 5-year-old daughter, Bernice. This photograph won the 1968 Pulitzer Prize for Feature Photography.

**1968: Martin Luther King Jr.'s funeral is held in Ebenezer Baptist Church Atlanta, GA,** a 7½-hour series of rites broadcast to 120 million U.S. television viewers and covered extensively in print media. Atlanta has set up a special airport hangar to welcome dignitaries. In the future, an Atlanta Journal columnist will say: "Everybody in the world had come here. That was pretty damn impressive," then add, "Atlanta still was a small town in a way." Other cities have burned, but Atlanta remains calm. Funeral attendees cram into the sanctuary, sitting in Ebenezer's worn wooden pews as crowds outside listen to the service being broadcast on speakers and millions watch on television. MLK's college professor, Harold DeWolf, says: "Martin Luther King spoke with the tongues of men and of angels. Now those eloquent lips are stilled." And yet, listeners are about to hear him again. A recording of his "Drum Major Instinct" sermon, which he had delivered at Ebenezer two months prior, is played. His voice resonates inside and outside the church. People are shaken. Some cry. Jet magazine's headline will sum it up like this: **"Rev. King Preached Own Funeral Before Death."**

## 10

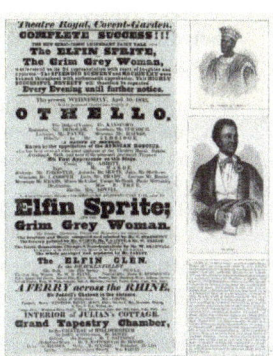

**1833: Ira Aldridge stars in Shakespeare's Othello** at the Theatre Royal, becoming the first African American to play Othello on a London stage.

Scan to learn more

**1947: Jackie Robinson signs his contract** to play for the Brooklyn Dodgers.

### The Slave Who Introduced Inoculation to America and Saved Lives

**April 1721-1722: During a smallpox outbreak, Onesimus, enslaved by Puritan minister Cotton Mather, saves hundreds of lives by teaching suspicious Bostonians a folk medicine procedure practiced for decades in Africa: inoculation.** He explains that rubbing an infected person's pus into the arm wound of an uninfected person can help prevent that person from contracting the disease. At first, Onesimus is ridiculed for his African "heathen practice." All Boston's physicians, except Zabdiel Boylston, refuse to perform the procedure. Boylston inoculated 286 people, and only six would die. George Washington would have his whole army inoculated in 1777. An English physician named Edward Jenner will finally develop a smallpox vaccine, but not for another 75 years.

**1881: Spelman College is founded** as Atlanta Baptist Seminary in the basement of Friendship Baptist Church in Atlanta, GA, by Baptist missionaries from Massachusetts, Harriet E. Giles and Sophia B. Packard. In 1884, the founders will change the name of their school to Spelman Seminary, and in 1924, it will become Spelman College.

1968: President Lyndon B. Johnson signs the **Civil Rights Act of 1968,** also known as the Fair Housing Act, into law.

1787: **Richard Allen and Absalom Jones found the Free African Society in Philadelphia,** a mutual aid organization that assists fugitive slaves and holds religious services for free Africans and their descendants.

1864: **Confederates massacre 250 unarmed Union soldiers, most of them Black, at Fort Pillow,** TN, after they surrender. Confederate General Nathan Bedford Forrest orders his troops to shoot Black soldiers "like dogs." As Union soldiers throw down their arms to surrender, Confederates target Black soldiers, killing 70 percent of them versus 20 percent of white Union soldiers. For the remainder of the war, Colored Troops will shout "Remember Fort Pillow!" before battle as a reminder that they do not have the same privilege of surrendering as their white Union counterparts.

1963: **Martin Luther King Jr. and at least 55 others are arrested and jailed in Birmingham, AL,** for "parading without a permit" during a nonviolent march against segregation. More than 1,000 activists had joined him. Commissioner Eugene "Bull" Connor issued orders to the police: "Stop them. … Don't let them go any further!" During his jailing, **Dr. King will draft "Letter from a Birmingham Jail."** He will be released on bond on April 20.

Scan to read the entire draft

1964: **Sidney Poitier** makes film history by becoming the **first Black actor to win the Academy Award for Best Actor** for his role as a construction worker who helps build a chapel in the 1963 film "Lilies of the Field."

ca. 1825: **Master Juba,** whose real name may be William Henry Lane, **is born** possibly in Providence, RI. He will become an international sensation, beginning his career by dancing for tossed coins, performing in the rough-and-tumble saloons and low-brow establishments of Manhattan's Five Points neighborhood, and working with white minstrel troupes. As perhaps the first African American to perform for white audiences and tour with white minstrel performers, he will mimic white dancers who imitate Black dancers, then close the show by dancing in his own style. His stage name probably derives from the juba dance, named for the African term *giouba*.

# Weekly Planner

**SUNDAY**

**MONDAY**

**TUESDAY**

**WEDNESDAY**

**THURSDAY**

**FRIDAY**

**SATURDAY**

"Invisible Man" manuscript by Ralph Ellison

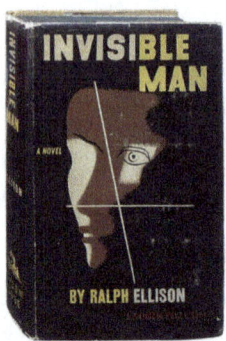

**1952: Ralph Ellison's novel "Invisible Man" is published** by Random House. In 1953, Ellison will win the National Book Award for Fiction, becoming the first African American to win it. The book will become a perennial choice for critics' lists of the best 100 novels.

Scan to read book preview

Back cover of Jackie Robinson comic book ca. 1951

**1889: A. Philip Randolph is born** in Crescent City, FL. He will be a hugely successful trade unionist and influential civil rights leader, including the founding president of the Brotherhood of Sleeping Car Porters in 1925, when other unions are closed to Blacks. His work will convince President Franklin D. Roosevelt to issue Executive Order 8802 on June 25, 1941, barring discrimination in defense industries and federal bureaus. He will also persuade President Harry S. Truman to issue Executive Order 9981, banning segregation in the armed forces. Randolph will lead the 1963 March on Washington for Jobs and Freedom, at which Martin Luther King Jr. will deliver his "I Have a Dream" speech.

**1894: Bessie Smith,** future "Empress of the Blues," **is born** in Chattanooga, TN.

**1915: Elizabeth Catlett,** future sculptor, painter, printmaker, and graphic artist, **is born** in Washington, D.C.

**1947: Jackie Robinson makes his Major League Baseball debut,** breaking the color barrier in professional baseball, as he steps onto Ebbets Field in Brooklyn to compete for the Brooklyn Dodgers before 26,623 fans. He scores the go-ahead run in a win against the Boston Braves. A few days later, more than 50,000 baseball fans will come to the Polo Grounds to see him play, and he will help draw over-capacity crowds at other ballparks, including Wrigley Field. But his move to MLB will involve harassment by fans, and some opposing players will threaten to strike if Robinson walks onto the field. Still, Robinson will win the first-ever Rookie of the Year Award and rank fifth in MVP voting, with 12 home runs, 48 RBI, 175 hits, and a .297 average. He will also lead the league with 29 stolen bases.

Kareem Abdul-Jabbar

**1947: Kareem Abdul-Jabbar** (birth name Lew Alcindor) **is born** in Harlem, NY.

Watch his high school highlights

**1955: DJ Kool Herc,** future father of hip hop, **is born** in Kingston, Jamaica.

## 100 Years Before Rosa Parks

1863: Charlotte L. Brown, a young Black woman, is forced off a San Francisco horse-drawn streetcar due to the company's segregationist policies. So she decides to sue the company, which argues that Black people should not be permitted to ride streetcars because they make white women and children feel "fearful and repulsed." Brown will ultimately win a $25 award, but appeals will tie her up in court for months, reducing the award to 5 cents. To make matters worse, she will be ejected again within days of winning her case. And so she will sue and win again. This time, she will be awarded $500. Private streetcars will finally be desegregated in 1893.

1903: W.E.B. Du Bois's **"The Souls of Black Folk" is published** by A. C. McClurg and Co. in Chicago. This book of essays and sketches, some of which had been published in The Atlantic Monthly, will become a cornerstone of African American literature.

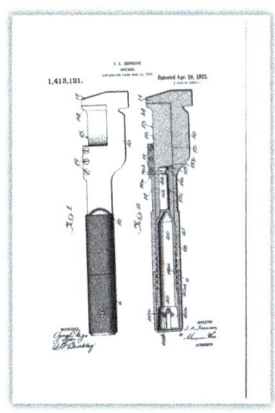

**The Jack Johnson Wrench**

1922: **Jack Johnson, the first African American heavyweight boxing champion, receives a patent for his wrench** (U.S. patent #1,413,121). He conceived and diagrammed the wrench while in prison for violating the Mann Act, a racially motivated conviction for traveling with his white girlfriend, Lucille Cameron, whom he later married. The wrench has slidable jaws that tighten and loosen via screw threads.

1775: **Free Black Minutemen fight in the first battles of the Revolutionary War,** the Battles of Lexington and Concord. It is this day that "the shot heard 'round the world" is fired from the musket of a Concord militiaman, as immortalized in a poem by Ralph Waldo Emerson.

**Scan below to read about 7 Black Heroes of the American Revolution**

# Weekly Planner

WEEK OF

**SUNDAY**

**MONDAY**

**TUESDAY**

**WEDNESDAY**

**THURSDAY**

**FRIDAY**

**SATURDAY**

### The Ku Klux Klan Act

1871: With the Ku Klux Klan terrorizing and murdering Blacks for seeking to exercise their right to vote, run for office, and serve on juries, President **Ulysses S. Grant signs the Ku Klux Klan Act, or Civil Rights Act of 1871, to curb racial violence in the South.** The act empowers Grant to use federal troops to protect African Americans' legal rights and to imprison people without a trial (or suspend the writ of habeas corpus). Grant will not hesitate to use this new authority. He will place nine counties in South Carolina under martial law, thousands will be arrested, and Klansmen will be prosecuted in federal courts, sometimes facing predominantly Black juries. Grant's actions will end the first era of the Klan. But in 1883, the U.S. Supreme Court will unanimously rule that it is unconstitutional for the federal government to penalize assault and murder—that local governments instead should exercise this power. With the end of the Grant Administration, the Ku Klux Klan Act will rarely be used. The Klan eventually will rise again.

1939: **Billie Holiday records the song "Strange Fruit,"** protesting against the lynching of Black people, with lyrics that liken victims to fruit hanging from trees. The 1939 recording will sell a million copies and become her biggest hit.

Read the Story of "Strange Fruit"

**90 Years Before 1619, Africans Revolt in America**

1529: **One hundred enslaved Africans, among the first brought to the North American continent, revolt,** run into the forest, and are never seen again by the Spanish, who brought them. Without the help of slaves, the Spanish settlement San Miguel de Gualdape (Tiera de Ayllón), situated between South Carolina's Pee Dee River and Georgia's Sapelo Island, is doomed, so the Spaniards sail away. There are no records of what happened to the fleeing Africans, but an indigenous group likely welcomed them. Legends will abound about "Black Indians" who do not fit neatly into America's racial categories. These groups will include the Brass Ankles of South Carolina, the descendants of runaway African slaves, white indentured servants, and Native Americans; and the 55,000 Lumbees of North Carolina, who will speak a unique English dialect and comprise the largest tribe east of the Mississippi River. The Lumbees will struggle in the 21st century for full recognition by the U.S. Congress.

### Bewitched?

1692: **Mary Black, a slave from Africa, is accused of witchcraft during the Salem witch trials.** She is arrested, indicted, imprisoned, and examined. When asked to re-pin her neckcloth, she does, and several people in the room cry out, claiming they have been pricked and are bleeding. Mary will be released on January 21, 1693, when no one comes forward to accuse her.

1922: **Charles Mingus Jr. is born** in Nogales, AZ.

# April

## 23

### The Black Edison

1856: **Granville T. Woods is born** in Columbus, OH. He will be nicknamed the "Black Thomas Edison." During his lifetime, he will secure more than 65 patents for electrical, communication, and mechanical devices, among them an electric rollercoaster, which he will first demonstrate at New York's Coney Island; the third rail, which will power trains without the need for exposed wires or batteries; automatic air brakes; and the railway telegraph.

## 24

1979: Ray Charles's song **"Georgia on My Mind,"** released in 1960, is decreed the **official state song of Georgia.** He performs it at the state capitol ceremony.

Ray Charles Plaza in Albany, GA, where he was born. The revolving, illuminated, bronze statue of Ray Charles is seated at a baby grand piano. Water flows down the sides of the statue as music by Charles plays on plaza loudspeakers.

## 25

Ella Fitzgerald ca 1946

1917: **Ella Fitzgerald is born** in Newport News, VA. She will become known as the First Lady of Song.

Ella Fitzgerald "A-Tisket-A-Tasket"

## UNITED NEGRO COLLEGE FUND
"A mind is a terrible thing to waste."

1944: The **United Negro College Fund is founded** by Frederick D. Patterson, then president of what will become Tuskegee University, college founder Mary McLeod Bethune, and others. In 1972 it will launch what will become one of the most widely recognized slogans in advertising history: "A mind is a terrible thing to waste." By 2023, the organization will raise $5 billion, helping more than a half-million students earn college degrees.

# Weekly Planner

**WEEK OF**_____

**SUNDAY**

**MONDAY**

**TUESDAY**

UNITED NEGRO
COLLEGE FUND
"A mind is a terrible thing to waste."

**WEDNESDAY**

**THURSDAY**

**FRIDAY**

**SATURDAY**

## 26

Soniakapadia

2018: The **National Memorial for Peace and Justice** (also called the National Lynching Memorial) opens in downtown Montgomery, AL, to commemorate the Black victims of lynching in the U.S. The Washington Post describes it as "one of the most powerful and effective new memorials created in a generation."

2012: The **Jim Crow Museum of Racist Memorabilia** opens on the campus of Ferris State University, telling a powerful story of oppression in the U.S. through a collection of 10,000 artifacts. Its mission is to use objects of intolerance to teach lessons of tolerance and to promote social justice.

## 27

Coretta Scott King in 1964

1927: **Coretta Scott King is born,** the third of four children, in Heiberger, AL, in her parents' home, with her paternal great-grandmother Delia Scott, a former slave, as midwife. Coretta will marry Martin Luther King Jr., and play a prominent role in the Civil Rights Movement of the 1960s. She will become friends with powerful politicians before and after her husband's assassination, among them Presidents John F. Kennedy and Lyndon B. Johnson. She will be creditedfor getting Black voters to the polls due to her telephone conversation with John F. Kennedy during the 1960 presidential campaign.

1945: **August Wilson** (Frederick August Kittel Jr.) **is born** in Pittsburgh, PA.

2023: **Fort Lee, VA, is renamed Fort Gregg-Adams,** honoring two Black officers, Lt. Gen. Arthur J. Gregg, the U.S. Army's first Black lieutenant general, and Lt. Col. Charity Adams, who led the first predominantly Black Women's Army Corps unit—**the storied 6888th (or Six Triple Eight)** Central Postal Directory Battalion, stationed in Europe during World War II, where it processed 17+ million pieces of mostly backlogged mail for military personnel. The military base is the first named for African Americans.

## 28

1967: **Muhammad Ali is stripped of his heavyweight boxing title** for refusing to be inducted into the U.S. Army. Ali, who is Muslim, cites religious reasons for his refusal.

The Passion of Muhammad Ali

**Scan to read full Esquire issue (Subscription needed)**

**Read the Story Behind Muhammad Ali's famous magazine cover**

## 29

1899: Edward Kennedy **Duke Ellington is born** in Washington, DC. He will write his first musical composition, "Soda Fountain Rag," in 1914 while working as a soda jerk. Three years later, he will become a sign painter and form his first group, The Duke's Serenaders, taking home 75 cents on his first play date. It will be the start of a long and fabulous career as a band leader. He will write or collaborate on more than 1,000 compositions and become a seminal, inventive, and charismatic figure in music history.

Admiral Michelle Howard, commander, U.S. Naval Forces Europe-Africa, returns a salute from Rear Adm. Thomas Ishee, as he assumes command of Submarine Group 8, during the Submarine Group 8 change of command ceremony at Naval Support Activity in Naples, Italy.

### Admiral Michelle Howard: Making Naval History

1960: **Michelle J. Howard is born** at March Air Force Base in California. She will achieve many firsts: the first African American woman to command a U.S. Navy ship, the USS Rushmore; the first Black woman to achieve two- and three-star rank; the first woman four-star admiral in U.S. Naval history; and the first to command operational forces—U.S. Naval Forces Europe and Naval Forces Africa. She will play a major role in rescuing Captain Richard Phillips, who is kidnapped by Somali pirates (the subject of a Hollywood film). In 2014, Admiral Michelle Howard will be appointed the 38th Vice Chief of Naval Operations, becoming the Navy's second-highest-ranking officer. In 2021, she will be sworn in as chair of the commission charged with recommending the removal of Confederate monuments from U.S. bases and renaming those bases named for Confederate soldiers.

May

SUN MON TUE WED THU FRI SAT

Frederick Douglass

# *May*

**WEEK 1**

_____
_____
_____
_____

**WEEK 2**

_____
_____
_____
_____

**WEEK 3**

_____
_____
_____

**WEEK 4**

_____
_____
_____
_____

**WEEK 5**

_____
_____
_____
_____

ALMOST ALWAYS, THE
CREATIVE DEDICATED
MINORITY HAS MADE THE
WORLD BETTER.
  MARTIN LUTHER KING JR.

**MAJOR**

**MINOR**

**HABIT TRACKER**     S   M   T   W   T   F   S

_____
_____
_____

**MISC**

# To-Do List

Date:

# NOTES

# Weekly Planner

_____ **WEEK OF** _____

**SUNDAY**

**MONDAY**

**TUESDAY**

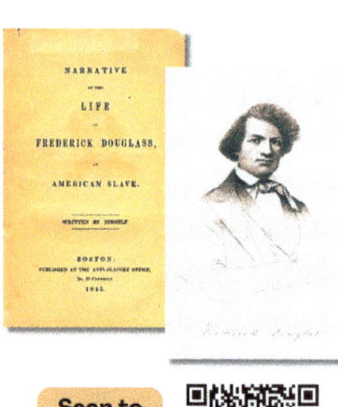

**WEDNESDAY**

Scan to read entire book (free)

**THURSDAY**

Scan to hear entire audiobook (free)

**FRIDAY**

**SATURDAY**

1

**1845: "Narrative of the Life of Frederick Douglass, an American Slave" is published** seven years after his escape. Douglass wrote the first of his three autobiographical narratives to demonstrate to skeptics that a slave could become an articulate orator and spokesman. The autobiography tells a powerful story of cruelty, violence, and oppression, recounting his life as a slave, his time with a "negro-breaker" who breaks the will of slaves, and Douglass's struggle for freedom. By 1860, 30,000 copies will be sold. Out of fear of being captured and re-enslaved, Douglass will sail to England and Ireland, where supporters will put up $710.96 to purchase his freedom. A neighbor of Douglass's former enslaver will criticize the book, describing Douglass as "an unlearned, and rather an ordinary negro," and doubting that he is the actual author. Others will admire the book and its author. Douglass will write two more autobiographies. (See below.)

Scan to read biography #2

Scan to read biography #3

### Slave as Author and Historian

By 1944, more than 6,000 formerly enslaved people will contribute to a new genre of American literature, the slave narrative; 150 of them will be published as books or pamphlets. The Workers Progress Administration, a New Deal agency, will collect and publish some 2,300 oral histories about life during slavery. These books and oral histories will be considered more than autobiographies; they will also serve as resources for reconstructing history. History, for them, is remembrance.

### Blacks Hold the First Memorial Day Service

1865: Three weeks after the surrender of Confederate General Robert E. Lee and two weeks after President Abraham Lincoln was assassinated, about 10,000 freed African Americans turn out at a former racetrack in Charleston, SC, to celebrate what may have been the nation's first Memorial Day celebration. They hold a parade led by 2,800 Black schoolchildren and place flowers on the unmarked graves of the 257 Union soldiers who helped free them. The Union soldiers were buried without coffins at the horse track, which had been converted into an outdoor prison for captured Union soldiers. The ceremony will not end until sundown, and mounds of flowers will cover the burial grounds. For more than a century, white Southerners will try to erase this ceremony from public memory. Southerners will gather at the graves of Rebel soldiers. On May 5, 1868, General John A. Logan will order the first national public holiday, celebrated on May 30, to honor war dead: Decoration Day.

1950: **Gwendolyn Brooks becomes the first African American to win the Pulitzer Prize** in any category. She wins the poetry award for her "Annie Allen" narrative published in 1949.

Scan to hear Gwendolyn Brooks read her poetry.

1971: Singer-songwriter **Bill Withers releases his debut album** on Sussex Records. It features "Ain't No Sunshine," which will rank high on lists of the greatest songs of all time. He wrote the song at age 31 when he worked in a factory making toilets for 747 airplanes. Even with a hit song, he refused to leave his job because he thought the music business was fickle. The song reached No. 6 on the U.S. R&B charts and was the first of his three gold records.

Scan to hear Bill Withers's debut album

1933: **James Brown is born** in Barnwell, SC.

1812: **Paul Cuffe meets with President James Madison at the White House.** They discuss the growing hostilities between the U.S. and Great Britain and the transatlantic emigration of African Americans to Africa. Cuffe is widely thought to be the first Black American to lead a Back-to-Africa effort. He is also likely the first person of color to formally meet with a sitting U.S. President.

**Scan to read the White House account**

**Cape Act**

**James Brown & The Famous Flames in a legendary performance** at the T.A.M.I. show (Teenage Awards Music International) in Santa Monica, CA, in 1964. Brown will later call it the "highest energy" performance of his career, saying, "I danced so hard my manager cried." This is reportedly the first time he used his "cape act," during which he drops to his knees, on the verge of collapse, and his valet drapes a cape over Brown's shoulders. Brown recovers and continues his passionate performance with abandonment. No one could outperform him. The Rolling Stones is the follow-up act. Lead guitarist Keith Richards will later comment that following James Brown was the biggest mistake of the Stones' career.

1891: **Daniel Hale Williams**, the son of a barber, founds the 12-bed Provident Hospital and Training School for Nurses, the first African-American-owned and -operated hospital in the U.S.

1961: **The first busload of Freedom Riders leaves Washington, D.C. for New Orleans,** intent on challenging segregated seating in the South by riding in interracial pairings and risking organized violence en route. From May to December, 436 people participate in 60 Freedom Rides; a bus is firebombed; 300 Riders are arrested; mobs of Ku Klux Klan members and their supporters brutally beat Riders with bats and pipes; many are shot at, jailed, and hospitalized.

Public Domain | Tommy Langston, Birmingham Post-Herald

A mob of racists beats Freedom Riders in Birmingham, AL, 1961

# Weekly Planner

WEEK OF

SUNDAY

MONDAY

TUESDAY

WEDNESDAY

THURSDAY

FRIDAY

SATURDAY

James Brown's silk and satin cape

Collection of the Smithsonian National Museum of African American History and Culture

May 1892: Composer **W.T. Talbert gives two recitals at Carnegie Hall,** becoming the first African American to perform there. A band of Black performers joins him. Little is known about Talbert, but the Carnegie Hall archivist believes he may have been Thad Talbert, the brother-in-law of Mary Burnett Talbert, a founder of the NAACP.

1905: **Robert S. Abbott publishes the first edition of The Chicago Defender,** which he founded with an initial investment of 25 cents and a press run of 300 copies. It will become the first Black publication with more than 10,000 readers. Abbott will herald it as "The World's Greatest Weekly."

May 1937: The first **Negro Motorist Green-Book is published** by African American mailman Victor Hugo Green. The book, which sells for 25 cents, is **a guidebook and veritable bible for Black (and all other non-white) travelers during the Jim Crow era.** It contains information on lodgings, businesses, gas stations, and auto repair shops that serve African Americans. Black travelers face a multitude of hardships and open racial discrimination because white-owned hotels, restaurants, and repair shops refuse to serve them. There is also the possibility of physical violence in whites-only "sundown towns," municipalities/neighborhoods that "colored people" must leave by sundown. **The Green Book, which will be published yearly until 1966, opens a pathway through a parallel universe, one where racial discrimination ceases to exist or is limited temporarily.**

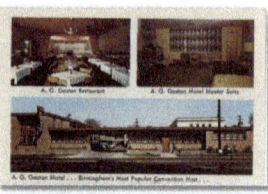

Postcard of the A. G. Gaston Motel in Birmingham, Alabama, circa 1960-1969.

### Southern Refuge

1954: The AG Gaston Motel in Birmingham, AL, a 32-room luxury motel with air-conditioned rooms and wall-to-wall carpeting, built by its namesake as a safe haven for Blacks in the segregated South, will soon open. Many famous guests will find refuge here, including Aretha Franklin, Harry Belafonte, Nat King Cole, and honeymooners Colin and Alma Powell. It will serve as a meeting place for civil rights leaders.

**Scan to see the A.G. Gaston Motel and more**

# May

## 8

1911: **Robert Johnson is born** in Hazelhurst, MS. He will become a legendary blues musician and composer and make landmark recordings of 29 songs in 1936 and 1937 that will influence generations of musicians. His songs will become blues standards. He will die of unknown causes at age 27 on August 16, 1938. Much about him will remain a mystery. (See the next page to hear his music.)

### Hair Like Mine

2009: Jacob Philadelphia's father, Carlton, a former Marine, is leaving the White House staff after serving a two-year stint on the National Security Council, starting in the Bush administration. The family asks for a family photograph with President Obama. The pictures are taken, but as the family is about to leave, Mr. Philadelphia tells President Obama that his son has a question, but he doesn't know what the question is. Jacob, then, speaks up …

**Jacob:** "I want to know if my hair is just like yours."

**Barack Obama:** "Why don't you touch it and see for yourself?" (Obama lowers his head; the boy hesitates.)

**Obama:** "Touch it, dude!" (The boy pats Obama's head.)

**Obama:** "So what do you think?"

**Jacob:** "Yes, it does feel the same."

Pete Souza, White House photographer

Oval Office, May 8, 2009 at 3:03 p.m.

## 9

1897: **Rudolph Fisher is born** in Washington, D.C. He will be an all-around talent and leading figure during the Harlem Renaissance—**physician, radiologist, scientific researcher, musician, composer, orator, short story writer, and dramatist.** (He will nickname his son Hugh "the New Negro.") In 1932, **Dr. Fisher will write the first detective novel with a Black detective,** "The Conjure-Man Dies," a murder mystery set in Harlem.

## 10

Anthony Barboza

1944: **Anthony Barboza is born** in New Bedford, MA. He will be a photographer, historian, artist, and writer, producing a range of traditional and innovative works that will be exhibited in galleries, national and international museums, and universities. In 1963, he will move to NYC to study photography, join the Kamoinge Workshop of Black photographers, begin a successful commercial career in fashion, journalism, and advertising, and pursue artistic endeavors. He will train a new generation of Black photographers.

Scan right to see photos

# Weekly Planner

WEEK OF_____

**SUNDAY**

**MONDAY**

**TUESDAY**

**Scan right to read Robert Johnson's obituary in the NY Times**

**WEDNESDAY**

**THURSDAY**

**FRIDAY**

*Downing Oyster jar*

**SATURDAY**

# May

## 11

1826: **Martin Henry Freeman is born** in Rutland, VT. In 1856, he will become the first African American president of a college, the Allegheny Institute (later Avery College), in Pittsburgh, PA. He was the second African American to graduate from Middlebury College in the class of 1849. In 1864, he moved to Liberia and served as president of Liberia College.

Marion S. Trikosko, Library of Congress

Bomb-damaged trailers at the Gaston Motel in Birmingham

### "Bombingham"

1963: After a May 10th compromise is announced between Birmingham, AL, white business owners, city officials, and civil rights leaders establishing a timeline to desegregate the city, segregationists respond with bombings. The bombings will set off weeks of protests across the nation.

Scan to see bombings captured in photographs

**There are 50 dynamite explosions in Birmingham between 1947 and 1965**

## 12

THOMAS DOWNING

1825: **Thomas Downing opens the luxurious Oyster House** in the heart of New York's financial district, creating New York's fine dining industry and restaurant culture two years before the opening of Delmonico, the Italian restaurant erroneously credited as the first fine dining establishment in the nation. Downing's waiters, armed with oyster knives and with towels draped over their arms, serve today's catch to a clientele of power brokers, aristocrats, and socialites in a fancy establishment decorated with damask curtains, gilded mirrors, and a crystal chandelier. The menu includes raw, fried, or stewed oysters, oyster pie, fine wine, and more. Downing will even ship oysters to England's Queen Victoria, who will send him a gold watch. He will also live an incredible double life. Beneath the fancy floorboards of Oyster House, not far from the wine cellar, Downing will operate a station of the Underground Railroad, hiding runaway slaves on their way to Canada and freedom.

Scan to read "The Double Life of New York's Black Oyster King"

*In 1842, as king of an oyster empire, Downing will cater the legendary Boz Ball, a multimillion-dollar feast in honor of Charles Dickens. Ball guests will consume 28,000 stewed oysters and 10,000 pickled oysters. Also, as one of the city's wealthiest men, he will save the New York Herald from financial ruin by loaning its owner $10,000.*

## 13

1862: **Robert Smalls, a 23-year-old slave, steals the Confederate ship Planter,** a steamer with a cargo of unmounted guns, in broad daylight from the dock in front of a Confederate general's home and office, **freeing 17 people—himself, his crew, and their families—from slavery.** He pilots the ship through a U.S. blockade of Charleston Harbor and into a Union-controlled enclave, where it will become a Union warship. This heroic act helps to convince President Lincoln to accept 5,000 Black recruits into the Union Army. Smalls himself will fight in 17 battles. After the Civil War, Smalls will return to Beaufort, SC, and be elected to the South Carolina Legislature. He will serve five terms in the U.S. Congress during the Reconstruction era and publish the Beaufort Southern Standard newspaper.

*"Good morning, sir! I've brought you some of the old United States guns, sir!"*
Robert Smalls, upon delivering a heavily armed Confederate ship to the Union Navy

## Freedom Riders Attacked, Bus Firebombed

1961: A Greyhound bus carrying Freedom Riders arrives at the Anniston, AL, bus station just after 1 p.m. The building is locked. Fifty men wielding bats, chains, and pipes appear, led by Ku Klux Klan leader William Chapel. They smash the bus windows, dent the bus, and slash its tires. Police are not at the scene, though police had been warning of a possible attack. The attackers ease up, and local police finally appear. They escort the bus to the Anniston city limit and then leave. More attackers materialize. They surround the bus and bash in windows as two highway patrolmen watch from a distance. The Freedom Riders refuse to deboard. Someone throws a firebomb through a window into the bus. The mob barricades the doors, trapping passengers inside the burning bus. The fuel tank explodes and some in the mob flee. Freedom Riders can finally escape, climbing out windows and rushing through the doors. The remaining members of the mob beat some.

Igbo Landing at Dunbar Creek

## The Flying Africans: Birth of the Legend

May 1803: A shipload of Africans, many of them Igbo people from present-day Nigeria, survive the Middle Passage and land in Savannah, GA, where they are auctioned off at a slave market. About 75 Igbo are purchased by enslavers, including U.S. Congressman Thomas Spalding, for $100 each. The slaves are chained and packed aboard the schooner York bound for Dunbar Creek on St. Simon's Island. But during the voyage, the Igbo tribesmen seize control of the ship, throw the crew overboard, and ground the ship in Dunbar Creek. Once ashore, the Igbo chief among them directs them to choose the protection of their god, Chukwu, over the living death of slavery. They walk hand-in-hand into the marshy waters, singing in the Igbo language, "The Water Spirit brought us, the Water Spirit will take us home." A dozen or so drown; some of the survivors are brought to Spalding's Sapelo Island plantation. (In 1830, Spalding will own 400 slaves.) This act of resistance will form the basis of the Flying Africans, the legend of enslaved Africans who could lift up and fly away—a story of escape from a life of slavery and a source of imagination that will find its way into spirituals and African American literature.

1872: **P.B.S. Pinchback becomes the first African American governor** in the United States, serving as governor of Louisiana for 35 days.

May 1962: **Herbie Hancock,** 22-year-old jazz pianist, keyboardist, and composer, **records his song "Watermelon Man"** for his debut album "Takin' Off." The 7-minute, 9-second song was inspired by the memory of a watermelon seller whose horse-drawn wagon ran over the streets of Chicago in the 1940s. "I'd heard the rhythmic clacking so many times, it was easy to turn it into a song pattern," he explains. "I wrote out a funky arrangement, with the melody lilting over a rhythmic pattern that represented the wagon wheels going over the cobblestones in the alley." The song will inspire a new music genre. On December 17, 1962, Cuban conga drummer Mongo Santamaria's band will record a three-minute, radio-friendly cover of "Watermelon Man," which will launch Latin boogaloo— the fusion of African American R&B rhythms and soul music with mambo and son montuno. In 1973, Hancock will record a funky version of the song for his "Head Hunters" album.

"Watermelon Man" 1962

"Watermelon Man / Head Hunters" 1973

Lawyers George E.C. Hayes, left, Thurgood Marshall, center, and James M. Nabrit outside the U.S. Supreme Court in Washington, D.C.

1875: Black jockey **Oliver Lewis** (above) **races H. Price McGrath's colt Aristides to victory** before a crowd of 10,000 spectators **at the first Kentucky Derby, winning $2,850 in prize money** for the horse's owner. Fourteen of the fifteen jockeys in the first Derby are African American. Lewis's winning time—2 minutes, 37.75 seconds—sets an American record for the 1.5-mile distance (which will be shortened to 1.25 miles in 1896). **Black jockeys will win 15 of the first 28 Derbys.**

Above: Jockey and horse trainer **James "Jimmy" Winkfield.** He will win the Kentucky Derby in 1901 and 1902 on His Eminence and Alan-a-Dale, respectively. **In 1901 alone, he will win 220 races.**

1954: The **U.S. Supreme Court rules in Brown v. Board** of Education of Topeka that racial segregation of children in public school is unconstitutional. At around 1 p.m., Chief Justice Earl Warren reads the Court's unanimous opinion aloud: "In the field of public education, the doctrine of 'separate but equal' has no place. Separate educational facilities are inherently unequal." The Court had listened to both sides argue for three days in December 1952 and reargue for three more days a year later. Thurgood Marshall, chief attorney for the plaintiffs, said: "In order to arrive at the decision that [the segregationsists] want us to arrive at, there would have to be some recognition of a reason why of all the multitudinous groups of people in this country you have to single out Negroes and give them this separate treatment. It can't be because of slavery in the past, because there are very few groups in this country that haven't had slavery someplace back in the history of their groups. It can't be color, because there are Negroes as white as the drifted snow, with blue eyes, and they are just as segregated as the colored man. The only thing it can be is an inherent determination that the people who were formerly in slavery, regardless of anything else, shall be kept as near that stage as is possible, and now is the time, we submit, that this Court should make it clear that that is not what our Constitution stands for." At the justices' private conference following the reargument, Warren challenged any fellow justice who believed Blacks were inferior to say so openly, and if no one would, he wanted a unanimous opinion. That is what he got for the first major decision of the Warren Court.

James Baldwin 1964

**1953: James Baldwin's masterpiece, the semi-autobiographical novel "Go Tell It on the Mountain,"** is published. It focuses on John Grimes and his experiences inside and outside the storefront church where his domineering father preaches. The story takes place within 24 hours, but the narrative voice shifts, moving through the recollections of others—John's mother, father, and aunt—over 70 years. Baldwin's novel is rich with biblical and religious references and full of tension and conflict involving poverty, race, violence, stigmas on sexuality, guilt, and spiritual awakening.

Scan to download free PDF of the book

2017: **Jean-Michel Basquiat's "Untitled"** (1982), an outlined skull against a blue background, **sells at a New York auction for $110.5 million.** It becomes the most expensive painting for a work by an American artist, by an African American artist, and the first work created after 1980 to sell for more than $100 million. Basquiat—who died at 27, six years after painting "Untitled"—joins the $100 million artists' club, which includes Picasso, Modigliani, Bacon, Munch, Warhol, and Giacometti.

# Weekly Planner

**WEEK OF**

**SUNDAY**

**MONDAY**

**TUESDAY**

**WEDNESDAY**

**THURSDAY**

**FRIDAY**

**SATURDAY**

# May

## 19

**1925: Malcolm X** (Malcolm Little) **is born** in Omaha, NE. The day will become an official holiday in Berkeley, CA, in 1979, with city offices and schools closed.

**1930: Lorraine Hansberry is born** in Chicago, IL. She will write the play "A Raisin in the Sun," which will open at the Ethel Barrymore Theatre on March 11, 1959. The first play produced on Broadway by an African American woman, it will have a run of 530 performances.

**2019: Robert F. Smith,** commencement speaker at Morehouse College, **announces to the nearly 400 graduating seniors that he will pay off their student loans, a gift that amounts to $34 million.** Smith, a billionaire technology investor and philanthropist, encourages the graduates to take his gift and pay it forward. Later, he will expand his philanthropy to include paying off the debts of those Morehouse graduates' family members. The gift is reportedly one of the largest philanthropic gifts made by an individual to a single institution in U.S. history.

> **Robert F. Smith's pledge**

## 20

**1865: Emancipation Day is celebrated in Tallahassee,** FL, 11 days after the end of the Civil War.

**"Little Red Corvette"**

1982: Accustomed to holding round-the-clock recording sessions in his basement studio to record his steady stream of musical ideas, **Prince** layers synth sounds over a drum machine beat and **captures the basic tracks for "Little Red Corvette."** Dez Dickerson then overdubs a guitar solo (which Guitar World magazine will later rank among the all-time best). The song, a euphemism for sex with a "much too fast" woman, will be released in the U.S. on February 9, 1983, and become the crossover hit he had been seeking.

## 21

**1955: Chuck Berry records "Maybellene."** It will sell over a million copies and reach No. 1 on the R&B charts. He will record "Roll Over Beethoven" in 1956, "Rock and Roll Music" in 1957, and "Johnny B. Goode" in 1958, and will be nicknamed the "Father of Rock and Roll." In 1977, NASA will immortalize "Johnny B. Goode" by launching it into space aboard both Voyager 1 and Voyager 2 to potentially entertain alien life forms.

**1971: Marvin Gaye's landmark album "What's Going On" is released** by Motown Records' subsidiary label Tamla. It is his 11th album, with songs that segue into others.

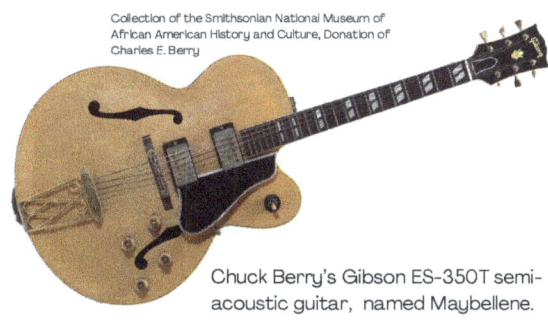

Collection of the Smithsonian National Museum of African American History and Culture, Donation of Charles E. Berry

Chuck Berry's Gibson ES-350T semi-acoustic guitar, named Maybellene.

# May

## 22

1848: **Lewis Temple, an African American blacksmith in the world's whaling capital, New Bedford, MA, invents a harpoon with a movable head: the Toggle-Iron** (later called Temple's Iron). It will be the single most important invention in the history of whaling and will capture a far greater proportion of whales struck by a harpoon than ever before.

1863: **The U.S. War Department issues General Order No. 143 establishing the Bureau of Colored Troops to recruit African American soldiers to fight for the Union Army.** Frederick Douglass will write a broadside calling all "men of color to arms." His sons will volunteer. A former slave named William Henry Singleton will help recruit 1,000 former slaves in New Bern, NC, for the First North Carolina Colored Volunteers. (Singleton will become a sergeant in the 35th U.S. Colored Troops.) About 175 regiments will be formed—including infantry, cavalry, engineers, light artillery, and heavy artillery units, together comprised of 179,000 free Blacks and formerly enslaved men, one-tenth of the Union army's manpower. Slightly more than 20 percent of these Black soldiers—some 36,000—will be killed in action, a mortality rate that is 35 percent higher than that of other troops. Sixteen Black soldiers will win the Medal of Honor.

## 23

1921: The jazz musical **"Shuffle Along" opens** at the 63rd Street Music Hall in NYC, bringing "electricity" to the sound of Broadway, per a New York Times writer in 2023, and putting sweat-inducing dance numbers on stage as never before. The show, with music composed by Eubie Blake and lyrics by Noble Sissle, will run for 504 performances, create curtain-time traffic jams, and launch the careers of legendary performers, including Josephine Baker, Florence Mills, Fredi Washington, Paul Robeson, and Adelaide Hall. (Author Caseen Gaines will note that one of its songs, "I'm Just Wild About Harry," will even help reelect a U.S. President.) "Shuffle" will change musical theater forever, bringing heart-stomping, toe-tapping, proto-jazz numbers to the Great White Way and establishing a "default musical style" for Broadway shows, according to the Times writer.

## 24

1797: Highly skilled **potter Thomas W. Commeraw opens the only Black-owned pottery business in Corlears Hook, a New York City neighborhood** just south of the present-day Williamsburg Bridge. He will turn out thousands of stoneware jars and jugs for storing beer, molasses, cider, preserves, milk, butter, salted meats, and pickled oysters. He will be among the first potters, if not the first, to stamp his work with his name and shop location, an early example of branding other potters will adopt as a standard feature. His competitors will include the descendant of Commeraw's former enslaver, a master potter. Commeraw's crescent- and bellflower-stamped vessels, painted with cobalt oxide, will reach South America, Europe, and Africa. Some will be traded for kidnapped Africans as his forebears had been bought with goods. His Black identity will be lost to history for almost two centuries due to the misspelling of his name as "Commerau" in city records. It will be assumed he was a craftsman of French descent until 2003, when a researcher comes across his name and race in a census.

# Weekly Planner

WEEK OF_____

**SUNDAY**

**MONDAY**

**TUESDAY**

**WEDNESDAY**

**THURSDAY**

**FRIDAY**

**SATURDAY**

Jesse Owens sets a world record in the 200-meter dash: 20.3 seconds

### 45 Greatest Minutes in Sports History

1935: **Jesse Owens,** the 21-year-old Ohio State University athlete, **averages a new world record every nine minutes**. He **sets five world records and ties a sixth in just 45 minutes** at the annual intercollegiate championship meet. This feat will go down in history as the greatest 45 minutes in sports.

1965: **Muhammad Ali and Sonny Liston meet for the second time for the heavyweight boxing title**, this time in Lewiston, ME. The knock-out is one of the fastest in heavyweight title history. The referee, former heavyweight champ Jersey Joe Walcott, later says: "[Ali] looked like a man in a different world. I didn't know what he might do. I thought he might stomp [Liston] or pick him up and belt him again."

Miles Davis

### Birth of the Cool

1926: **Miles Davis is born** in Alton, IL. He will become one of the most important jazz innovators in history, changing the course of jazz several times.

1956: **Althea Gibson wins at the French Open,** becoming the first Black athlete to triumph in a Grand Slam tournament.

### Who Cooked Up the Chitlin Circuit?

During 1911: Vaudeville performer Sherman Dudley establishes S.H. Dudley Theatrical Enterprises, the first Black vaudeville circuit, by buying and leasing theaters in Washington, D.C., Virginia, and, the following year, Baltimore. By 1914, the Dudley Circuit will consist of over 20 entertainment venues, "all owned and operated by blacks as far south as Atlanta." It will thrive until the white-owned-and-managed Theater Owners Booking Association (TOBA) out-competes Dudley in southern states. Dudley will sell his venues to TOBA, whose business will eventually plummet during the Great Depression. Two siblings, Denver and Sea Ferguson, will then directly book Black artists for a national network of venues: the Chitlin Circuit. It will cater to Black audiences, provide work Black artists couldn't get in white-owned venues, and launch the careers of many legendary Black performers. Chitlins will be the meal of choice.

Sherman Dudley 1900

Denver Ferguson 1950s.

# May

## 28

1970s: Fashion designer **Stephen Burrows invents the lettuce hem** by mistake when his assistant overstretches a jersey hem. Burrows likes the look and makes it his signature element. He will use it in bright-colored garments that drape unconventionally, have stretched edges, and are cut at various angles. Burrows will become the first Black fashion designer to sell internationally.

## 29

1851: **Sojourner Truth delivers her speech "Ain't I a Woman?"** at the Women's Rights Convention in Akron, OH.

**Scan to compare speech versions**

## 30

**Stepin Fetchit: Racial Stereotype ... or Trickster?**

1902: **Lincoln Perry, who will be known by his stage name Stepin Fetchit, is born** in Key West, FL. He will adopt the stage name as a contraction of "step and fetch it," a lucky racehorse he supposedly bet on. During an era rife with derogatory black-face, he will be the first Black actor to become a millionaire and the first to receive a screen credit. His shuffling, bumbling character will epitomize the laziest man in the world and be ridiculed as a racial stereotype. But years later, some will regard his screen persona as a trickster who plays dumb to forfeit responsibility, disobey authority, and escape backlash.

## 31

May 31-June 1, 1921: The **Tulsa Race Riot takes place** in Tulsa, OK. In two days, 800+ people will be treated for injuries, 100-300 people will be massacred, 35 city blocks will lay in ruins, and Tulsa's thriving Black Wall Street district will be destroyed.

# June

| SUN | MON | TUE | WED | THU | FRI | SAT |
| --- | --- | --- | --- | --- | --- | --- |
| | | | | | | |
| | | | | | | |
| | | | | | | |
| | | | | | | |
| | | | | | | |

Harriet Tubman

# June

**WEEK 1**

_____

_____

_____

_____

**WEEK 2**

_____

_____

_____

_____

**WEEK 3**

_____

_____

_____

**WEEK 4**

_____

_____

_____

_____

**WEEK 5**

_____

_____

_____

_____

**IN RECOGNIZING THE
HUMANITY OF OUR
FELLOW BEINGS, WE
PAY OURSELVES THE
HIGHEST TRIBUTE.
THURGOOD MARSHALL**

**MAJOR**

**MINOR**

**HABIT TRACKER**       S   M   T   W   T   F   S

**MISC**

# To-Do List

Date:

# NOTES

# Weekly Planner

**WEEK OF**_____

**SUNDAY**

**MONDAY**

**TUESDAY**

**WEDNESDAY**

**THURSDAY**

**FRIDAY**

**SATURDAY**

Missy Elliott - The Rain (Supa Dupa Fly) [Official Music Video]

**Supa Dupa Debut**

**1980: CNN debuts with Bernard Shaw as chief anchor.** He will co-anchor three newscasts daily and become CNN's first chief anchor. His coverage of the attempted assassination of President Ronald Reagan in 1981 will put CNN on the map as a worthy news source. At the beginning of the Persian Gulf War, Shaw, a Vietnam veteran and former Marine corporal, will report from a Baghdad hotel room as CNN broadcasts live footage of airstrikes and anti-aircraft fire. "I've never been there," he will say, "but this feels like we're in the center of hell." Years later, he will tell an interviewer: "In all of the years of preparing to being anchor, one of the things I strove for was to be able to control my emotions in the midst of hell breaking out. And I personally feel that I passed my stringent test for that in Baghdad."

## Tubman Leads the Combahee Raid

**1863: Harriet Tubman leads Union soldiers in the Combahee Ferry Raid, becoming the first woman to lead a major U.S. military operation,** a lightning raid to free slaves in the breadbasket of the Confederacy. Tubman guides Union gunboats through mine-filled waters and comes ashore at dawn with 150 African American troops to rescue 756 slaves from South Carolina plantations, transport them to freedom, set fire to buildings and granaries, destroying 10,000 bushels of rice while dodging bullets fired by Confederate soldiers and the slave owner. She falls and tears her dress but doesn't lose a man. Many of the former slaves will join the Union Army. The Combahee Raid causes millions of dollars in damage, lays waste to nine plantations, including some of the South's grandest, strikes terror into the heart of the Confederacy, and underscores the prowess of Black troops. Tubman's raid will go down in history as having freed the most enslaved African Americans at any one time.

1906: **Josephine Baker** —Freda Josephine McDonald—**is born** in St. Louis, MO.

### Birth of "The Rain (Supa Dupa Fly)"

1997: The **Hype Williams-**directed **music video for Missy Elliot's debut single, "The Rain (Supa Dupa Fly)," is released.** Missy's first solo video is styled by **music's "Secretary of Style," June Ambrose,** who pushes the envelope by dressing Missy in a **patent-leather blow-up suit** (it will be mistakenly referred to as a humongous trash bag). As Missy dances, Ambrose stands nearby pumping air into the suit, which has a slow leak. The video captures Missy Elliot's bodacious style. It also pushes the boundaries of music videos while proving Missy can wear a so-called "garbage bag" with more style than many musicians exude in designer wear.

2019: **Jay-Z,** who once rapped, "I'm not a businessman, I'm a business, man," **is now the first hip-hop artist to accumulate a fortune that conservatively totals $1 billion,**\* according to Forbes. His kingdom includes liquor, art, real estate, and stakes in companies like Uber. He has also accumulated 22 Grammy Awards—thus far.

\*Forbes reports Jay-Z is worth $2.5 billion as of January 2025.

# June

## 4

**1940: Charles R. Drew is awarded his Doctor of Science degree** from Columbia University. His research and his dissertation, "Banked Blood: A Study in Blood Preservation," will revolutionize blood storage, standardizing blood collecting, processing, and storage while dramatically increasing the shelf life of plasma. Drew will direct blood collection from 100,000 donors for the U.S. military, saving countless lives during World War II and afterward. But in June 1942, the American Red Cross will announce it would segregate blood collected from African Americans, including Drew's blood. Drew will object, calling the policy insulting and saying there's no scientific evidence of any difference between the blood of different races.

**1967: Twelve Black men (11 athletes, 1 politician) gather for the Muhammad Ali Summit** in East Cleveland to express support for his decision not to serve in the Vietnam War. His boxing license has been revoked, and he faces a possible five-year prison sentence. The summit is an act of courage for participants—they put their careers on the line—and a turning point in sports history as athletes transcend sports to focus public attention on civil rights.

Scan

## 5

1773: George Leile becomes the first African American licensed by the Baptists to preach to slaves in plantations along the Savannah River. He will baptize and convert slaves, form a congregation of 30 members, and cofound the **First African Baptist Church in Savannah, GA.** It will be called the **Mother Church of Black Baptists.** The First African Baptist Church eventually will be led by a slave, Andrew Bryan. He will be severely whipped and imprisoned for preaching to large gatherings, which enslavers suspect are meetings to plot a slave rebellion. Once found innocent and released from prison, Bryan will preach from sunrise to sunset, and the congregation will grow to 69 members in 1788, to over 400 in 1794, and 700 in 1800. On June 1, 1790, with 27 pounds sterling, Bryan, who has secured his freedom, will purchase the land for the new church building. Reverend Bryan will live until age 92.

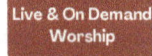

| Visit the Church | Live & On Demand Worship |
|---|---|

## 6

James Meredith pulls himself across Highway 51 after being shot in Hernando, MS. The gunman, Aubrey James Norvell, is visible in the bushes on the left. This photograph will win the 1967 Pulitzer Prize for photography.

1966: Civil Rights activist **James Meredith is shot and wounded** by a sniper just one day into his 220-mile solo "March Against Fear" from Memphis, TN, to Jackson, MS, to inspire Black Mississippians to register to vote and dismantle the culture of fear stirred up by white supremacists.

**Martin Luther King Jr.** and other Civil Rights leaders, including **Stokely Carmichael, continue Meredith's 220-mile march,** registering 4,000 African American voters in the Delta. They will reach Jackson on June 16. **Carmichael will capture the nation's attention using the term "Black Power."**

# Weekly Planner

**WEEK OF**_____

**SUNDAY**

**MONDAY**

First African Baptist Church in Savannah, GA

**TUESDAY**

**WEDNESDAY**

TO THE GLORY OF GOD

THIS BUILDING WAS ERECTED IN 1859 BY THE MEMBERS OF THE CONGREGATION DOING THE WORK THEMSELVES. IT IS RATED EXCELLENT IN ARCHITECTURE AND LISTED IN THE NATIONAL REGISTER OF HISTORIC PLACES.

THIS IS THE FIRST BUILDING CONSTRUCTED OF BRICK IN THE STATE OF GEORGIA OWNED BY BLACKS.

**THURSDAY**

**FRIDAY**

**SATURDAY**

# June

## 7

Photo of the stamp that the United States Postal Service issued in 2012 to commemorate Pulitzer Prize-winning poet Gwendolyn Brooks.

**1917: Gwendolyn Brooks is born** in Topeka, KS.

**1958: Prince** (Prince Rogers Nelson) **is born** in Minneapolis, MN.

## 8

Left to right: Stokely Carmichael, Gwendolyn Green, and Joan Trumpauer Mulholland.

**1961: Freedom Riders are arrested in Jackson, MS, and taken a week later to the notorious Parchman State Penitentiary.** They had traveled from New Orleans to test the enforcement of the Supreme Court's decision in Morgan v. the Commonwealth of Virginia, outlawing segregation in interstate travel. Among those arrested are Stokely Carmichael, Gwendolyn Green, Joan Trumpauer Mulholland, Jan Triggs, Rev. Robert Wesby, Helen Wilson, Terry Perlman, Jane Rosett, and Travis Britt. At one point, 300 Freedom Riders will be imprisoned at Parchman, drawing media attention to their fate and to the inhumane conditions there. Modeled after a southern plantation, the complex extends for tens of thousands of acres and is surrounded by uninhabitable swampland. A visiting lawyer in 1971 will witness conditions and call prisoner treatment at Parchman the last legal vestiges of slavery.

## 9

**2020: Four-star General Charles Q. Brown Jr. is confirmed unanimously by the U.S. Senate to become Chief of Staff of the U.S. Air Force.** He will be the first African American to lead a branch of the U.S. Armed Forces. President Joseph Biden will eventually nominate him as Chairman of the Joint Chiefs of Staff, the highest ranking and most senior military officer in the U.S. Armed Forces and the chief military advisor to the President, the National Security Council, the Homeland Security Council, and the Secretary of Defense. He will be sworn in as the 21st Chairman of the Joint Chiefs of Staff on October 1, 2023.

June 1921: **The Crisis** Magazine, the publication of the NAACP, publishes **Langston Hughes's "The Negro Speaks of Rivers,"** the poem he had written a year earlier on the back of an envelope in 10-15 minutes. It will jumpstart his literary career.

1910: **Howlin' Wolf** (Chester Arthur Burnett) **is born** in White Station, MS. He will grow up on a plantation, and at age 18, his father will give him his first guitar. Howlin' Wolf (the name given to him for killing his grandmother's chicks) will become a protégé of Charley Patton, who is often called the "father of the Delta blues." Wolf will drive to Chicago in 1952, join the Chess Records stable, and develop a legendary rivalry with fellow Mississippian Muddy Waters (see April 4). Wolf will help to transform acoustic Delta blues into electric Chicago blues. He will record blues, rhythm and blues, rock and roll, and psychedelic rock and sing with what will be described as a "sandpaper-growl of a voice." "[N]o one could match Howlin' Wolf for the singular ability to rock the house down to the foundation while simultaneously scaring its patrons out of its wits," musician-critic Cub Koda will write.

1963: **Alabama Governor George Wallace stands defiantly at the door of the University of Alabama** in Tuscaloosa to prevent two Black students, Vivian Malone and James Hood, from enrolling. President John F. Kennedy's administration orders the U.S. Army's 2nd Infantry Division from Fort Benning, GA, to enforce racial integration of the university.

Vivian Malone enters Foster Auditorium to register for classes at the University of Alabama.

Five months earlier, Governor **George Wallace** took his oath of office and delivered his **inaugural address,** promising **"Segregation Forever."**

Archives and Records Services Division, Mississippi Department of Archives and History

1963: **Medgar Evers, a Civil Rights activist, is shot** while emerging from his car at his home in Jackson, MS. He staggers 30 feet, collapses at his door, and is rushed to a hospital, which initially refuses to treat him, but finally does. He dies within the hour. It is the first murder of a nationally known Civil Rights movement leader.

**Medgar and Myrlie Evers Home National Monument**

# June

## 13

Frank Wolfe / LBJ Library

Thurgood Marshall, the great-grandson of a slave and son of a dining car waiter, in the Oval Office with President Lyndon B. Johnson on June 13, 1967.

1967: President **Lyndon B. Johnson nominates Thurgood Marshall to be the nation's first Black U.S. Supreme Court justice.**

> **"Sometimes history takes things into its own hands."**
> *Thurgood Marshall*

Scan to read text

## 14

1916: **Saint Elmo Brady becomes the first African American to receive his doctorate in chemistry,** at the University of Illinois.

"Twenty Whites & One 'Other': St. Elmo Brady, ...

**Ralph Ellison Hears the Tale About a Man Who Could Make Himself Invisible**

1938: **Ralph Ellison interviews Leo Gurley** on the corner of 135th Street and Lenox Avenue in Harlem, who tells **the story of "Sweet-the-monkey,"** a badass man who gave folks hell, escaped Jim Crowism, let the police arrest him and lead him to jail, and then "turn hisself invisible and disappear," leaving them with "nothing but the handcuffs."

## 15

1877: **Henry O. Flipper,** born into slavery in Georgia, **becomes the first African American to graduate from the U.S. Military Academy at West Point.** He will become the first nonwhite officer to lead the Buffalo Soldiers of the U.S. Army's 10th Cavalry.

1921: **Bessie Coleman becomes the first African woman and first Native American to earn a pilot license and the first Black person to earn an international pilot's license.** She will become known as Queen Bess and Brave Bessie and will inspire others to earn their pilot's license.

Bessie Coleman

# Weekly Planner

SUNDAY

MONDAY

TUESDAY

WEDNESDAY

THURSDAY

FRIDAY

SATURDAY

WEED (N)—marijuana, reefers.

WHIPPED UP (ADJ)—worn out, exhausted, beat for your everything.

WREN (N)—a chick, a queen.

WRONG RIFF—saying, or doing the wrong thing. Ex.—"You're coming up on the wrong riff."

Y

YEAH, MAN—an exclamation of assent.

Coming!

## CAB CALLOWAY
and his
## COTTON CLUB ORCHESTRA

*Exclusive Management:*
MILLS ARTISTS, Inc.
799 Seventh Avenue
New York, · N. · Y.

TOGGED TO THE BRICKS—dressed to kill, from head to foot.

TOO MUCH (ADJ)—term of highest praise. Ex.—"You are too much."

TRICKERATION (N)—struttin' your stuff, muggin' lightly and politely.

TRILLY (V)—to leave, to depart. Ex.—"Well, I guess I'll trilly."

TRUCK (V)—to go somewhere. Ex.—"I think I'll truck on down to the gin-mill (bar)."

TRUCKING (N)—a dance introduced at the Cotton Club in 1933.

TWISTER TO THE SLAMMER (N)—the key to the door.

TWO CENTS (N)—two dollars.

U

UNHIP (ADJ)—not wise to the jive, an icky, a jeff, a square.

V

VIPER (N)—one who smokes reefers, a tea-hound.

V-8 (N)—a chick who spurns company, is independent, is not amenable.

W

WHAT'S YOUR STORY?—what do you want, what have you got to say for yourself, how are tricks, or what excuse can you offer? Ex.—"I don't know what his story is".

**Don't igg me. Get hip and collar this jive.**

Cab Calloway's Cat-ologue: a Hepster's Dictionary (June 1938)

# June

## 16

1938: **Cab Calloway,** the first Black American to have a million-record hit, **publishes the first dictionary compiled by an African American**: "Cab Calloway's Cat-ologue: A Hepster's Dictionary." According to the foreword, it contains "colorful and unique words, phrases and expressions employed by Harlem musicians and performers. ..." (More editions will follow.) Cab documented what Black folks ordinarily do with language: stretch it, bend it, break it, and put it back together again, customized just right for Black folks.

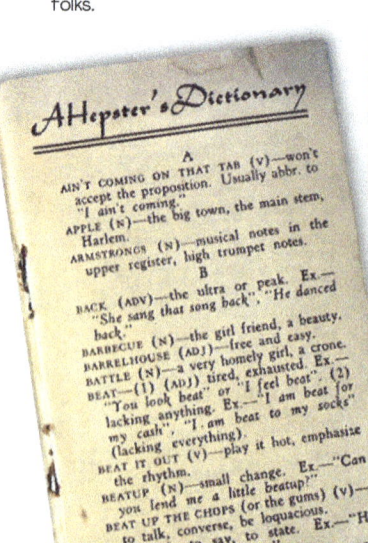

## 17

1775: **Peter Salem, an enslaved patriot, fires the shot that kills British Major John Pitcairn at the Battle of Bunker Hill, according to eyewitnesses.** He will become a Revolutionary War hero, and his owner will grant him his freedom so he can continue to fight in the war.

Venus Williams's debut at the US Open in 1997

1980: **Venus Williams is born** in Lynwood, CA.

1987: **Kendrick Lamar is born** in Compton, CA.

## 18

1953: **Martin Luther King Jr. and Coretta Scott marry** in her childhood home in Marion, AL.

See wedding photos

1967: **Jimi Hendrix performs** many of his most popular songs, including "Purple Haze" and "Hey Joe," at the **Monterey Pop Festival** in Monterey, CA. There are an estimated 10,000-15,000 people in the audience.

Boston News-Letter advertisement,
June 19, 1704

### Newspaper Ties to Slavery

1704: Boston Postmaster John Campbell, founder of the first regularly published American newspaper, places an advertisement in the Boston News-Letter: "A Negro Woman about 16 Years Old, to be Sold by John Campbell Post-master, to be seen at his house next door to the Anchor Tavern." This ad would serve as a template for early American editors, who would fund their newspapers by publishing thousands of slave-brokering ads and connecting buyers with sellers. Benjamin Franklin's Pennsylvania Gazette will publish the following ad: "To be SOLD, A Negro Man Twenty-two Years of Age, of uncommon Strength and Activity, very fit for a Farmer, or a laborious Trade, he understands the best Methods of managing Horses, and is very faithful in the Employment: Any Person that wants such a one may see him by enquiring of the Printer hereofr" [sic]. In the mid-1700s, Franklin will publish at least 277 slave-for-sale ads and earn 90 pounds in brokering fees. He will list himself as broker in 113 of these ads, some of which list the sale of young mothers and children either together or by breaking up the family "as the Buyer pleases."

Scan for more

Courtesy of Nicholls State University

Frank Campbell in a photograph taken in 1906. He was sold in 1838 at age 19 along with 271 other slaves to keep Georgetown University financially afloat.

### University Ties to Slavery

1838: **Jesuit priests sell 272 slaves** from six Maryland plantations to three Louisiana sugar plantations for $115,000 (equivalent to $3.8 million in 2023) **to rescue the Jesuit college now known as Georgetown University from bankruptcy.** Almost 100 of these slaves will survive the Civil War, but all will be lost to history until the 21st century, when the Georgetown Memory Project will rediscover the identities of many. By 2021, **the project will find 11,000 direct descendants of Georgetown slaves, among them actress S. Epatha Merkerson, of television's "Law & Order" fame**. Georgetown University, which will have an endowment of $3.3 billion in 2024, will take steps to atone for the sins of the sale via an apology, philanthropy, a slavery institute, university partnerships, and more. Other universities, including Brown, Harvard, Yale, and the University of Virginia, will publicly acknowledge their ties to slavery. Harvard will pledge $100 million to address its injustices.

Scan to read Harvard's Ties to Slavery

The Galveston Daily News.

### Juneteenth

1865: Major General Gordon Granger arrives in Galveston, TX, with some 2,000 Union troops and **announces that the more than 250,000 enslaved Black people in Texas are free by executive decree.** Their freedom comes two and a half years after President Lincoln's Emancipation Proclamation became official (January 1, 1863). June 19th will become known and celebrated as Juneteenth.

### Keeping Freed People Enslaved

Many white former slave owners in Texas used deceit and violence to force runaways to return and keep Blacks enslaved. Former Confederate soldiers tracked down these runaways, shot them dead, or punished them and returned them to their former owners, though it was illegal to do so.

Temple Cummins (right), enslaved on a Texas plantation, tells the story of how her mother eavesdropped on her master's dinner conversation and learned the slaves had been freed but that **her master refused to inform them so they could harvest "another crop or two."** Upon hearing she was free, Temple's mother ran into the fields to spread the news to 20-40 other slaves, who rejoiced and stopped working. When she returned to get Temple, the master shot at her, just missing her head.

Scan for more

# June

## 20

Family, French Cuisine, and Freedom
THE LIFE OF JAMES HEMINGS
Plantation Owner's Enslaved Son · Brother
French Chef · Internationa...
Negotiator
Teacher
Free Man

**America's Culinary Founding Father**
**1790: James Hemings, Thomas Jefferson's Black chef, cooks a dinner that unites the nation.** He prepares food for the momentous "Dinner Table Bargain," during which Jefferson, James Madison, and Alexander Hamilton strike a grand bargain: the national government will assume all state debts to finance the Revolutionary War in return for settling on Jefferson's and Madison's choice to situate the capital city on a site by the Potomac River. The menu, Hemings's declaration of culinary independence, includes capon stuffed with Virginia ham, chestnut purée, artichoke bottoms, and truffles served with Calvados sauce, and boeuf à la mode with French-style boeuf bouillon instead of gravy. Six years earlier, Jefferson selected Hemings, the half-brother of Sally Hemings, out of his 600 slaves to accompany him to Paris, where Jefferson would serve as U.S. minister to the French court while Hemings trained as a chef at the Château de Chantilly. Hemings then supervised the French-speaking staff at Hôtel de Langeac, which served as Jefferson's Paris residence and the American embassy. Though legally free in France, Hemings returned to the U.S. with Jefferson in 1789 and became one of the most influential chefs in U.S. history. He introduced "macaroni pie" (macaroni and cheese), ice cream, crème brûlée, meringue, whipped cream, and French fries to Americans.

## 21

1861: **Harriet Jacobs publishes "Incidents in the Life of a Slave Girl, written by herself,"** becoming the first formerly enslaved African American to publish an autobiography. She hid in a tiny crawl space under the roof of her grandmother's house. She stayed there for seven years, finally escaping to the free North, where she was reunited with her children.

1964: CORE members James Chaney, Andrew Goodman, and Michael Schwerner are stopped for speeding in Mississippi. The three, participants in the 1964 Freedom Summer voter registration campaign, had visited a Black church in Longdale, MS, which the Ku Klux Klan had burned. Police escort Chaney, Goodman, and Schwerner to jail and hold them for hours. When they're allowed to leave, police officers and others follow them and force them to pull over. The three are then abducted, driven to a different location, shot at close range, and buried. Their burnt-out car will be found near a swamp three days later. Seven weeks later, their bodies will be found in an earthen dam. The federal government will indict 19 men for civil rights violations. Seven will be convicted and receive minor sentences. The deaths will spur the passage of the Civil Rights Act of 1964. More than four decades later, one killer will be charged and convicted of three counts of manslaughter and sentenced to 60 years in prison, where he will die in 2018.

## 22

1909: **Katherine Dunham is born** in Glen Ellyn, IL. She will be among the 20th century's most renowned dancers and choreographers. She will be called the "matriarch and queen mother of Black dance," and the Washington Post will call her "dancer Katherine the Great." She will merge cultural dance with ballet components, become a leading dance anthropologist, and choreograph over 90 dances in her career. The Dunham Technique, will consist of movements and exercises rooted in traditional African dances.

1938: **Joe Louis TKOs German boxer Max Schmeling** in their rematch, at Yankee Stadium in NYC, 2 minutes and 4 seconds into round one, with 41 punches. An estimated 70 million people listened to the radio broadcast of the fight.

# Weekly Planner

WEEK OF ____________

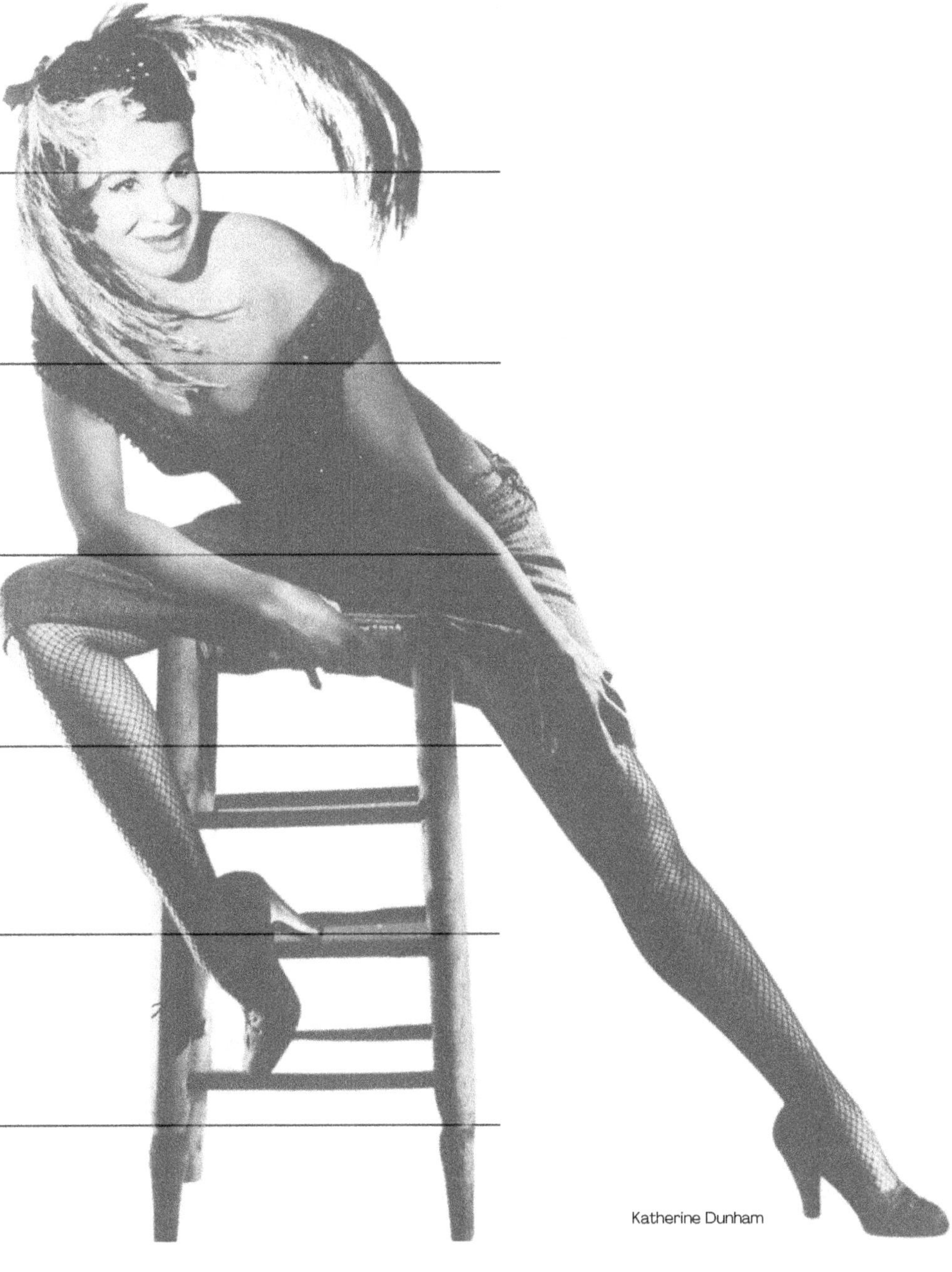

Katherine Dunham

SUNDAY

MONDAY

TUESDAY

WEDNESDAY

THURSDAY

FRIDAY

SATURDAY

# June

## 23

**1940: Wilma Rudolph is born** in Saint Bethlehem, Clarksville, TN, the 20th of 22 children in a blended family. She will be the first American woman to win three gold medals in a single Olympic Games, when, in 1960, she sets three world records—in the 100- and 200-meter individual events and the 4 × 100-meter relay.

## 24

**1936: Mary McLeod Bethune,** founder-president of Bethune-Cookman College, is appointed director of Negro Affairs of the National Youth Administration, becoming **the first Black woman to head a department of a federal agency.** She will organize the Federal Council on Negro Affairs, which will become known as President Franklin Delano Roosevelt's **Black Cabinet.**

Wilma Rudolph crosses the finish line at the Olympic 100m event, winning and setting a new world record on September 2, 1960.

## 25

**1971:** The **blaxploitation film "Shaft" is released,** directed by Gordon Parks, starring Richard Roundtree, and featuring Isaac Hayes's Grammy-winning soundtrack.

**2013:** The **U.S. Supreme Court invalidates a key provision in the Voting Rights Act of 1965** with a 5 to 4 ruling in Shelby County v. Holder. The ruling strikes down the requirement that states must obtain pre-approval—or "preclearance"—before changing their voting laws and maps. (Preclearance is a process the federal government has used to block state-sponsored discrimination before it could occur.) The conservative justices concluded that the formula used to determine the need for preclearance is "based on 40-year-old facts having no logical relationship to the present day" and that subjecting a state to preclearance based on its past discrimination is unconstitutional because it infringes on states' rights. In a dissenting opinion, Justice Ruth Bader Ginsburg writes: **"Throwing out preclearance** when it has worked and is continuing to work to stop discriminatory changes **is like throwing away your umbrella in a rainstorm because you are not getting wet."**

# June

## 26

2015, President **Barack Obama** delivers the eulogy and **sings "Amazing Grace" at the funeral of Rev. Clementa Pinckney, who was gunned down with eight others** by a racist terrorist during Bible study in Charleston, SC's Emanuel African Methodist Episcopal Church.

## 27

1919: **Marcus Garvey's Black Star Line is incorporated,** becoming a major symbol for his followers and for Pan-Africanists. In three years, the first of four ships will be purchased, a reconditioned coal boat formerly used in World War I. It will sail for three years between the U.S. and the West Indies as the first Black Star Line ship with an all-Black crew and Black captain.

2003: **Barry C. Black,** Chief of Chaplains of the U.S. Navy, **is named the 67th chaplain of the U.S. Senate,** becoming the first African American and first Seventh-day Adventist to hold the post.

2023: The **International African American Museum opens** at Gadsden's Wharf in Charleston, SC, where hundreds of thousands of enslaved Africans landed. The museum tells the story of the journey of the millions of Africans captured and forced across the Atlantic in the Middle Passage, how they arrived in Atlantic ports, and how "their labor, resistance and ingenuity" and that of their descendants "shaped our world." The museum's mission is "to foster empathy and understanding," empower "visitors with knowledge of the past," and "challenge, illuminate, inspire and ultimately … move people to action."

## 28

1977: **Measha Brueggergosman** (née Gosman) **is born** in New Brunswick, Canada. She will become **the most recognizable opera singer in Canada,** performing internationally. Her paternal 4x great-grandparents escaped slavery in Connecticut and Rhode Island during the American Revolution and were listed in the Book of Negroes, a record book that documented the names of escaped slaves, before being transported to freedom in Canada.

# Weekly Planner

**SUNDAY**

**MONDAY**

**TUESDAY**

**WEDNESDAY**

**THURSDAY**

**FRIDAY**

**SATURDAY**

# June

## 29

1874: The **Freedman's Bank fails.** The savings bank system (37 branches in 17 states and D.C.) was incorporated in 1865 to help the formerly enslaved bridge the gap to freedom and economic independence.

1916: The 369th Infantry Regiment is reorganized and will become known as the **Harlem Hellfighters.** It will spend 191 days under fire in World War I, longer than any other U.S. regiment. The **French government will award the Croix de Guerre** to 170 members for their valor.

1969: The 1969 **Harlem Cultural Festival begins at Mount Morris Park** (now Marcus Garvey Park) in Harlem. It will take place over six Sundays between June 29 and August 24, and become known as Black Woodstock (the Woodstock festival will take place during the same summer, drawing most of the music media attention). **Ahmir "Questlove" Thompson will win the Academy Award for Best Documentary Feature** at the 94th Oscars for "Summer of Soul (... Or, When the Revolution Could Not Be Televised)" in 2022.

2023: The **U.S. Supreme Court bans affirmative action in American universities** in the case Students for Fair Admissions, Inc. v. President and Fellows of Harvard College.

## 30

1917: **Lena Horne is born** in Bedford-Stuyvesant, Brooklyn. Her career will span 70 years, from the Cotton Club chorus line in Harlem at age 16 to night clubs to Broadway and Hollywood.

1967: The USAF selects **Robert H. Lawrence Jr.,** a highly experienced pilot with a doctorate in physical chemistry, for its Manned Orbital Laboratory, making him **the first Black astronaut.**

2015: **Misty Copeland becomes the first African American woman to be promoted to principal dancer in the 75-year history of American Ballet Theatre,** among the nation's top three classical ballet companies. Time magazine has just named her one of the 100 most influential people in the world, featuring her on its cover.

2022: **Ketanji Brown Jackson is sworn in as an associate justice of the U.S. Supreme Court,** making history as the **first African American woman** to sit on the highest court in the land.

# July

| SUN | MON | TUE | WED | THU | FRI | SAT |
| --- | --- | --- | --- | --- | --- | --- |
|  |  |  |  |  |  |  |
|  |  |  |  |  |  |  |
|  |  |  |  |  |  |  |
|  |  |  |  |  |  |  |
|  |  |  |  |  |  |  |

Langston Hughes (c. 1925) by Winold Reiss

# July

**WEEK 1**

_____
_____
_____
_____

**WEEK 2**

_____
_____
_____
_____

**WEEK 3**

_____
_____
_____
_____

**WEEK 4**

_____
_____
_____
_____

**WEEK 5**

_____
_____
_____
_____

**IF THERE IS NO STRUGGLE,
THERE IS NO PROGRESS.
FREDERICK DOUGLASS**

**MAJOR**

**MINOR**

**HABIT TRACKER**   S  M  T  W  T  F  S

**MISC**

# To-Do List

Date:

# NOTES

# Weekly Planner

**WEEK OF**

**SUNDAY**

**MONDAY**

**TUESDAY**

**WEDNESDAY**

**THURSDAY**

**FRIDAY**

**SATURDAY**

Composite image by Clarice
Bajkowski/The 19th/Wiki Commons

# July

## 1

1893: **Walter White is born** in Atlanta, GA. He will join the NAACP in 1918, and because he is fair-skinned, he will sometimes pass as white in the South in order to investigate lynchings. In 1929, he will lead the NAACP and achieve many successes. He will work with President Harry S. Truman to desegregate the armed forces, and create the NAACP Legal Defense Fund, which will win a nation-changing legal victory: the 1954 Supreme Court decision in Brown v. Board of Education, the legal basis for school desegregation. According to his family's oral history, White's maternal great-grandmother was Dilsia, the slave of William Henry Harrison, who fathered six children with her. Because it would have been politically unwise for Harrison to run for president while "bastard slave children" lived in his home, he gave four of Dilsia's children to his brother, who sold them off. Harrison was elected President in 1840.

1917: **Race Riot in East St. Louis, IL:** White-led mobs rush into Black neighborhoods in East St. Louis, IL, and beat and shoot Blacks indiscriminately, including women and children, and lynch many others. Whites murder 39-150 African Americans, destroy the equivalent of millions of dollars worth of property, and leave 6,000 Black people homeless.

## 2

1777: **Vermont becomes the first colony to ban slavery.** It also moves to provide full voting rights for Black men.

1822: **Denmark Vesey and five slaves are hanged for allegedly plotting a slave revolt** in Charleston, SC. They had been accused of planning to kill slaveholders, liberate thousands of slaves, and sail to Haiti.

1839: Led by **Joseph Cinqué, 53 Africans aboard the slave ship Amistad,** sailing from the coast of Cuba, kill the captain and two crew members and take control of the vessel. Two months later, the U.S. Navy will seize the ship off Long Island, NY, and tow it to New London, CT. The Spanish embassy will demand that the slaves be returned to Cuba, but a federal trial will take place in 1840 to determine the Africans' fate. The judge will rule in their favor, and the U.S. Supreme Court will uphold his decision.

1956: In RCA's New York recording studio Elvis Presley records **two songs written by songwriter Otis Blackwell: "Don't Be Cruel" and "All Shook Up."** The songs will be million-sellers, though Blackwell and Presley will never meet. **Blackwell will go on to write 1,000+ other songs, including "Return to Sender,"** also recorded by Presley. Blackwell's songs will define pop music.

1964: **President Lyndon B. Johnson signs the Civil Rights Act** of 1964 into law, prohibiting discrimination on the basis of race, color, religion, sex, or national origin.

1991: **John Singleton's** film **"Boyz n the Hood" premieres in Los Angeles.** He developed the idea to fulfill an application requirement for film school in 1986 and sold the script to Columbia Pictures in 1990 upon graduation. At 24, he will become the youngest person and the first African American to be nominated for Best Director. He will also be nominated for Best Original Screenplay.

## 3

Summer 2014: **Nine-year-old** Sofia Bernstein from Cambridge, MA, **writes President Barack Obama requesting he put a woman on "dollors/coins"** "because if there where no Woman there wouldnt be Men." She lists a few suggestions. President Obama thanks her for her letter the following year, and a year afterward, **Treasury Secretary Jack Lew announces the proposal to replace President Andrew Jackson with Harriet Tubman on the $20 bill,** which would make her the first African American woman to appear on U.S. currency.

1976: **Tina Turner, bruised, walks out on her abusive husband, Ike, as he sleeps in their Hilton Statler Hotel room.** With just 36 cents and a Mobil gasoline card in her pocket, she sprints across Interstate 30 in Dallas, seeking refuge at the nearby Ramada Inn. She will stay at the Ramada for three days, hiding from Ike but able to see from her window. **Her "escape" will be a turning point in her life.** She will divorce Ike two years later and build a second career. Her room at the Ramada eventually will be renovated and called the Cake Suite. The **"Escape Suite" down the hall will be filled with photos and memorabilia** from her career.

1881: **Tuskegee University** (formerly known as the Tuskegee Institute) **opens** for the training of Black teachers**.**

1910: In a boxing match billed as "the fight of the century," **Jack Johnson, the first African American world heavyweight boxing champion, beats the previously undefeated champion James J. Jeffries,** who came out of retirement not just to challenge Johnson but to "retrieve the honor of the white race." The fight takes place in Reno, NV, before nearly 20,000 people. In 15 rounds, Johnson knocks Jeffries down twice. Jeffries had never been knocked down. His corner then "throws in the towel," ending the fight and preventing him from having a KO on his record. The fight will silence Johnson's critics but **trigger race riots in more than 25 states and 50 cities** across America. At least 20 people will be killed and hundreds injured.

Samuel J. Miller, Daguerreotype
Art Institute of Chicago

Frederick Douglass, 1852

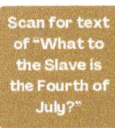
Scan for text of "What to the Slave is the Fourth of July?"

1852: **Frederick Douglass delivers** the keynote address at an Independence Day celebration in Rochester, NY— a biting speech in which he asks, "**What to the Slave is the Fourth of July?"** He then says: "This Fourth of July is *yours,* not *mine. You* may rejoice, *I* must mourn," and adds: "I say it with a sad sense of the disparity between us. I am not included within the pale of glorious anniversary! Your high independence only reveals the immeasurable distance between us."

1975: **Arthur Ashe becomes the first Black man to win** the **Wimbledon** men's singles championship.

1957: **Althea Gibson wins the women's singles tennis title at Wimbledon, becoming the first African American to win** a championship at London's All England Lawn Tennis and Croquet Club.

1975: **50 Cent** (Curtis James Jackson III) **is born** in South Jamaica, Queens, NY. He will adopt the nickname "50 Cent" as a metaphor for change.

1979: **Kevin Hart is born** in Philadelphia, PA.

# Weekly Planner

**WEEK OF**

**SUNDAY**

**MONDAY**

**TUESDAY**

**WEDNESDAY**

**THURSDAY**

**FRIDAY**

**SATURDAY**

# July

## 7

**1915:** **Margaret Walker is born** in Birmingham, AL. In 1942, **she will become the first African American to win a national writing prize,** the Yale Series of Younger Poets Competition.

**July 1995:** **Oseola McCarty, an 87-year-old retired laundress** in Hattiesburg, MS, **announces that she has used a portion of her life's savings to establish a trust of $150,000 that will go to the University of Southern Mississippi to provide scholarships** for students in financial need. Her gift will forever change philanthropy at the university. McCarty quit school in the sixth grade to care for her aunt, became a washerwoman, and lived frugally. Over the years, she opened several bank accounts, saving money as her mother Lucy taught her to. She never married, never had children, never owned a car, and she pushed a cart nearly a mile to the grocery store. After her announcement, over 800 people from across the nation will make donations, more than tripling her original gift. By 2023, the endowment will provide $631,397 in scholarships to 130 students.

## 8

**1860:** **The slave ship Clotilda arrives in Mobile, AL, illegally and on a Sunday night, 52 years after the United States abolished international slave trading.** Cudjo Lewis, along with 109 others torn from West Africa, are aboard the ship. Cudjo was a member of the Yoruba people in what is now eastern Benin, and his Yoruba name was Oluale Kossola. Kidnapped in April, he was imprisoned in a slave pen known as a barracoon and then shipped, naked, on the Clotilda, **the last recorded slave ship to arrive in the U.S.,** a 45-day journey across the Atlantic Ocean. The Clotilda's captain will burn and scuttle the ship to hide evidence of his illegal trade. Cudjo will be enslaved by a ship captain named James Meaher for five years. In 1865, Cudjo and the others will be freed by Union soldiers. He will marry Abile, who also arrived on the Clotilda. They and the others will fail to raise enough money to return to Africa, so they will stay in Alabama and establish Africatown, just north of Mobile. Those who arrived on the Clotilda will die off by the early 1920s. Cudjo will be the last survivor. He will die on July 26, 1935, at about 94. His descendants will live in Mobile.

 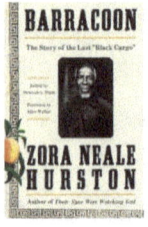

*Zora Neale Hurston will interview Cudjoe Lewis to write a nonfiction work, "Barracoon: The Story of the Last 'Black Cargo.'"*

## 9

**1868:** The **14th Amendment to the U.S. Constitution, considered among the most consequential amendments, is ratified.** It defines and grants citizenship to all persons born or naturalized in the U.S., including formerly enslaved people, and guarantees equal protection under the laws.

**14th Amendment**
**Explained**
(Scan)

 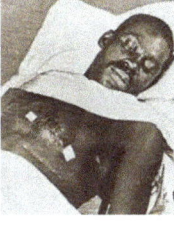

**1893: Daniel Hale Williams performs the first successful open-heart surgery.** The patient, James Cornish, who had been stabbed in the chest, will walk out of the hospital in 51 days and live for more than 20 years.

The cabin where Mary McLeod was born and raised in Mayesville, SC.

**1875: Mary McLeod Bethune is born** in Mayesville, SC.

Circa 1910

John Taylor Jr. competing for the University of Pennsylvania track team

**First African American Olympic Champion**

July 1908: **John Taylor Jr.,** the son of former slaves, **becomes the first Black American to win an Olympic gold medal.** He competes at the London Summer Games as a member of the U.S. 1600-meter relay team. Dr. Taylor wins the medal within weeks of earning his degree in veterinary medicine. He will earn 45 trophies and 70 medals during his brief athletic career. He will die of typhoid pneumonia at age 24, within five months of winning Olympic gold.

**1976:** Texas Congresswoman **Barbara Jordan,** the first African American woman from the South elected to the House of Representatives, **becomes the first African American and the first woman to deliver the keynote address at the Democratic National Convention.**

# Weekly Planner

**WEEK OF**_____

## SUNDAY

## MONDAY

Gift of Jowcol Music LLC

## TUESDAY

## WEDNESDAY

## THURSDAY

John Coltrane's tenor saxophone,
made by Selmer in Paris in 1965

## FRIDAY

## SATURDAY

# July

## 13

John Coltrane and bandmembers in the U.S. Navy.

**1946:** **Seaman 1st Class John Coltrane makes his first recording of jazz standards and bebop tunes in Hawaii with other Navy musicians.** He also does kitchen duty and works on the security detail. He enlisted on August 6, 1945, the day a U.S. B-29 bomber dropped the atomic bomb on Hiroshima.

**2013:** **Alicia Garza plants the idea for Black Lives Matter** with a Facebook post containing the phrase "Black lives matter" upon news of the acquittal of Trayvon Martin's murderer. Garza, Patrisse Cullors, and Opal Tometi create the BLM movement, which grows after the 2014 deaths of Michael Brown in Missouri and Eric Garner in NY. In 2021, a Norwegian member of parliament will nominate BLM for the Nobel Peace Prize.

**Scan for Time's Women of the Year article**

## 14

**1943:** The **George Washington Carver National Monument** in Newton County, MO, a unit of the National Park Service, is founded during President Franklin D. Roosevelt's administration. It is **the first national monument dedicated to an African American** and the first to someone other than a president.

George Washington Carver

## 15

**1870:** **Georgia becomes the last former Confederate state readmitted to the Union.** It had rejoined the Union two years earlier but was expelled because African Americans were removed from the state legislature.

Ernie Barnes, no. 61 of the San Diego Chargers, in action., 1961-62 NFL season.

**1938:** **Ernie Barnes is born** in Durham, NC. He will be a professional football player, actor, author, and artist. He will be best known for his paintings featuring elongated figures in movement.

## 16

1929: **Pig Foot Mary** (Lillian H. Dean), one of the wealthiest women in America, dies in Los Angeles. Born in the Mississippi Delta in 1870, she **migrated to NYC and sold pigs' feet out of a repurposed baby carriage** in the San Juan Hill neighborhood in front of a saloon from early morning until late at night. Customers traveled from as far as New Jersey and Long Island to eat her boiled-then-fried specialty, which many migrants from the South missed. In 1917, Mary **set up a stand at the corner of 135th Street and Lenox Avenue,** where the aroma of her yams, pigs' feet, chitlings, hog maws, roasted corn, and fried chicken lured long lines of customers. When her husband, John Dean, a postal worker and newsstand owner, suggested investing in real estate, she **became the first Black woman to purchase property in Harlem.** In 1917, she bought a five-story apartment building at the corner of 137th Street and Lenox Avenue for $42,000 (about $650,000 today). She **sold it in 1923 for $72,000 ($1.26 million in 2023).** While still selling pigs' feet, she bought and sold other buildings. She sold one to the **Harlem YMCA,** which became a dormitory. Another property became **Harlem Hospital.** The world-famous **Schomburg Center for Research in Black Culture, a branch of the New York Public Library, now stands on the corner where she sold pigs' feet.** At her death, her net worth was equivalent to about $6.5 million in 2023.

1943: The film **"Stormy Weather," starring Lena Horne, Bill Robinson, and Cab Calloway** and his band, **is released.** It features what is perhaps **the greatest dance sequence in film history,** performed by the Nicholas Brothers in one take.

### FloJo the Unbeatable

1988: Florence Griffith Joyner, aka FloJo, sets the first of her three world records, sprinting 100 meters in 10.49 seconds in the quarterfinals of the U.S. Olympic Trials. She will win Olympic gold in this event in Seoul two months later. She will set a second world record at the Seoul Olympic games in September, running 200 meters in 21.56 seconds in the quarterfinal race. But she will improve on this record by setting a world record in the same event on the same day, sprinting 200 meters in 21.34 seconds in the final race. She will win a third Olympic gold medal in the 4x400 meter relay in Seoul. Her world records will still stand in 2024. FloJo is known for her athletic prowess and her bold style. She runs in bikini-bottom running suits emblazoned with lightning bolts, one-legged suits, or speed-skating suits. Her six-inch fingernails are painted and bejeweled. In 2020, Time Magazine will list FloJo as one of the most influential women of the past century.

## 17

1794: **Richard Allen founds the nation's first Black Episcopal church,** the African Episcopal Church of St. Thomas, in Philadelphia. He called the congregation the African Methodist Episcopal Church (A.M.E.). The church building, **Mother Bethel African Methodist Episcopal Church,** will be the oldest real estate property continuously owned by African Americans.

# July

## 18

William H. Carney

1863: Suffering from several gunshot wounds, Sergeant **William H. Carney** catches the falling flag from the dying color guard during the Battle of Fort Wagner, which guards the Port of Charleston, and climbs up the hill to the walls of the fort, urging his fellow troops from the 54th Massachusetts Infantry Regiment to follow. He plants the flag in the sand at the base of the fort and holds it upright until he is rescued. Carney will become the first African American recipient of the Medal of Honor on May 23, 1900, for his conspicuous gallantry.

Mast Sgt. William Carney: The first African American Medal of Honor recipient

## 19

Ralph Ellison

1995: Donald Katz, a white author and journalist, **launches Audible, a provider of audiobooks in digital format, partly due to the influence of his college professor, Ralph Ellison.** Katz will credit Ellison for teaching him that Americans work "to create an identity from a synthesis of divergent cultures," and have a distinctive way of talking and telling stories. "Because of Ralph I always heard the sound of what I read and what I wrote," Katz says. "Well-composed words sound like music to me, and after being a writer for 20 years, this led directly to an idea that became Audible.com." Audible will become a membership platform that offers access to 68,000 hours of content and 11,000+ titles, including Ralph Ellison's.

Scan for more

## 20

1914: **Marcus Garvey, age 28, founds the Universal Negro Improvement Association,** a Black nationalist fraternal organization, in Jamaica. He will establish a branch in Harlem in 1916 and in 1919 become president of the Black Star Line, a shipping company that moves goods and people between North America and Africa.

Anthony Barboza

Members of the Kamoinge Workshop in 1973. Back row, from left: Albert R. Fennar, Ray Francis, Herbert Randall, C. Daniel Dawson, Beuford Smith, Herb Robinson, Adger Cowans and Anthony Barboza. Front row, from left: Herman Howard, Ming Smith, James Mannas Jr., Louis Draper, Calvin Wilson, and Shawn Walker.

1963: **Kamoinge Workshop, a Black photography collective, is founded in NYC.** Roy DeCarava will be its first director. (Kamoinge is "a group of people who are working together" in the Kikuyu or Gikuyu language, spoken mainly in Kenya.) The group is a supportive yet critical artistic community intent on capturing Black life through a lens and creating a Black aesthetic in photography. Kamoinge photographers' work will eventually be exhibited in leading museums and displayed and archived in the Smithsonian Institution. The group will become the longest continuously running non-profit group in the history of photography.

# Weekly Planner

WEEK OF_____

SUNDAY

MONDAY

TUESDAY

WEDNESDAY

THURSDAY

FRIDAY

SATURDAY

1896: **The National Association of Colored Women (later to become the National Association of Colored Women's Clubs) is established** in Washington, DC. It adopts the motto "Lifting as we climb." Its **founders are Harriet Tubman, Ida B. Wells, Mary Church Terrell, Francis E.W. Harper, Margaret Murray Washington, Victoria Earle Matthews, and Josephine Silone Yates.** It will campaign for women's suffrage and against lynching, and support efforts for improving education. The organization will grow from 5,000 members around the turn of the century to 100,000 in 1924.

1981: **Luther Vandross records** his debut song **"Never Too Much."** It will be the lead song on his debut album of the same name, released on August 12, 1981

1939: New York Mayor Fiorello La Guardia appoints 31-year-old **Jane Bolin** as a judge of the Domestic Relations Court, making her **the nation's first Black female judge.** Bolin, the first Black woman to graduate from Yale Law School (class of 1931), will be the nation's only Black female judge for twenty years. As a judge, she will help end the race-based assignments of probation officers, and help to end segregated childcare facilities and blood donations. She will also influence Mayor Robert F. Wagner Jr. to integrate public housing in 1957. After reaching the mandatory retirement age of 70, she will volunteer as a reading instructor in NYC public schools. Constance Baker Motley, the civil rights lawyer and the first African American woman appointed to the federal judiciary, will cite Bolin as a role model.

Scan for full report

Scan for W.E.B. Du Bois's "Address to the Nations of the World" (p. 124)

1872: **Elijah McCoy,** born free in Colchester, Ontario, to parents who escaped enslavement in Kentucky, **receives U.S. patent No. 129,843 for "Improvement in Lubricators for Steam-Engines," an automatic lubrication system he invented in his home machine shop** in Ypsilanti, MI. The automatic system will save time and money for railroad companies. It enables trains to run faster with little need to stop for lubrication. **Nearly every railroad company in North America will want his system, asking for "the real McCoy"** to avoid inauthentic copies. In all, McCoy will obtain 57 patents, more than any other African American in his day, including patents for a folding ironing board and a lawn sprinkler. **McCoy is unique in American history. His name will come to mean "the genuine article."** Few other Americans' names live on as an expression in the English language.

1900: The **First Pan-African Conference opens in London's Westminster Hall.** W.E.B. Du Bois plays a leading role. He drafts "Address to the Nations of the World," an appeal to fight against racism, request that European countries grant self-governance to their African and the West Indies colonies, and demand rights for Black Americans.

# July

## 24

July 1919: **Claude McKay's sonnet "If We Must Die" is published** in the July issue of The Liberator magazine. He wrote it in response to white mob attacks on Black Americans during the Red Summer of 1919, when race riots occurred in more than three dozen cities in the U.S. and one rural county in Arkansas. Winston Churchill will supposedly quote the sonnet during World War II.

## 25

1916: **Garrett A. Morgan,** the self-taught inventor of the gas mask, hauls to safety eight men who were trapped in a new waterworks tunnel 120 feet below the waves of Lake Erie when a natural gas pocket exploded. Morgan **invented the gas mask** several years earlier, after learning about the 1911 fire that killed 146 workers locked inside New York's Triangle Shirtwaist Factory. Morgan set out to solve a problem—suffocation from smoke inhalation. He designed a hood with a low-hanging tube that draws air at foot level because he knew carbon monoxide lingers at head level. He drew inspiration from circus elephants he'd seen stick their trunks out of tents to draw fresh air. Due to racism, he knew whites would doubt his invention, so in 1914 he hired a white actor to pose as its inventor. While the actor entertained a crowd, Morgan strapped on his "safety hood," entered a smoke-filled tent, and stayed inside a half-hour before reemerging safely. Sales followed, but it wasn't until the tunnel explosion and the failure of two rescue parties to save anyone that Morgan's patented gas mask got proper attention.

## 26

1948: President **Harry S. Truman signs Executive Order 9981, desegregating the armed forces.**

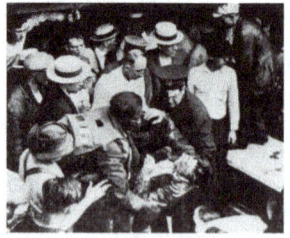

Garrett Morgan brings the first man out of the tunnel.

# Weekly Planner

**SUNDAY**

**MONDAY**

**TUESDAY**

## If We Must Die!

If we must die, let it not be like hogs
    Hunted and penned in an inglorious spot,
While round us bark the mad and hungry dogs,
    Making their mock at our accursed lot.
If we must die, let it not be like hogs
    So that our precious blood may not be shed
In vain; then even the monsters we defy
    Shall be constrained to honor us, though dead!

Oh, kinsman! We must meet the common foe;
    Though far outnumbered, let us still be brave,
And for their thousand blows deal one deathblow!
    What though before us lies the open grave?
Like men we'll face the murderous, cowardly pack,
    Pressed to the wall, dying, but—fighting back!
               —*Claude McKay.*

**WEDNESDAY**

**THURSDAY**

**FRIDAY**

**SATURDAY**

### Obama's National Introduction

2004: **Barack Obama delivers the keynote speech at the 2004 Democratic National Convention** in Boston, introducing himself as a skinny kid with a funny name while planting his name in the nation's political landscape. Three months later, he will be elected U.S. Senator from Illinois.

### The Silent Parade

1917: The National Association for the Advancement of Colored People, church, and community leaders organize the Silent Parade, a silent march, during record summer heat, by some 10,000 Black people along Fifth Avenue in New York City to protest violence toward African Americans, including lynchings in Waco and Memphis, and riots in East St. Louis, where white mobs killed 40 Blacks. This was the first such protest in NYC and the second public protest by African Americans for civil rights. The first involved picketing against the 1915 film "The Birth of a Nation."

1909: **Chester Himes is born** in Jefferson City, MO. He will start his writing career while in prison, publishing in national magazines. Upon his release, Langston Hughes will introduce him to literary figures and help his career. Himes will work in Los Angeles as a Warner Bros. screenwriter, which will end when Jack L. Warner hears about him and says, "I don't want no niggers on this lot." Himes's major works will include the novel "If He Hollers Let Him Go" and the hard-boiled Harlem Detective Series, including "A Rage in Harlem" and "Cotton Comes to Harlem." He will be regarded a literary light as influential as Dashiell Hammett and Raymond Chandler. His circle of friends will include Richard Wright, Malcolm X, Picasso, Nikki Giovanni, Ishmael Reed, Melvin Van Peebles, and James Baldwin.

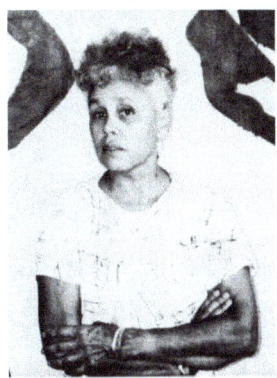

1926: **Betye Saar is born** in Los Angeles, CA.

July 1933: **Lead Belly,** a prisoner in Louisiana's Angola prison, among the most notorious penitentiaries in the South, **sings several songs while playing a 12-string guitar, including "Good Night, Irene," as ethnomusicologist John Lomax records them for the Library of Congress.** Lead Belly will be released from prison, sign with Capitol Records, and eventually be inducted posthumously into the Rock and Roll Hall of Fame.

1921: **Whitney Young Jr. is born** in Lincoln Ridge, KY. He will become a major civil rights movement leader and head the National Urban League from 1961 to 1971, working for equal opportunity for African Americans in both the public and private sectors. He will propose a domestic "Marshall Plan" calling for $145 billion in federal aid to cities, which will in part be incorporated into President Lyndon B. Johnson's War on Poverty.

# August

| SUN | MON | TUE | WED | THU | FRI | SAT |
|-----|-----|-----|-----|-----|-----|-----|
|     |     |     |     |     |     |     |
|     |     |     |     |     |     |     |
|     |     |     |     |     |     |     |
|     |     |     |     |     |     |     |
|     |     |     |     |     |     |     |

Aretha Franklin | Photo by Anthony Barboza

# August

**WEEK 1**

_____

_____

_____

_____

**WEEK 2**

_____

_____

_____

_____

_____

**WEEK 3**

_____

_____

_____

_____

**WEEK 4**

_____

_____

_____

_____

_____

**WEEK 5**

_____

_____

_____

_____

**YOU CAN'T SEPARATE PEACE FROM FREEDOM BECAUSE NO ONE CAN BE AT PEACE UNLESS HE HAS HIS FREEDOM.**
**MALCOLM X**

**MAJOR**

**MINOR**

**HABIT TRACKER**    S  M  T  W  T  F  S

_____

_____

_____

_____

**MISC**

# To-Do List

Date:

# NOTES

# Weekly Planner

**WEEK OF**_____

**SUNDAY**

**MONDAY**

**TUESDAY**

Map of the Underground Railroad

**WEDNESDAY**

**THURSDAY**

**FRIDAY**

**SATURDAY**

# August

## 1

1960: **Chuck D** (Carlton Douglas Ridenhour) **is born** in Long Island, NY. He will cofound the hip hop group **Public Enemy with Flavor Fav** in 1985.

1834: Britain's **Slavery Abolition Act takes effect, freeing more than 800,000** enslaved Africans in the British Empire, including those enslaved in Canada. The act makes Canada a free territory, and so between 1834 and the early 1860s, **Canada will draw over 30,000-40,000 fugitive slaves and free Blacks** from the U.S.

1863 North Star with star and Argyle stocking. Legend has it this token offered advice to escaping slaves "to leave quietly carrying shoes if necessary and follow the North Star."

## 2

1790: **The first U.S. census begins,** with Thomas Jefferson as census bureau director. It will take months to collect data from households in the Union, and Jefferson will share a concern with President George Washington that the census significantly undercounts the population. What is clear from the start is that the census separates "free whites" from any other free citizen. Slaves will be counted separately. Sixty years later, census takers will sort race by color (Black or white) and document any trace of African ancestry using the term "mulatto." In 1890, African heritage will be a matter of mathematics: "Black" for 100 percent African heritage, "mulatto" for 50 percent African ancestry, and "quadroon" and "octoroon" for one-fourth and one-eighth African heritage, respectively. In 1970, people will get to self-identify their race. (Barack Obama, born to a white woman from Kansas and a Black man from Kenya, will mark himself as "Black.")

2000: **"Cha-Cha Slide,"** the single by DJ Casper (Willie Perry Jr.), **is released. This infectious song will become a line-dance craze and a global phenomenon** played at birthday parties, dance clubs, roller rinks, weddings, family cookouts, bar mitzvahs, Quinceaneras, sports events, health clubs, senior citizen homes —wherever people want to move.

Anthony Barboza

1924: **James Baldwin is born** in Harlem Hospital in NYC. His mother, Emma Berdis Jones, is a cleaning woman; he will never learn the identity of his biological father. The eldest of nine children, he is reared by his mother and his stepfather, David Baldwin, a preacher. At age 14, James will become a preacher at the Fireside Pentecostal Assembly. His experience in the pulpit will last three years and ultimately impact his rhetorical style, writing themes, and stance on religion.

**1936: Jesse Owens wins the first of four gold medals at the Summer Olympics in Berlin,** crushing Adolf Hitler's myth of Aryan superiority. Owens will win four gold medals—in the 100-meter and 200-meter races, the long jump, and the 4 x 100-meter relay. His record-winning performance would not be equaled for another 48 years. During his lifetime, he is considered the greatest track and field athlete in history.

2001: With her hit movie "The Princess Diaries," starring Julie Andrews and Anne Hathaway, **motion film and television producer Debra Martin Chase becomes the first African American to produce a movie that grossed over $100 million.** The film will eventually gross more than $165 million worldwide. This is not Chase's first major success. She ran actor Denzel Washington's production company, Mundy Lane Entertainment, in the mid-1990s, when she executive produced an Oscar- and Emmy-nominated documentary on Hank Aaron. She also executive produced ABC's "The Wonderful World of Disney," the television musical starring Brandy, Whitney Houston, and Whoopi Goldberg, watched by more than 60 million people. She even hired future showrunner Shonda Rhimes as her intern (see March 27). Chase cast Anne Hathaway for her feature film debut, the lead role in "The Princess Diaries." It will be the breakthrough role for the future Academy Award winner.

1901: **Louis Armstrong is born** in New Orleans, LA. He will spend his youth in poverty in the neighborhood known as the Battlefield, drop out of school at 11, sing in the streets for money, and be sent to the Colored Waif's Home, which is run like a military camp. He will eventually play in brass bands and tour on a steamboat up and down the Mississippi River before moving to Chicago and New York to play with the greatest musicians of his day. In the 1950s, **Armstrong will become a "jazz ambassador," a beloved American icon, and one of the most influential musicians of all time.** He will tour the world, record chart-topping songs and albums, appear in over 30 films, and play more than 300 performances per year for three decades. His home in Queens, NY, will become a museum.

1961: **Barack Obama is born** in Honolulu, HI, to an American mother and a Kenyan father. He is the only president born outside of the 48 contiguous states.

Jack Daniel is in the white hat. The Black man on the left is either Nathan "Nearest" Green or his son George.

**The Master Stiller Behind Jack Daniel's? A Slave**

c.1856: **Jasper "Jack" Daniel, a farm-chore boy, is introduced to Nathan "Nearest" Green,** an enslaved man **who teaches Daniel how to make Tennessee sour mash whiskey.** Jack Daniel will sell Nearest's whiskey, the finest around, and earn enough money to buy the distillery. After the Civil War, **Nearest will work for Daniel as "master stiller," but the whiskey will be Jack Daniel's.** Daniel's family will sell the company in 1956 for $20 million. Nearest's family will not see any of the money even though the brand, which uses Nearest's distilling methods, has become the world's top-selling whiskey. Nearest Green knew how to give whiskey a distinctive smoothness—by filtering it through 10 feet of sugar maple charcoal to remove impurities and impart a hint of sweetness. This charcoal-mellowing process intertwines whiskey-making with slavery. Enslaved Africans carried with them the tradition of purifying water by filtering it through charcoal.

# Weekly Planner

WEEK OF_____

**SUNDAY**

**MONDAY**

**TUESDAY**

19th century Jack Daniel bottle jug stencil found
where Nearest Green distilled whiskey
in the mid-to-late 1800s.

**WEDNESDAY**

**THURSDAY**

**FRIDAY**

**SATURDAY**

# August

## 6

## 7

## 8

**Voting Rights Act of 1965 – Definition, Summary & Significance**
The Voting Rights Act of 1965, signed into law by President Lyndon B. Johnson, aimed to overcome legal barriers at the state and local levels that prevented African Americans from exercising their right to vote as...

**1965:** **President Lyndon B. Johnson signs into law the Voting Rights Act of 1965,** prohibiting discriminatory voting practices used to disenfranchise African American voters. Within three years, Black voter registration in the South will increase by 1.3 million. Black voter registration will change dramatically in Mississippi. In 1965, just 7 percent of eligible Black voters are registered. In 1968, the number will rise to 60 percent.

**NATIONAL ARCHIVES**

**The Voting Rights Act of 1965, August 6, 1965**
By July 1965 each chamber of Congress had passed its own voting rights bill. The two bills were merged in a conference committee as S. 1564. The House passed the bill on August 3, 328-74. The Senate...

**1904:** **Ralph Bunche is born** in Detroit, MI. In 1950, he will become the first African American and the first person of African descent to win a Nobel Prize.

**1968.** A few months after MLK was assassinated, **James Brown records** the song **"Say it Loud – I'm Black and I'm Proud"** in LA's Vox Studios with a chorus of 30 young people from Watts and Compton. It will soar to the top of the charts and become **an anthem of Black pride and empowerment.**

**1871:** The formerly enslaved Samuel Johnson organizes Tennessee's first Emancipation Day. Eight years earlier to the day, he had been freed by his owner, Andrew Johnson, who was then military governor of Tennessee and would later become U.S. President. Emancipation Day will spread to surrounding states like Kentucky, Missouri, and Virginia, where it is celebrated as a special day with reunions, cookouts, and homecomings in the same spirit as Juneteenth, now nationally recognized.

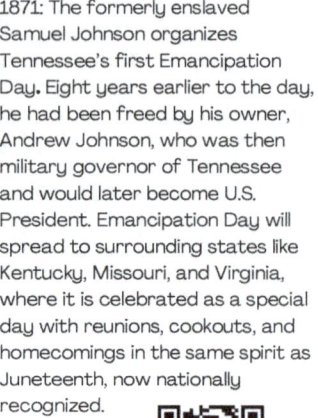

**Andrew Johnson and the 8th of August -**
**Andrew Johnson National Historic Site (U.S. ...**

**2024:** **Sydney McLaughlin-Levrone set a world record in the 400-meter hurdles with a time of 50.37 seconds at the Paris Summer Olympics, winning a gold medal and shaving 0.28 seconds off the world record time she set in June.** Today, she crossed the finish line a comfortable 1.5 seconds ahead of silver medalist Anna Cockrell, McLaughlin-Levrone's teammate. The feat is astonishing since it can take years for hurdlers to eclipse records by mere fractions of a second. Her win also sets a new Olympic record, one she herself had set at 51.46. In Paris, McLaughlin-Levrone will also run the final leg of the 4x400-meter relay for the U.S. women's relay team, which will bring her Olympic medal tally to four golds.

**NEW WORLD RECORD!**
**WOMEN'S 400M HURDLES**

### The Ultimate Femme Fatale

**1930: Betty Boop debuts in a cartoon short, "Dizzy Dishes," performing at a jazz club.** The producer, Max Fleischer, does not credit the person who inspired the *Boop-oop-a-doop* character with puppy-dog eyes and an hourglass figure. **Her sexy style is derived from Black female stars of the day, but Betty Boop's scat singing is based on a stage character created by Esther Jones, a child entertainer from Chicago who is Black** and who performed in the U.S. and for royalty across Europe.

Esther Jones

The front page of the Tocsin of Liberty on August 10, 1842, the issue in which Thomas Smallwood makes the first published reference to the "underground railroad"

**1842: Thomas Smallwood, who set up the first station on the Underground Railroad steps away from the U.S. Capitol, will coin the term "underground railroad" on this day** in an abolitionist newspaper as a joke to demoralize slaveholders. In a letter published under the pen name Sam Weller in the Tocsin of Liberty in Albany, NY, Smallwood tells slaveholders their "walking property walked off." "It was your cruelty to him, that made him disappear by that same 'under ground rail-road' or 'steam balloon,' about which one of your city constables was swearing so bitterly a few weeks ago, when complaining that the 'd----d rascals' got off so, and that no trace of them could be found!" Smallwood tells slaveholders they may request information about their lost property by writing to him at the "office of the underground railroad." The first party of fugitives to escape via Smallwood's mythical transportation network was a group of 15 men, women, and children. Escapes were dangerous and daring. Smallwood and white abolitionist Charles Torrey would hide enslaved people in covered wagons and head north in the middle of the night. One wagonload might be worth $200,000 in today's dollars. Smallwood will flee to Canada on Independence Day, July 4, 1843.

### Father of the Underground Railroad

August 1850: **William Still meets a former slave from Alabama** searching for his family, whom he hadn't seen in 40 years. **"Suppose I should tell you that I am your brother," William tells the man,** who is stunned. William takes his brother to meet their parents, who had escaped slavery years earlier. "O, Lord," his mother cries. "How long have I prayed to see my two sons!" This unexpected reunion inspires Still to keep detailed records to facilitate the reunion of families torn apart by slavery. From this day forward, Still will keep records of the 1,000 fugitives he will shepherd to freedom through the Anti-Slavery Society.

### Mother of Black Feminism

1858: **Anna Julia Cooper is born a slave** in Raleigh, NC. Either her owner, George Washington Haywood, or his brother Fabius, is probably her father. She will work as a domestic servant, but win scholarships and go on to receive a Ph.D. from the Sorbonne, University of Paris, becoming the fourth African American woman to earn a doctorate. She will move to Washington, D.C., and in 1892 complete her first book, "A Voice from the South: By a Black Woman of the South." She will be called the Mother of Black Feminism. That same year, she will cofound the Colored Women's League along with Helen Appo Cook, Ida B. Wells, Charlotte Forten Grimké, Mary Jane Peterson, Mary Church Terrell, and Evelyn Shaw. In 1930, she will be named president of Frelinghuysen University in Washington, D.C.

# Weekly Planner

WEEK OF _____

**SUNDAY**

**MONDAY**

**TUESDAY**

**WEDNESDAY**

**THURSDAY**

**FRIDAY**

**SATURDAY**

1873: **J. Rosamond Johnson is born** in Jacksonville, FL. He will become a successful composer and singer during the Harlem Renaissance and write the tune for the hymn "Lift Every Voice and Sing." His older brother, James Weldon Johnson, will write the lyrics.

### The Birth of Hip Hop

1973: DJ Kool Herc, whose name alludes to the Greek god of strength, Hercules, is the DJ at his sister's back-to-school party in the Bronx. He uses two record players to extend the beat of a record while using a mixer to switch between the records and isolate the percussion. His turntable manipulation, the beginning of "scratching," will become a component of hip hop.

### King of Wings

1961-1964: Alabama-born **John Young creates the chicken wing, which the world will devour by the billions.** In his Buffalo, NY, restaurant Wings N Things, he does what African American cooks have done for centuries—find a way to use an animal part that white cooks discard—the boniest piece of the chicken: the wing. Young whips up "mumbo sauce," a tangy, sweet, spicy tomato-based sauce, adds some tropical fruit and slathers it on uncut wings. Once a throwaway part, chicken wings will become the chicken's most expensive (and arguably the tastiest) part.

### 58 Jazz Giants Say, "Cheese!"

1958: At 10 a.m., **58 jazz giants gather at 17 East 126th Street in Harlem for a group photograph** by Art Kane. The historic photograph will appear in the January 4, 1959, issue of Esquire Magazine.

Big Mama Thornton (r) with Little Brother Montgomery 1980

1952: **Willie Mae "Big Mama" Thornton records the song "Hound Dog"** in Los Angeles for Peacock Records. The song is written for a woman berating her selfish man. The record will sell over a half-million copies, reach No. 1 on the R&B charts, be listed by the Rock and Roll Hall of Fame as one of the "500 songs that shaped rock and roll," and be inducted into the Grammy Hall of Fame. Four years later, Elvis Presley will record his version of "Hound Dog," which will sell 10 million copies globally.

# August

## 14

**1942: Molefi Kete Asante,** who will be a leading figure in African American studies, **is born** in Valdosta, GA. **He will be the father of Afrocentricity,** an academic approach that focuses on the centrality of the African experience for people of African heritage and draws on history, art, culture, mythology, spirituality, philosophy, and sociology. He will propose the nation's first doctoral program in African-American Studies at Temple University.

Scan for Temple U. Afrocentricity Guide

Scan left to read "The 1619 Project"

2019: The first edition of **The 1619 Project,** a journalism project developed by the New York Times' Nikole Hannah-Jones and other Times writers, **is published in the Times Magazine.** Its aim is "to reframe the country's history by placing the consequences of slavery and the contributions of Black Americans at the very center of the United States' national narrative." It is published to commemorate the 400th anniversary of the arrival of the first Africans in Virginia.

## 15

Brothers Isaac and Joe Clark, two of the men who incorporated the town in 1887

1887: **27 Black voters create Eatonville, Florida's first all-Black incorporated municipality,** on 100 acres of land a former slave had purchased. In 1897, John Hurston, father of author Zora Neale Hurston, will become mayor. Zora's Eatonville experiences will be ingrained in her work, notably her 1928 essay "How It Feels to Be Colored Me" and her 1937 novel "Their Eyes Were Watching God," often listed among the 100 best novels.

1933: **Satchel Paige uses his soon-to-be-famous "hesitation pitch" while playing integrated baseball in Bismarck, ND.** The local newspapers describe it as a "tricky delayed delivery" used "with great effectiveness." He will be inducted into the Baseball Hall of Fame in 1971.

## 16

Woody Strode poster for the 1936 Berlin Olympics. Eighteen African Americans will participate in the games. Inset: Woody Strode as star of the 1960 Western film "Sergeant Rutledge."

August 1936: Woody Strode likely becomes the first Black man to appear on an Olympic games poster. He poses nude for one poster in a series of 55 for the 1936 Berlin Olympics, the first games in which the Olympic torch is brought by relay runners from Greece and the first to be televised (via 25 large screens set up in Berlin). Strode will become a world-class decathlete, NFL football star, champion wrestler, and film actor. The Nazis, eager to push the racial myth of Aryan superiority, will close the exhibit because it includes posters of naked Black and Jewish athletes.

2009: **Usain Bolt,** the Jamaican sprinter and world record holder in several events, **sets a new world record of 9.58 seconds in the men's 100-meter final** at the world track and field championships in Berlin. Considered the greatest sprinter of all time, he is the world record holder in the 100-meter, 200-meter, and 4 x 100-meter relay. He is an eight-time Olympic gold medalist.

# Weekly Planner

**SUNDAY**

**MONDAY**

**TUESDAY**

**WEDNESDAY**

**THURSDAY**

**FRIDAY**

**SATURDAY**

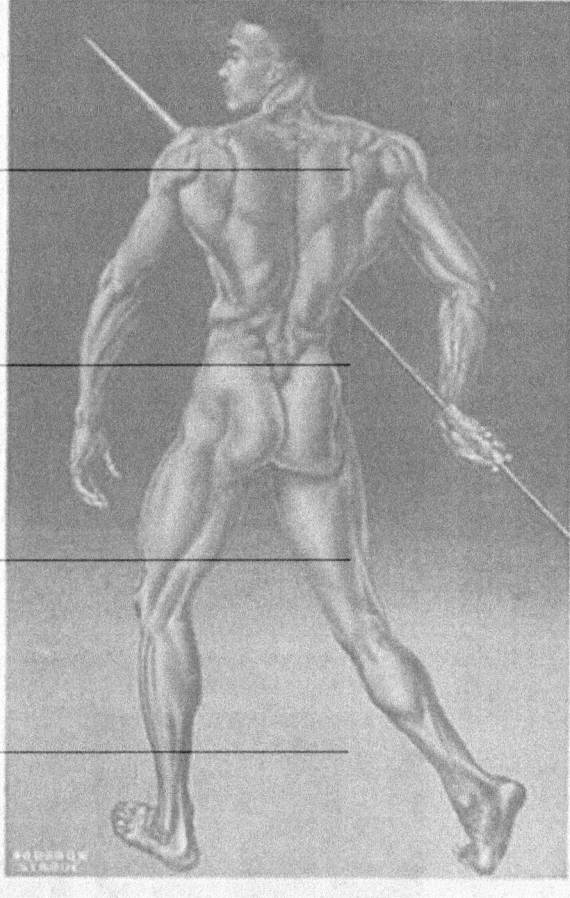

UNTER DEM PROTEKTORAT DES AMERIKANISCHEN BOTSCHAFTERS
UND MITWIRKUNG DER VEREINIGUNG CARL SCHURZ
ANLÄSSLICH DER XI. OLYMPIADE
SPECIAL SPORT EXHIBITION
# AMERICAN CHAMPIONS

FIFTY PORTRAITS OF AMERICAN ATHLETES
BY
## STOWITTS
TIERGARTENSTRASSE 21A · BERLIN · 9.–15. SEPTEMBER 1936
GEÖFFNET VON 10–21 UHR          SONNTAGS VON 10–18 UHR
EINTRITTSPREIS 0.50 RM

Woody Strode poster for the 1936 Berlin Olympics.

# August

## 17

**1959: "Kind of Blue," jazz trumpeter Miles Davis's album, is released. It will become the best-selling instrumental jazz album in history,** with 5 million copies sold. Critics will regard it as his masterpiece. It will be called the greatest jazz album ever recorded and one of the best and most influential albums ever made. One critic will pronounce it a "defining moment of 20th-century music." The album features Davis's sextet: John Coltrane and Julian "Cannonball" Adderley (saxophonists), Bill Evans (pianist), Paul Chambers (bassist), Jimmy Cobb (drummer), and Wynton Kelly (pianist).

**1976: "Roots: The Saga of an American Family," a novel by Alex Haley, is published,** telling the seven-generation story of an American family, from the kidnapping of a 17-year-old Mandinka man in 18th century Africa through enslavement and down to Haley's search for his ancestral roots. The book will spend 46 weeks on The New York Times best-seller list, spawn a 12-hour, 8-episode television miniseries that draws 130 million viewers, and inspire millions of African Americans to trace their family history.

Scan to read "Roots"

## 18

**1920: The 19th Amendment to the United States Constitution is ratified,** guaranteeing women the right to vote. It was first introduced to Congress in 1878. Black women will vote and hold political offices, but many states will pass laws discriminating against African Americans and prevent them from exercising their rights.

James Meredith walking to class at University of Mississippi, accompanied by U.S. marshals.

**1963: James Meredith fulfills his childhood dream of becoming the first African American to graduate from the University of Mississippi,** majoring in political science. He will graduate from Columbia Law School in 1968.

**1969: Jimi Hendrix performs at the Woodstock Festival.** In an uninterrupted set that lasts nearly two hours, he plays "Hey Joe," "Purple Haze," "Star Spangled Banner," "Voodoo Child (Slight Return)," and other songs.

## 19

Frederick Douglass   John Brown

**August 19-21, 1859: John Brown and Frederick Douglass meet** at a quarry near Chambersburg, PA. **Brown tells Douglass his plan to capture the federal armory at Harpers Ferry,** free the enslaved, and lead a rebellion. Douglass warns that Brown is "going into a perfect steel trap" from which he will "never get out alive."

"Come with me, Douglass; I will defend you with my life," John Brown says. "When I strike, the bees will begin to swarm, and I shall want you to help hive them." Frederick Douglass refuses, preferring political action instead of bloodshed.

Weeks later, Brown will attack Harpers Ferry and be arrested by Robert E. Lee (who would later commit treason against the U.S. by joining the Confederacy). Brown will be hanged on December 2.

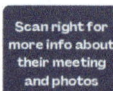
Scan right for more info about their meeting and photos

**1971: Sammy Davis Jr. records "The Candy Man."** He will admit to disliking the song, but it will be his only No. 1 hit.

1619: A year before the Mayflower arrives in New England, **"20 and odd" Angolans arrive in the English-speaking colony of Virginia.** They had been **captured in Angola** by slave raiders, **packed aboard a Portuguese slave ship** bound for the coast of present-day Mexico, **stolen on the high seas,** packed aboard the White Lion, a Dutch warship commanded by an Englishman, and finally **brought to Point Comfort** in Virginia (modern-day Hampton Roads), **where White Lion captain John Colyn Jope sells them for food.**

Emmett Till and his mother Mamie

1955: **Emmett Till, age 14, travels by train from Chicago to Mississippi, where he plans to spend two weeks visiting family.** A few days later, Emmett, his cousins, and friends go to a nearby store to buy candy. Emmett will be accused of acting "familiar" with white storekeeper Carolyn Bryant. Two white men will abduct and kill Emmett, then roll his corpse into a river.

Nat Turner's Bible, which he was holding when captured

### The Bloodiest Slave Revolt in U.S. History

1831: **Nat Turner, a fiery preacher** who believed in signs and heard divine voices, **leads a rebellion of about 75 enslaved people** in Southampton County, VA, murdering 55-65 white people and spreading fear among whites across the South. Turner will hide for two months before he is caught, convicted, and hung; 56 enslaved people will also be tried and executed. White mobs will retaliate, killing 200 enslaved and free Blacks, most of whom were not involved in the rebellion. Some are beheaded and their heads are put on roadside stakes as a warning to Blacks. Laws will be changed to deny Blacks trials by jury and send criminals to Africa. South Carolina will build arsenals to make weapons readily available in the event of another revolt.

1966: **GZA (Gary Grice, a.k.a The Genius),** who will be a rapper, producer, and songwriter, **is born** in NYC. **He will be a founding member of the Wu-Tang Clan** along with his cousins RZA and Ol' Dirty Bastard. GZA will drop out of school in the 10th grade and work as a bicycle messenger while nurturing an interest in science. His rap stories will favor science and philosophy. As a rapper, he will meet scientists and lecture on science and hip hop at Harvard, MIT, NYU, Oxford, USC, and Cornel.

GZA freestyles about the …

**1978: Kobe Bryant is born** in Philadelphia, PA. Regarded as one of the greatest basketball players of all time, Bryant will win five NBA championships, become an 18-time NBA All-Star, an NBA Most Valuable Player, a two-time NBA Finals MVP, and an Olympic gold medalist on the 2008 and 2012 U.S. Olympic teams. He will be the all-time leading scorer in Los Angeles Lakers history, with a career high of 81 points in a single game, second in the NBA only to Wilt Chamberlain's 100-point game.

August 24-30, 1971: **Donny Hathaway records** side one of his "Live" album at The Troubadour in Hollywood, including **"The Ghetto."** He will record side two on October 7 at The Bitter End in Greenwich Village, NY. The album, his most influential, will be released in 1972.

Pullman porter making an upper berth aboard the Capitol Limited, Chicago-bound, 1942

1925: Labor advocate and editor **A. Philip Randolph founds the Brotherhood of Sleeping Car Porters,** the first predominately African American labor union, in New York City. Its members are employees of the Pullman Company, whose owner invented the overnight sleeping train car in the 1880s. The company's Blacks employees, echoing the master-servant dynamics of slavery, shine shoes, make up beds, wake passengers, and do other menial tasks to ensure passenger comfort. The porters endure poor working conditions and long hours and are often summoned with racial slurs, including "boy." The company requires them to travel 11,000 miles and work 400 hours per month, to earn basic wages. The union will play a significant role in the labor and Civil Rights movements.

1997: **Arthur Ashe Stadium opens.** The world's largest tennis stadium, with a capacity of 23,771 seats, is named for Arthur Ashe (1943–1993), the first winner of the men's singles tournament at the U.S. Open in 1968. The stadium hosts the U.S. Open. The first official match is between Tamarine Tanasugarn of Thailand and Chanda Rubin of the United States in the 1997 U.S. Open. Tanasugarn wins in two sets. The first champions in the stadium will be Patrick Rafter of Australia and Martina Hingis of Switzerland.

# Weekly Planner

WEEK OF

**SUNDAY**

**MONDAY**

**TUESDAY**

**WEDNESDAY**

**THURSDAY**

**FRIDAY**

**SATURDAY**

Kobe Bryant

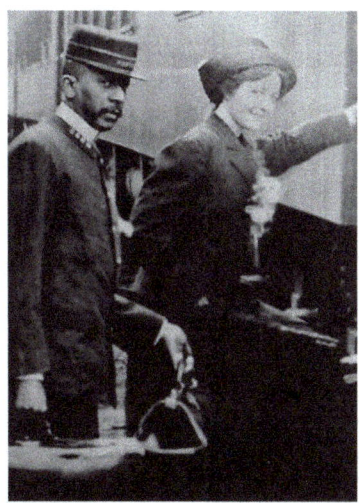

Pullman porter helping a woman, 1880s

## 26

**1918:** **Katherine Johnson is born** in White Sulphur Springs, WV. As a NASA mathematician, **her orbital mechanics calculations will be critical to the success of crewed spaceflights.** She will be nicknamed "human computer."

### "Take My Hand, Precious Lord"

**1932:** Thomas A. Dorsey's wife, Nettie, dies during childbirth, and their child dies days later, throwing composer **Thomas A. Dorsey**'s life into crisis. In his grief, he **writes the song "Take My Hand, Precious Lord,"** which comes direct from God, he says. It will become the favorite song of Martin Luther King Jr., who will ask Dorsey to play it for him on the eve of King's assassination. The father of gospel music, Dorsey will write 3,000 songs and train the first generation of gospel singers, including Mahalia Jackson and James Cleveland.

## 27

Barack Obama accepts his party's nomination

**2008:** **Barack Obama becomes the first African American nominated for the office of President of the United States** by a major political party, the Democratic Party.

## 28

### "I Have a Dream"

**1963:** Standing before the Lincoln Memorial, **Martin Luther King Jr. delivers his historic speech "I Have a Dream"** to a crowd of 250,000 people **at the March on Washington** for Jobs and Freedom. King delivers the first seven-and-a-half paragraphs of a speech written by his attorney, Clarence B. Jones. But when gospel singer Mahalia Jackson shouts, "Tell 'em about your dream, Martin! Tell 'em about your dream!" King lays aside the prepared text and looks out over the crowd. Jones, standing behind King, whispers to a neighbor, "These people [out there] don't know it, but they're about to go to church." King then takes an oratorical detour to describe his "dream" (which he'd mentioned months earlier in Boston) while rubbing his right foot over the back of his left leg. Considered one of the greatest pieces of oratory in U.S. history, the speech, delivered in part like an extemporaneous jazz riff, will galvanize public opinion before Congress votes on society-shaking legislation, the Civil Rights Act of 1964 and the Voting Rights Act of 1965.

## 28

**1955: Emmett Till,** a 14-year-old boy from Chicago, **is abducted from his great-uncle's home, tortured, and shot dead** by two white men, Roy Bryant and J.W. Milam, for allegedly flirting with, touching, or whistling at a young white female storekeeper while buying candy in Money, MS. The killers chain Till to a 74-pound fan and dump his corpse into the Tallahatchie River.

"[T]hey marched him out of the house into a truck that was waiting outside."

**Emmett Till's Casket Goes to the Smithsonian**
Simeon Wright recalls the events surrounding his cousin's murder and the importance of having the casket on public display

## 29

1920: **Charlie Parker is born** in Kansas City, KS.

*Watercolor generated by Midjourney AI*

1958: **Michael Jackson, who will be called the "King of Pop," is born** in Gary, IN.

The roofs of submerged homes east of downtown New Orleans

**2005: Hurricane Katrina makes landfall as a category 3 hurricane near New Orleans, LA,** overwhelming levees and **flooding 80 percent of the city.**

## 30

1901: **Roy Wilkins is born** in St. Louis, MO. He will play a pivotal role in the Civil Rights Movement, serving as executive secretary and executive director of the NAACP. A spokesperson for the movement, he will be called "Mr. Civil Rights." Due to his support for nonviolent activism, he will strongly oppose the militancy of the Black Power Movement. He will help organize the 1963 March on Washington, participate in the Selma-to-Montgomery marches in 1965, confer with Presidents Kennedy, Johnson, Nixon, Ford, and Carter, and testify before Congress.

1967: The **U.S. Senate confirms Thurgood Marshall as the first African American to serve as a U.S. Supreme Court Justice,** in a 69-11 floor vote.

August 30-September 5, 1983: **Guion Bluford becomes the first African American astronaut to fly into space.** He is a mission specialist aboard the Space Shuttle Challenger on its third flight. It is the Space Shuttle program's first night launch and night landing. It will complete 98 orbits of the earth in 145 hours before landing at Edwards Air Force Base in California.

The Tallahatchie River near Glendora, Mississippi, where Till's body is found.

1955: The **corpse of Emmett Till is discovered in the Tallahatchie River**, his face unrecognizable.

**"What else could I do? He thought he was as good as any white man."**
*J.W. Milam's response when asked why he killed Emmett Till*

Mamie Till looks over the body of her son Emmett Till at the morgue before his funeral. With her is her fiancé, Gene Mobley. In 2016, Time Magazine named this photo one of the 100 most influential photos of all time.

At left is a partial photo. The complete photo is disturbing to view. To see it, scan the QR code below.

**Warning**
View at your own discretion

**Mamie Till insisted that her son have an open casket so the world "could see what they did to my baby."**

# September

| SUN | MON | TUE | WED | THU | FRI | SAT |
|-----|-----|-----|-----|-----|-----|-----|
|     |     |     |     |     |     |     |
|     |     |     |     |     |     |     |
|     |     |     |     |     |     |     |
|     |     |     |     |     |     |     |
|     |     |     |     |     |     |     |

George Washington Carver

# September

**WEEK 1**

_____
_____
_____

**WEEK 2**

_____
_____
_____

**WEEK 3**

_____
_____
_____

**WEEK 4**

_____
_____
_____

**WEEK 5**

_____
_____
_____

> IF YOU'RE GOING TO HOLD SOMEONE DOWN YOU'RE GOING TO HAVE TO HOLD ON BY THE OTHER END OF THE CHAIN. YOU ARE CONFINED BY YOUR OWN REPRESSION.
>
> TONI MORRISON

**MAJOR**

**MINOR**

**HABIT TRACKER**   S   M   T   W   T   F   S

**MISC**

# To-Do List

Date:

# NOTES

# Weekly Planner

_____WEEK OF_____

**SUNDAY**

**MONDAY**

**TUESDAY**

**WEDNESDAY**

**THURSDAY**

**FRIDAY**

**SATURDAY**

# September

## 1

**1773: Phillis Wheatley becomes the first African American to publish a book of poetry,** "Poems on Various Subjects, Religious and Moral."

**1967: Louis Armstrong's song "What a Wonderful World" is released.** It was recorded in United Recording Studio in Las Vegas after Armstrong's midnight show. Armstrong completed the recording session at 6 a.m. The song will become a standard, ranked among the best of all time.

**1975: Daniel "Chappie" James** of the U.S. Air Force becomes the first African American to be promoted to four-star general in the U.S. military. He is named commander in chief of the North American Aerospace Defense Command, which gives him operational command of all U.S. and Canadian strategic aerospace defense forces.

## 2

Anthony Barboza

Romare Bearden, 1976

**1911: Romare Bearden is born** in Charlotte, NC. The New York Times will describe him as "**the nation's foremost collagist.**" He will be a man of many talents, however. He **will write or co-write several books and plays and compose music.** His song "Sea Breeze" will become a jazz classic recorded by Billie Eckstine and Dizzy Gillespie. He will pitch in the Negro leagues and **receive an offer to play for a Major League Baseball team,** the Philadelphia Athletics, **15 years before Jackie Robinson becomes MLB's first Black player.** Bearden will enjoy Harlem in an era when the Savoy attracts several thousand "happy feet" every night and Pig Foot Mary's food cart spreads the aroma of roasted pigs' feet across city blocks. Bearden will serve in the U.S. Army on the European front during World War II, study at U.S. art schools and the Sorbonne in Paris, talk shop with Picasso, and host a group of talented artists in his Harlem studio. In July 1963, he will cofound The Spiral, an art collective committed to the civil rights struggle and intrigued by aesthetic problems. His art will be exhibited in leading museums, and in 1987, he will be awarded the National Medal of Arts. One hundred years after his birth, the U.S. Postal Service will release Forever stamps of his art so customers can adorn letters and packages with miniature facsimiles of his work.

## 3

Anthony Barboza

James Van Der Zee 1980

**1916: James Van Der Zee opens the Guarantee Photo Studio in Harlem**, launching decades of photography that documents the life of Harlem and notable Black figures. His work will include studio portraits, funeral portraits, and street scenes. **He will become a famous photographer and a leading figure in the Harlem Renaissance.** Among his subjects: Joe Louis, Countee Cullen, Bill Robinson, A'Lelia Walker, Daddy Grace, Florence Mills, and Marcus Garvey.

# September

## 4

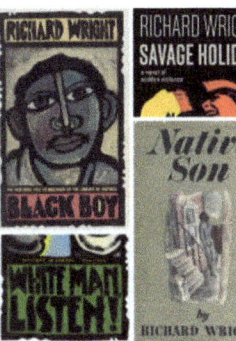

1908: **Richard Wright is born** in Roxie, MS.

Scan to read Richard Wright sampler

1981: **Beyoncé** (Beyoncé Giselle Knowles) **is born** in Houston, TX. She will become a cultural icon who is sometimes called Queen Bey. Her voice will be "one of the most compelling instruments in popular music," according to a critic. NPR will rank her **No. 1 on its list of the 21st century's most influential women musicians.**

## 5

Nerissa Ward

Jesmyn Ward

2017: **Jesmyn Ward's novel "Sing, Unburied, Sing" is published. It will win the National Book Award for Fiction, making her the first African American to win twice.** She first won the award in 2011 for her novel "Salvage the Bones."

Scan to read book preview
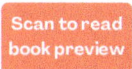

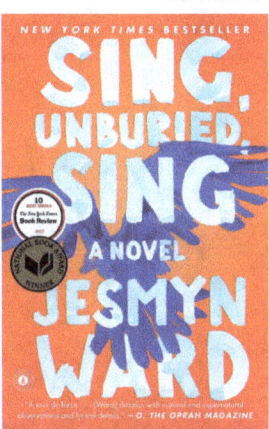

NEW YORK TIMES BESTSELLER
SING, UNBURIED, SING
A NOVEL
JESMYN WARD

Jesmyn Ward's 'Sing, Unburied, Sing' is a ghost st...

## 6

Frances E.W. Harper

September-October 1859: **Frances E.W. Harper** published her story "The Two Offers" in the Anglo-African Magazine, becoming **the first African American woman to publish a short story.** Five years earlier, she published "Poems of Miscellaneous Subjects," which included her most famous poem, "Bury Me in a Free Land." Harper was steadfast and courageous. In 1858, she refused to give up her seat on a segregated Philadelphia trolley car—nearly a century before Rosa Parks's refusal to move would send tremors through the segregated South. The anti-slavery newspaper "The Liberator" published Harper's account. "I did not move, but kept the same seat," she wrote. "When I was about to leave, [the conductor] refused my money, and I threw it down on the car floor, and got out, after I had ridden as far as I wished. Such impudence!"

Scan to read "The Two Offers"

Weekly Planner

WEEK OF _____

SUNDAY

MONDAY

TUESDAY

WEDNESDAY

THURSDAY

FRIDAY

SATURDAY

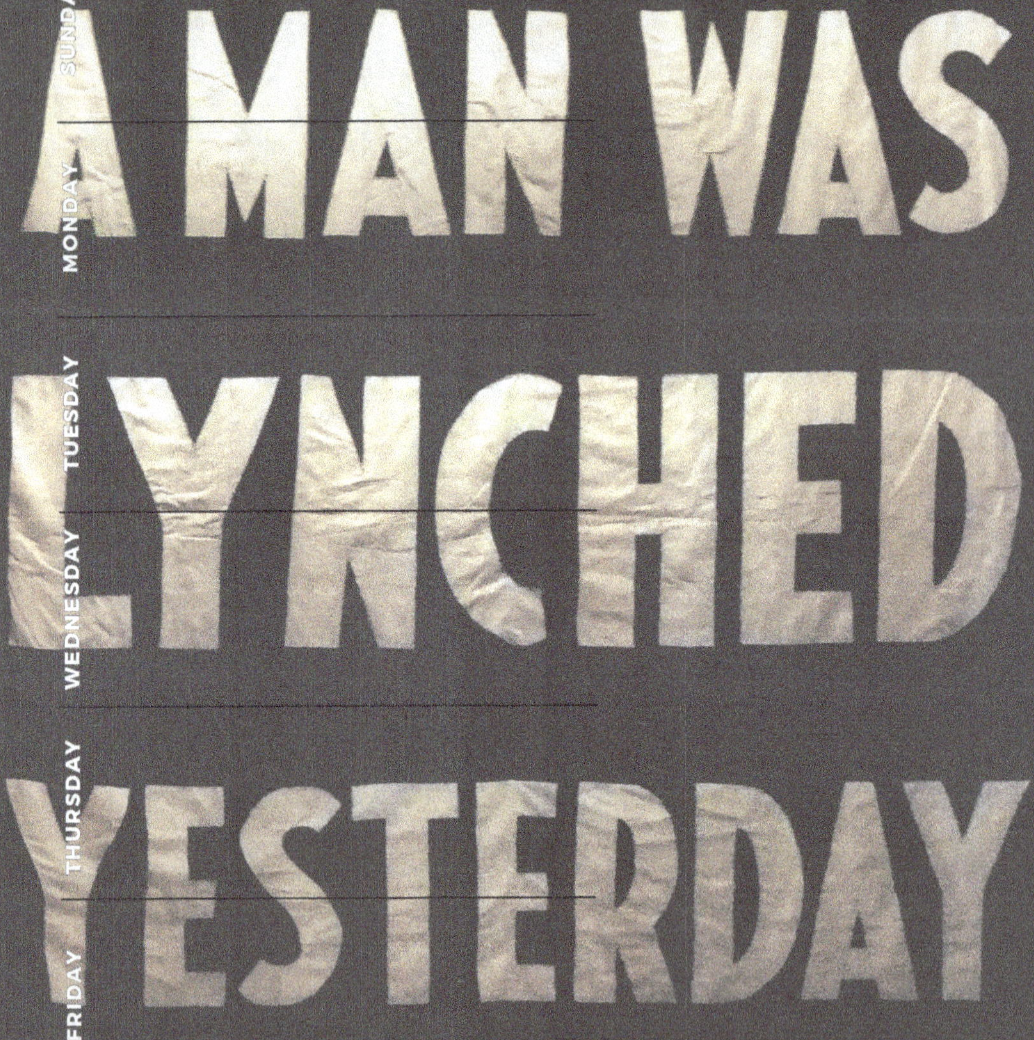

A MAN WAS LYNCHED YESTERDAY

Replica of the 1920 flag flown by the NAACP when a lynching occurred in the United States

# September

## 7

Anthony Barboza

**1917:** **Jacob Lawrence is born** in Atlantic City, NJ. He will become **the first Black artist featured in New York's Museum of Modern Art.** His art will hang in the White House.

**2010:** **Isabel Wilkerson's nonfiction book "The Warmth of Other Suns" is published,** its title derived from a Richard Wright poem. The book tells the story of the Great Migration of Black Americans from Southern states to the Midwest, Northeast, and West from 1915 to 1970. It will win many honors, including the National Book Critics Circle Award.

Scan to read book preview

## 8

Seeking Sanctuary

**1565:** **St. Augustine is founded by Don Pedro Menéndez de Avilés, who arrived from Spain with 800 colonists,** including free and enslaved Africans. **Juanillo, a castaway captured in 1562, becomes the first recorded Black resident of St. Augustine.** Due to his knowledge of Indigenous languages, he serves as an interpreter.

**1936:** As part of its anti-lynching campaign, **the NAACP flies a 6-by-10-foot flag from its headquarters at 69 Fifth Avenue in Manhattan to mark the lynching of A.L. McCamy in Dalton, GA: "A Man was Lynched Yesterday."** The NAACP will raise the flag for two years—until the landlord threatens eviction. The original flag will be stored in the Library of Congress collection.

*"Honestly, thank you to the people who didn't believe in me … To those who thought you were putting water on my fire, you were really adding gas to it, and I'm really burning so bright right now."*
*Coco Gauff*

Scan to watch

## 9

**1739:** **The Stono Rebellion, a deadly slave uprising, begins.** A literate slave named Jemmy (in some accounts, Cato) leads 20 armed Africans (perhaps former Congolese soldiers) on a 15-mile march south from the Stono River toward Spanish Florida, where freedom is promised to slaves from British North America. The Africans recruit others en route, kill 20 whites, and are defeated by the South Carolina militia a week later. Most of the Africans will be executed; others will be sold in slave markets in the West Indies.

**1969:** **Maya Angelou's autobiography, "I Know Why the Caged Bird Sings," is published.** The first in a series of seven autobiographical works, it chronicles her often traumatic early life, from age 3 to 16.

*"The needs of a society determine its ethics."*
*Maya Angelou*

**2023:** **Coco Gauff, age 19, wins her first grand slam tennis title, the US Open,** beating Aryna Sabalenka in three sets to become the first teenager to win the US Open since one of her idols, Serena Williams, won in 1999. In 2019, at age 15, Gauff beat her other tennis idol, Venus Williams, in straight sets at Wimbledon.

# September

## 10

W.E.B. Du Bois

1899: **W.E.B. Du Bois's "The Philadelphia Negro" is published by the University of Pennsylvania.** It is the first sociological case study of an African American community, a systematic investigation of Blacks' social conditions at the end of the century in the city's Seventh Ward. Over three years, Du Bois mapped every Black residence, business, and church in the community, conducted interviews, and gathered statistics. The text reveals a Philadelphia borough where Black citizens endure racial discrimination and poverty.

The Philadelphia Negro A Social Study (1899)

**Scan for full text**

W.E.B. Dubois

## 11

William Parker's house, site of the Christiana Rebellion

### Pre-Civil War September 11th

1851: **The Christiana Resistance, an armed resistance by free Blacks and escaped slaves, prevents slaveowner Edward Gorsuch of Maryland and a federal marshal from capturing four of Gorsuch's six runaway slaves.** The resistance takes place in the early morning at the home of William Parker, where two of Gorsuch's runaways are staying. Parker, an escaped slave, leads his household up to the second floor, where they plan to defend themselves with guns. Gorsuch, federal marshals, and other slave catchers surround Parker's house. Parker's wife, Eliza, blows a horn, signaling neighbors for help. Both Blacks and whites arrive, many of them armed. Gorsuch enters the house. He is shot and killed. The rest of Gorsuch's party gallop off on horseback. The Christiana Resistance gains national attention. To appease the South, President Millard Filmore calls out the Marines, who arrest 141 Blacks and whites. They are charged with treason. Jury deliberation in the first trial lasts only 15 minutes before charges are dropped. Eventually, all 141 are released. The rebellion arouses anger in the South, helping to ignite the Civil War.

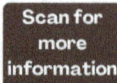
**Scan for more information**

## 12

### Society's Best-Kept Secret

1953: For her wedding, future First Lady Jacqueline Bouvier Kennedy wears an ivory silk taffeta wedding dress designed by Ann Lowe, the first African American to become a noted designer, with a shop on ritzy Madison Avenue and customers such as the Roosevelts, du Ponts, Rockefellers, and Whitneys. However, she will remain their secret. Ten days prior to the Kennedy wedding, Lowe's workroom flooded. She and her staff had to recreate months of work in under two weeks. Despite wedding dress descriptions in the press, Lowe will not receive credit for her Kennedy gown for a decade. In 1964, a Saturday Evening Post article will call her "Society's Best-Kept Secret." Her wealthy clientele realized they could get Dior quality at rock-bottom prices, so they would talk down Lowe's prices, and after paying seamstresses, Lowe would lose money. At the height of her career, she will be penniless.

Aboard the Endeavor, Mae Jemison orbits the earth 127 times, logging 190 hours, 30 minutes, and 23 seconds.

September 12-20, 1992: **Mae Jemison becomes the first Black woman to travel into space,** aboard the space shuttle Endeavor.

# September

## 13

Lewis Latimer

**1881: Lewis Latimer receives a patent** for a cardboard-encased carbon filament, **which makes incandescent lighting practical and affordable and is longer-lasting than earlier filaments.** In 11 months, he will receive another patent for the filament-manufacturing process. **He'd already drawn the original plans for Alexander Graham Bell's telephone** and invented the toilet for railroad cars. **He will go on to design and patent the threaded lightbulb socket, develop a forerunner to the air conditioner** ("Apparatus for cooling and disinfecting"), **seek a patent for a safety elevator that prevents riders from falling into the shaft, write the first book on electrical lighting, and supervise the installation of all public lighting in New York, Philadelphia, Montreal, and London.**

**1994:** The **Notorious B.I.G.'s debut studio album, "Ready to Die," is released** by Bad Boy Records and Arista Records. It will spawn three singles: "Juicy," "Big Poppa," and "One More Chance."

## 14

Constance Baker Motley in 1965

**1921: Constance Baker Motley is born** in New Haven, CT. She will become a front-line lawyer for the NAACP Legal Defense and Educational Fund and will be the first Black woman to argue before the U.S. Supreme Court, arguing 10 cases and winning nine of them. She will handle hundreds of Civil Rights cases from 1945 through the mid-1960s. She will personally lead the litigation to integrate the Universities of Georgia, Alabama, Mississippi, and other schools, and will play a pivotal role in Brown v. Board of Education, the landmark school desegregation case. In 1964, she will become the first Black woman elected to the New York State Senate. The following year, she will serve as the first woman President of the Borough of Manhattan. In 1966, President Lyndon B. Johnson will appoint her to the federal bench in the Southern District of New New York, making her the first African American woman to serve as a federal judge.

Some Fun Tonight

**1955: Little Richard, considered the "architect of rock and roll," records "Tutti Fruitti"** in New Orleans, LA. The wild but irresistible refrain of this major hit, his first, is: "A-wop-bop-a-loo-mop-a-lop-bam-boom!" Some think it's the best, most inspired rock lyric ever recorded. The hard-driving song will receive top billing among the 100 records that changed the world.

### *A-wop-bop-a-loo-mop-a-lop-bam-boom!*

# Weekly Planner

WEEK OF _____

**SUNDAY**

**MONDAY**

Scan below to read preview

**TUESDAY**

Nathan & Polly Johnson House - Video ...

**WEDNESDAY**

Scan above to tour the Nathan and Polly Johnson House, where Douglass lived and where three of his children were born.

**THURSDAY**

**FRIDAY**

**SATURDAY**

# September

## 15

**Birmingham Post-Herald** HOME EDITION

# BOMB BLAST KILLS 4 CHILDREN, INJURES 17 AT CHURCH HERE

The four girls killed in the bombing, clockwise from top left: Addie Mae Collins (14), Cynthia Wesley (14), Carole Robertson (14), and Carol Denise McNair (11).

1963: Days after Birmingham, AL, schools are integrated, Ku Klux Klan members plant 19 sticks of dynamite on a timing device outside the basement of the 16th Street Baptist Church. Unaware that their lives are about to end or change forever, five children put on choir robes in the basement. **At 10:22 a.m., an anonymous caller phones the church and warns, "Three minutes." Less than a minute later, the bomb explodes, killing four of the five children and injuring twenty-two others.** "It was just a matter of time," Pastor John H. Cross will say. "We've been expecting this all along." It is the city's 41st bombing within the past 16 years.

Scan to see the results of other Birmingham bombings

## 16

1896: **Freddie Stowers is born** in Barnwell, SC. He will become **the most decorated African American soldier in World War I.** He will be awarded the Medal of Honor posthumously for his actions in the Champagne-Marne defensive and the Aisne-Marne offensive in 1918.

Scan left to read Medal of Honor Citation

1925: **B.B. King (Riley B. King) is born** in Berclair, MS. He will be crowned the **King of the Blues** and become one of the most influential guitarists of the last half of the 20th century.

1987: **"Beloved," Toni Morrison's fifth novel, is published** by Alfred A. Knopf. Its haunting story is derived from the tragic real-life story of Margaret Garner, a slave who escaped Kentucky and fled to the free state of Ohio in 1856 (see January 27). When U.S. marshals broke into her house to return her to slavery, she was attempting to kill her children to spare them from slavery. She had already killed her youngest daughter. "Beloved" will win the Pulitzer Prize for Fiction, and critics will list it among the 100 most influential novels. Yet, in the 2021-22 school year, at least 11 U.S. schools will ban it for various censorship reasons.

## 17

1821: The **African Grove Theatre, a 300-seat venue on Mercer and Bleecker Streets in NYC, debuts its first production,** the opera "Richard III," with Black actors and crew. The Grove, the nation's first Black theater, founded by William Henry Brown, will produce classical plays, ballet, music, and opera to entertain Black New Yorkers, free or enslaved.

### From Frederick Bailey to Frederick Douglass

1838: Frederick Bailey and his bride Anne, who helped him escape slavery, arrive via stagecoach at the New Bedford, MA, home of Nathan and Polly Johnson, free black abolitionists in the city, which harbors 300-700 fugitive slaves on any given day. Nathan suggests Frederick change his surname to Douglas, a character in Walter Scott's poem "The Lady of the Lake." Frederick likes the idea and adds a second "s" to the name. He shovels coal, reads the abolitionist paper The Liberator, registers to vote, and attends abolitionist meetings. Douglass will become a lay preacher in the African Methodist Episcopal Zion Church, where he will develop oratorical skills. A white banker will invite him to speak at the Massachusetts Anti-Slavery Society's 1841 convention in Nantucket. The speech will launch his career as an antislavery lecturer.

# September

## 18

1850: **Congress passes the Fugitive Slave Act of 1850, which requires that slaves be returned to their owners, even if they flee to a free state.** It also makes the U.S. government responsible for finding, returning, and trying escaped slaves.

1895: **Booker T. Washington gives his Atlanta Compromise speech** at the opening of the Atlanta Exposition before a predominantly white audience. It is the first speech delivered by an African American to a racially mixed audience in the South. In it, Washington says Blacks shouldn't agitate for political and social equality but should work hard and earn whites' respect by acquiring job skills. Only then will white society grant them full citizenship.

Scan to hear Booker T. Washington recite his speech

## 19

1865: **Atlanta University is founded by ex-slaves** James Tate and Grandison Daniels as the first HBCU in the Southern U.S. It will be the nation's first graduate school to award degrees to African Americans and the first Southern institution to grant bachelor's degrees to African Americans. In 1988 it will consolidate with Clark College, founded in 1869 as the nation's first four-year liberal arts college to serve African American students. The consolidated schools will become Clark Atlanta University.

### Camilla Massacre

1868: After fulfilling Congress's Reconstruction requirements by giving Blacks the right to vote after the Civil War, Georgia is readmitted to the Union. But the state legislature expelled 33 newly elected members because they were at least one-eighth Black. Philip Joiner, one of those expelled, leads several hundred Blacks and a few whites on a 25-mile march from Albany, GA, to Camilla, GA, a majority-white town and the Mitchell County seat, where they plan to hold a political rally. Camilla's sheriff warns the marchers that they will meet violence in the town. Marchers arrive and enter the courthouse square, where whites deputized by the sheriff open fire. The marchers retreat to the swamp and are chased for miles. An estimated 9-15 Blacks are killed, 40 more are wounded. Whites then beat Blacks and warn them they will be killed if they show up at the polls on election day. The massacre will intimidate African Americans from voting, and election fraud will ensure victory for white Democrats, the racial minority in southwest Georgia.

## 20

**Mitchelville Founded**
September 1862: Union Army General Ormsby Mitchell proposes the construction of a village on Hilton Head Island, SC, for slaves fleeing Confederate-held territory. Within a few months, **Mitchelville, the first Black self-governed town in the U.S., is founded.** It has patterned streets, quarter-acre plots, houses constructed with material provided by the army, an elected government, laws, a church (the First African Baptist Church), schools, and stores. White visitors need passes.

Scan to Explore Mitchelville

2023: The **U.S. Senate confirms U.S. Air Force General Charles Q. Brown, the 22nd Chief of Staff of the Air Force, as Chairman of the Joint Chiefs of Staff,** the highest ranking and most senior military officer in the U.S. Armed Forces and the chief military advisor to the President, the National Security Council, the Homeland Security Council, and the Secretary of Defense. He will be the second Black chairman of the Joint Chiefs; the first was Colin Powell, who took office in 1989. With General Brown as the new chairman and Lloyd J. Austin III as Secretary of Defense, the top two U.S. military positions will be held by Black men for the first time in history. Forty-three percent of the 1.3 million men and women on active duty in the military are people of color. General Brown will be sworn in on September 29, 2023.

WEEK OF

SUNDAY

MONDAY

TUESDAY

WEDNESDAY

THURSDAY

FRIDAY

SATURDAY

# September

## 21

**Buffalo Soldiers**

1866: The **U.S. Army forms an African American unit, the 10th Cavalry, one of the original Buffalo Soldiers regiments in the post-Civil War Regular Army.** The members will be nicknamed Buffalo Soldiers by Native American tribes in the Indian Wars. The members of all African American regiments formed in 1866 will become known as Buffalo Soldiers: the 9th and 10th Cavalry Regiments, the 24th and 25th Infantry Regiments, and the Second 38th Infantry Regiment.

## 22

1862: **President Abraham Lincoln issues the preliminary Emancipation Proclamation** declaring that on January 1, 1863, all those enslaved in rebellious states "shall be then, thenceforward, and forever free." The decree applies only to those enslaved in Confederate states, not to those enslaved in states loyal to the Union.

Mary Lou Willia...

**For Mary Lou Williams, Piano Is Key**

During 1916: Mary Lou Williams, age six, learns that the piano is key to survival. To stop her white neighbors from throwing bricks into her home, Williams gives them private piano concerts. When she breaks her arm, her white neighbors knock on her door and ask where their music has gone. She will become known as the first lady of the jazz keyboard. At age 13, Mary Lou Williams will play with Duke Ellington's band, the Washingtonians. She will also arrange and compose several tunes for Ellington and Benny Goodman, Earl Hines, and Tommy Dorsey; host a weekly radio show ("Mary Lou Williams's Piano Workshop"); mentor and collaborate with Thelonious Monk, Charlie Parker, Miles Davis, and Dizzy Gillespie; compose the bebop hit "In the Land of Oo-Bla-Dee"; play gigs with Bud Powell, Art Blakey, and Ben Webster; write liturgical music ("I am praying through my fingers when I play"); teach at Duke University; form her own record label and publishing company; perform at the White House; and record more than 100 records.

## 23

1863: **Mary Church Terrell** (Mary Eliza Church) **is born** in Memphis, TN. She will be **among the first African American women to earn a college degree.** She will become **a national activist for civil rights and suffrage**. At 17, she will meet Frederick Douglass at President James Garfield's inaugural gala and work with him on civil rights issues. In 1892, **she will cofound the Colored Women's League and serve as the first president of the National Association of Colored Women.** She will publish articles on the African American Women's Club Movement and **become a founding member of the NAACP.**

1926: **John Coltrane is born** in Hamlet, NC.

1930: **Ray Charles is born** in Albany, GA.

1946: **Paul Robeson**, singer, actor, and civil rights activist, **sings in the rain at a Lincoln Memorial rally calling for President Harry Truman and Congress to create federal legislation to end lynching.**

Anthony Barboza

1935: **Louis H. Draper, future photographer, is born** in Richmond, VA. In 1963, **he will cofound the Kamoinge Workshop, a Black photography collective.**

2016: The **National Museum of African American History and Culture,** the 19th museum of the Smithsonian Institution, **opens to the public in Washington, DC.**

Plan Your Visit

AP

Black student Elizabeth Eckford is jeered by white student Hazel Bryan as Eckford attempts to enter Little Rock Central High School.

**Little Rock Nine**

1957: **Escorted by troops from the 101st Airborne Division, nine young black girls enter—and integrate—the all-white Central High School in Little Rock, AR,** three weeks after Arkansas Governor Orval Faubus ordered National Guard troops to surround the school and prevent its federal court-ordered integration.

Collection of the Smithsonian National Museum of African American History and Culture, Gift of Carlotta Walls LaNier

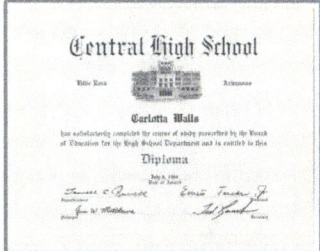

Carlotta Walls's Little Rock Central High School diploma, 1960

1981: **Serena Williams, among the greatest tennis players of all time, is born** in Saginaw, MI.

First-round doubles action from the Women's draw at the 2013 US Open. Serena and Venus Williams defeat Silvia Soler-Espinosa and Carla Suarez Navarro; 6-7(5), 6-0, 6-3

**WEEK OF**_____

SUNDAY

MONDAY

TUESDAY

WEDNESDAY

THURSDAY

FRIDAY

SATURDAY

# September

## 27

1827: **Hiram R. Revels,** future African Methodist Episcopal Church minister and college administrator, **is born** in Fayetteville, NC. The **Mississippi legislature will elect him to represent the state in the U.S. Senate** in 1870 and 1871 during the Reconstruction era, making him **the first African American to serve in either house of the U.S. Congress.**

**Scan above for more about Hiram Revels in the U.S. Senate**

## 28

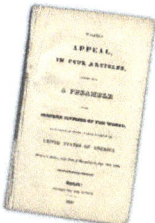

1829: David Walker publishes "Appeal to the Colored Citizens of the World," calling for the immediate abolition of slavery.

**Scan to read it**

1980: The new, five-story **Schomburg Center for Research in Black Culture opens in Harlem** near the geographic heart of the Harlem Renaissance. It **houses 10 million objects** of national and international significance, including a signed first edition book of poems by Phillis Wheatley, and the **papers, manuscripts, files, rare recordings, or archival material** of John Henrik Clarke, Lorraine Hansberry, Langston Hughes, Malcolm X, Nat King Cole Ralph Bunche, William Pickens, Paul Robeson, Booker T. Washington, Toussaint Louverture, and Marcus Garvey. The **ashes of Langston Hughes will be buried under the lobby floor**, beneath an inlaid mosaic cosmogram with lines from his poem "The Negro Speaks of Rivers."

**Scan left to see which two poets danced over Langston Hughes's ashes buried at the Schomburg**

## 29

**Scan**

**A Black Founding Father?**

1784: **Prince Hall** founds African American Freemasonry.

1910: The **National Urban League,** originally named the Committee on Urban Conditions Among Negroes, **is founded in New York City.**

**©CBS NEWS**

1998: Gordon Parks photographs 177 hip hop artists, producers, and influencers at 17 East 126th Street in Harlem for the cover of XXL Magazine. "A Great Day in Hip-Hop" is Parks's homage to Art Kane's historic photo of 58 jazz greats in front of the same Harlem brownstone for the January 4, 1959 issue of Esquire Magazine. Kane's photograph is entitled "A Great Day in Harlem." (See Kane's photograph on August 12.)

2023: **General Charles Q. Brown,** an Air Force fighter pilot with 130 combat flying hours in his military career, is sworn in as Chairman of the Joint Chiefs of Staff.

## 30

1859: The **inventor Benjamin Boardley** (also known as Bradley) **purchases his freedom using the $1,000 he had earned by developing and building the U.S. Navy's first steam-powered warship.** He was unable to patent his work while enslaved. He will go on to be an instructor at the Naval Academy.

**Scan to see Boardley's steam engine**

# October

| SUN | MON | TUE | WED | THU | FRI | SAT |
|-----|-----|-----|-----|-----|-----|-----|
|     |     |     |     |     |     |     |
|     |     |     |     |     |     |     |
|     |     |     |     |     |     |     |
|     |     |     |     |     |     |     |
|     |     |     |     |     |     |     |

Model: Pat Evans                    Photo: Anthony Barboza

# October

**WEEK 1**

_____
_____
_____
_____

**WEEK 2**

_____
_____
_____
_____

**WEEK 3**

_____
_____
_____

**WEEK 4**

_____
_____
_____
_____

**WEEK 5**

_____
_____
_____

**THE COST OF LIBERTY
IS LESS THAN THE
PRICE OF REPRESSION.
W.E.B. DUBOIS**

**MAJOR**

**MINOR**

**HABIT TRACKER**      S   M   T   W   T   F   S

_____
_____
_____
_____

**MISC**

# To-Do List

Date:

# NOTES

# Weekly Planner

_____ **WEEK OF** _____

**SUNDAY**

**MONDAY**

**TUESDAY**

FOLIES-BERGÈRE

JOSÉPHINE BAKER

HYPER-REVUE

UN VENT DE FOLIE

**WEDNESDAY**

**THURSDAY**

1927 poster advertising a Josephine Baker
performance at the Folies Bergère

**FRIDAY**

**SATURDAY**

## 1

September 30-October 1, 1962: **James Meredith becomes the first African American student to enroll at the University of Mississippi.** Twenty-four federal marshals escort him; 538 federal law enforcement officers also arrive. **A mob of 2,500 whites riot, throwing Molotov cocktails and acid.** Someone drives a stolen bulldozer into the line of marshals; 26 are wounded, and two civilians are killed. **President Kennedy orders the U.S. military to respond; 31,000 troops arrive in the largest mobilization for a single disturbance in U.S. history.** Troops on campus outnumber students 5-to-1.

**Thrilla in Manila**

1975: **Muhammad Ali and Joe Frazier meet in the boxing ring in their third and final match** for the world heavyweight boxing championship. The fight, billed as the "Thrilla in Manila," is held at the Araneta Coliseum in metro Manila, Philippines. **Ali wins in 14 rounds after Frazier's corner asks the referee to stop the fight.** An estimated 1 billion view the fight, which will be remembered as one of the most brutal in boxing history. Ali has now won two of the boxers' three bouts. (See March 8 for bout #1 and January 28 for #2.)

1989: Four-star General **Colin Powell becomes the youngest officer and the first Black American to be sworn in as Chairman of the Joint Chiefs of Staff,** the highest-ranking and most senior military officer in the U.S. Armed Forces.

## 2

Josephine Baker visits a Paris nightclub

**Paris Adores La Baker**

1925: Josephine Baker makes her Paris debut in La Revue Nègre at the Théâtre des Champs-Élysées at the height of the Jazz Era. She captivates the audience with a new dance, the Charleston, and Paris falls in love. The papers proclaim, "The Black Venus in Paris," and La Baker becomes the toast of the town and the high priestess of jazz. Hordes of Parisians adore her.

1935: **Robert Henry Lawrence Jr. is born** in Chicago, IL. He will become a major in the U.S. Air Force, earn a Ph.D. in physical chemistry from Ohio State University, complete test flights that contribute "greatly to the development of the Space Shuttle," and become **the first Black astronaut.**

## 3

Mary McLeod Bethune (2nd from left) with teachers, male helpers, students, cows, mule, and horse. The Institute is established with five girls in a rented cabin. By 1918, there will be a four-story building called Faith Hall, a two-story building used for a kitchen and a new $40,000 auditorium on 20 acres.

1904: With just $1.50, **Mary McLeod Bethune establishes the Daytona Literary and Industrial Training Institute for Negro Girls.** She uses charred wood for pencils and elderberries for ink. The school has just six pupils, including her son, but in two years, it will grow to 250, and **in 1923, it will merge with another institution and become Bethune-Cookman College.** She will open a hospital and nursing school, found the National Council of Negro Women, become an advisor to Franklin D. Roosevelt, create his unofficial Black Cabinet and serve as its only woman, and cofound the United Negro College Fund.

**WERD**

ATLANTA—1949

Frequency: 860 Kc.....Power: 1000 Watts d.
Owned-Operated By......Radio Atlanta, Inc.
Business-Studio Add...274½ Auburn Ave., NE
Phone Number...............Lamar 0566-7-8
Transmitter Location...Fairmount Street, NW
Air Time ............................Daytime

1949: **WERD, the first radio station owned and programmed by African Americans, begins broadcasting** (on 860 AM). Jessie B. Blayton Sr., a bank president and Atlanta University professor, purchased WERD for $50,000 and changed its format to become a voice for Black folks in an era when Black views on the dial were scarce.

# October

## 4

1951: **Henrietta Lacks,** the great-great-granddaughter of a slave, **dies at age 31** of aggressive cervical cancer in Baltimore and will be buried in an unmarked grave, but only after **a patch of skin is harvested** from her cervix without her permission or her family's. **Cells in the patch will thrive inexplicably and grow trillions of more cells, which will be bought, sold, labeled, and stored in labs and biotechnology companies globally. They will spawn thousands of patents and launch a medical revolution.** A cell line will be named for Henrietta Lacks: HeLa (pronounced hee-lah). It will become the most wondrous and widely exploited human cell line in science, leading to treatments for hemophilia, herpes, influenza, leukemia, and Parkinson's disease, and to the polio vaccine, a cancer drug (tamoxifen), chemotherapy, gene mapping, and in vitro fertilization. Lacks's cells will generate millions of dollars in profits, and the Lacks family will see none of it. Lacks will otherwise be forgotten, and an obituary will not be written for decades. But 22 years after Lacks's death, her daughter-in-law will learn from a cancer researcher that Henrietta's cells are the subject of cancer research. She will race home to tell her husband, "Part of your mother, it's alive!"

## 5

1795: **Sally Hemings, Thomas Jefferson's slave and possibly the half-sister of his deceased wife, gives birth** to Harriet at his ancestral home, Monticello. Jefferson is likely the father of this child. Harriet is Sally's second child; the first, born in 1790, lived only a few days. Harriet, too, will die in infancy, but five more children will be born, **each birth listed in Monticello records, each linked genetically to Sally Hemings and Thomas Jefferson. Their descendants will gather at Monticello after a DNA study is published in 1998 indicating a genetic link to both Jefferson and Hemings.** However, Jefferson's acknowledged white descendants will continue to deny that Jefferson and Hemings ever had a sexual relationship.

2001: **The film "Training Day" is released, starring Denzel Washington, who will win the Academy Award for Best Actor in a Leading Role** at the 74th Oscars in 2002, becoming the second African American to win the award. The first, Sidney Poitier, won it in 1964.

## 6

Anthony Barboza

### 81 Jazz Stars Say, "Cheese!"

October 1983: Anthony Barboza photographs the largest assemblage of jazz musicians to appear in a group photograph. Eighty-one musicians (and three offspring) pose on the roof of Barboza's photo studio at 108 East 16th Street in Manhattan, including **Billy Taylor; Bobby Watson; Jay Hoggard; Oliver Lake; Kevin Eubanks,** who will lead "The Tonight Show Band"; **Big Nick Nicholas** (who played with Duke Ellington, Cab Calloway, Charlie Parker, and Charles Mingus and for whom John Coltrane composed a tribute entitled "Big Nick"); and **Henry Threadgill,** who will win the Pulitzer Prize for Music in 2016. (See Art Kane's photo of 58 jazz musicians in Harlem on August 12; also see Gordon Parks's photo of 177 hip hop artists, producers, and influencers on September 29.)

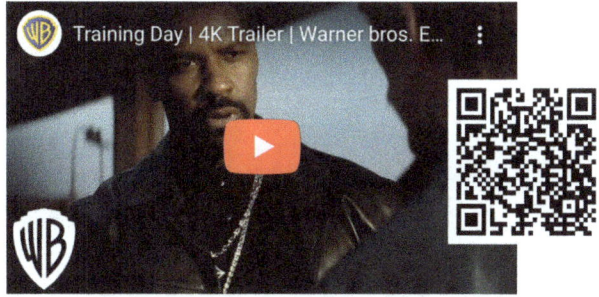

# Weekly Planner

_____ WEEK OF _____

**SUNDAY**

**MONDAY**

**TUESDAY**

**WEDNESDAY**

**THURSDAY**

**FRIDAY**

**SATURDAY**

## 7

1891: **Archibald Motley Jr. is born** in New Orleans, LA. As a major artist, he will visually chronicle the African American experience in Chicago and in the Harlem Renaissance, although he will never actually live in Harlem.

Anthony Barboza

1934: **Amiri Baraka** (Everett LeRoi Jones) **is born** in Newark, NJ. He will write several volumes of poetry, drama, essays, fiction, and music criticism, including "Blues People," considered a seminal book on jazz. His career will span five decades, and he will become the second Poet Laureate of New Jersey. His son, Ras J. Baraka, will be elected mayor of Newark in 2005 and serve several terms.

1969: **The Jackson 5 releases the song "I Want You Back."** It will be this Motown group's first No. 1 hit and will eventually sell six million copies worldwide. It will be one of the greatest debut singles of all time.

## 8

Anthony Barboza

Faith Ringgold

1930: **Faith Ringgold is born** in Harlem, NYC. She will become a major American artist who practices in multiple media, from painting and quilts to sculptures and books. Inspired by the works of James Baldwin, Amiri Baraka, and Jacob Lawrence, **she will paint a political collection named the American People Series,** exploring the charged atmosphere of race, politics, and gender in America. **It will include** two attention-grabbing large-scale murals: **"The Flag Is Bleeding, U.S. Postage Stamp Commemorating the Advent of Black Power,"** which will explore race and national identity (the National Gallery of Art will acquire it); **and "Die," a sort of modern American "Guernica"** in which bloodied Blacks and whites fight and die and run and tumble. "Die" will hang next to Picasso's painting "Les Demoiselles D'Avignon" in New York's Museum of Modern Art. Ringgold will also write and illustrate 17 children's books, including "Tar Beach," the magical story of Cassie Louis Lightfoot, whose dreams come true on the roof of her Harlem apartment building when the stars lift her and she flies over the city.

## 9

George Washington Carver as a child

1855: Enslaver **Moses Carver purchases George Washington Carver's parents, Mary and Giles, for $700.** Mary will give birth to George, who will be born into slavery. His birthdate will never be known. Giles will die before George is born. **When George is one week old, he, his mother, and his sister will be kidnapped by night raiders** in Arkansas. **Only George will be found alive.** Moses will raise him. **He will** go on to study agriculture at Iowa State University, teach at the Tuskegee Institute, **promote alternative crops to cotton and methods to prevent soil depletion, and become the father of organic agriculture.** U.S. presidents will publicly express admiration for him. Henry Ford will build a replica of his birth cabin in Ford's Michigan museum. And schools, museums, bridges, even **a nuclear submarine will bear his name.**

## 10

The Baldwin grand piano owned and used by Thelonious Monk (above) is now in the National Museum of African American History and Culture.

**1917: Thelonious Sphere Monk is born** in Rocky Mount, NC. The future pianist and composer will become a pioneer of modern jazz with a signature playing style featuring dissonances and melodic twists. He will develop this unique style as the house pianist at the Manhattan nightclub Minton's Playhouse, where he will participate in cutting contests. He will be fiercely independent. During performances, he will stop playing, stand up and dance for a time, and then rejoin the band. His style of dress will be cool: suits, hats, sunglasses. His style of improvisation will be playful, unorthodox, and dramatic—with hesitations and silences. His records will be under-appreciated, his style will be ridiculed, but his compositions will be looted. His contributions to jazz will be immense, including such compositions as "Round Midnight," "Straight, No Chaser," and "In Walked Bud." He will be recognized as a founding father of bebop, and his compositions will be recorded more often than any other jazz composer's except Duke Ellington.

## 11

**Lip Takedown**
**1931: Bulldogging, bringing down a steer by biting its lip, was invented by Bill Pickett**, perhaps in 1903, but no one knows for sure exactly when. No matter. An eyewitness in Oklahoma on this day watches Bill Pickett in action and describes it this way: "The steer lunged into the arena. … [Pickett's] horse plunged full speed after it … the rider leaped from the saddle. He turned a complete somersault along the length of the steer's back, flying out and down over the curved horns to fasten his teeth in the side of the steer's mouth. With sheer strength, he dragged the running behemoth's head to the tanbark, thrust its horn in the ground, and forward momentum threw the steer hocks over horns in a somersault of its own."

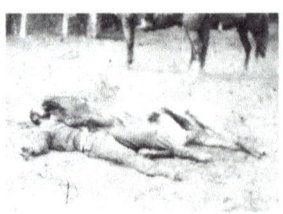

## 12

"President of the United States in Exile," Dick Gregory

**1932: Dick Gregory is born** in St. Louis, MO. He will be a trailblazing comedian who tackles issues, including race, using a satirical, no-holds-barred approach. He will also become a bestselling author, businessman, vegetarian, feminist, lecturer, Civil Rights activist, fasting advocate, and presidential candidate (in 1968, he will receive 47,097 write-in votes). Gregory will be a crossover star, a Black comedian who can make both Blacks and whites laugh by "just talking about what I read in the newspaper." His activism will provide material with a hard edge. Gregory, a friend of MLK, will be arrested many times but claim he got "the first really good beating I ever had in my life" in a Birmingham jail in 1963.

Political leaflet in the form of a counterfeit dollar

# Weekly Planner

WEEK OF _____

**SUNDAY**

**MONDAY**

**TUESDAY**

**WEDNESDAY**

**THURSDAY**

**FRIDAY**

**SATURDAY**

"Trying to explain music is like trying to dance architecture."

*Thelonious Monk*

"Political promises are much like marriage vows. They are made at the beginning of the relationship between candidate and voter, but are quickly forgotten."

*Dick Gregory*

# 13

October 1927: **A'Lelia Walker, philanthropist and arts patron, opens** her redesigned double townhouse at 108-110 West 136th Street, NYC, as a private membership club, the **Dark Tower. Artists, musicians, writers, actors, newspaper publishers, and Civil Rights leaders attend invitation-only, salon-like parties,** including W.E.B. Du Bois, Countee Cullen, Zora Neale Hurston, Andy Razaf, Fredi Washington, Carl Van Vechten, Clarence Darrow, Alberta Hunter, Paul Robeson, James Weldon Johnson, and Langston Hughes.

1962: **Jerry Rice, a future wide receiver in the NFL, is born** in Starkville, MS. The Pro Football Hall of Fame will call him "the most prolific wide receiver in NFL history with staggering career totals." He will set the record for the most career touchdowns (208), career receiving touchdowns (197), career receptions (1,549), and career receiving yards (22,895). He will win three Super Bowl titles with the San Francisco 49ers. As a youth, he will learn to catch by snatching bricks tossed to him as he stood atop scaffolds, making sure his father, a brick mason, had enough bricks to lay as he builds houses by hand.

# 14

## White House, Black Hands

1792: After the previous day's Masonic ceremony to lay the cornerstone of the White House, enslaved labor digs in to construct the home of the President of the United States. The White House will become a beacon of democracy built with the bricks of liberty, bound by the mortar of freedom and the ideals enshrined in the nation's founding documents, and yet forbidden to the builders themselves. Over the next eight years, enslaved people will be deeply involved in every aspect and stage of construction: clearing the land; felling trees; building roads, bridges, and wharves; quarrying, cutting, and moving stone; sawing timber; building kilns; making bricks; laying floors; raising the roof and the walls.

Scan to learn more about the building of the White House

"I wake up every morning in a house that was built by slaves."

*First Lady Michelle Obama (2016)*

# 15

Dancing in Congo Square

## Congo Square: The Heart of New Orleans

1817: The mayor of New Orleans issues a city ordinance restricting gatherings of slaves to one location: Place des Nègres, a grassy commons behind the original city rampart (which will become Rampart Street). Here, on "free Sundays," enslaved Africans will freely enjoy music and dance, set up markets, trade handmade goods, practice their religious traditions, and eat African foods, including calas—hot, deep-fried rice fritters sold out of covered baskets balanced on women's heads. (Calas resemble beignets). As many as 600 slaves and free people of color will congregate in the "place"—which will eventually be called Congo Square, likely because most slaves in the area are of Congolese or Angolan descent. Voodoo will evolve here, and jazz will be born from African rhythmic patterns played here. New Orleans is the only place in America where Africans can own drums. (Elsewhere, slave masters banned drumming by slaves due to a fear of the communicative powers of drums. Slaves in the Stono Rebellion of 1739 used drums to signal one another and recruit others to join the revolt. (See September 9.)

1966: **Huey Newton and Bobby Seale found the Black Panther Party for Self-Defense** in Oakland, CA.

# October

## 16

1859: At about 11 p.m., **John Brown** (see portrait below) **and a band of 21 men raid the arsenal at Harpers Ferry,** VA (now WV), believing 200-500 slaves would join the fight. By morning, they will be surrounded. On the 17th, 10 of the band will be killed, and the rest will be captured by U.S. Marines commanded by Col. Robert E. Lee and Lieut. J.E.B. Stuart. **The raid will be called a prelude to the Civil War**; Northerners will view Brown as a hero; Southerners will consider him a traitor and outlaw.

Gold medalist Tommie Smith (center) and bronze medalist John Carlos (right) raise fists on the podium.

1968: Olympians Tommie Smith and John Carlos raise black-gloved fists in protest during the playing of the U.S. national anthem, "The Star-Spangled Banner," during the medal ceremony at the Summer Olympics in Mexico City, bringing attention to civil rights issues.

1995: The **Million Man March is held in Washington, D.C.** Black men attend as a demonstration of unity of purpose and family values. Estimates of the number of marchers range from 400,000 to 1.1 million.

## 17

1961: **Bill Russell and four other Black Boston Celtics players boycott an NBA exhibition game against the St. Louis Hawks in Lexington, KY, after a hotel coffee waitress says: "I'm sorry, but we don't serve Negroes."** The coach drives them to the airport, and they fly back to Boston, where fans supported the move. "Negroes are in a fight for their rights, a fight for survival in a changing world," Russell told news outlets. It was the first boycott of a game due to a Civil Rights protest. Years later, an NBA Commissioner will say: "Bill stood for something much bigger than sports: the values of equality, respect, and inclusion that he stamped into the DNA of our league."

## 18

1775: **Phillis Wheatley,** the first African American poet to publish a book, **is freed from slavery.**

Anthony Barboza

1948: **Ntozake Shange is born** in Trenton, NJ. She will become an influential poet, playwright, and spoken-word artist—the author of 15 plays, 19 poetry collections, 6 novels, 5 children's books, and 3 essay collections. Her best-known work will be "for colored girls who have considered suicide / when the rainbow is enuf," which will open on Broadway in 1976 when she is 27. The play—which she will call a choreopoem because it blends poetry, dance, and music—will feature a series of monologues delivered by seven Black actresses, each named for a color of the rainbow. She will play the Lady in Orange. Born Paulette Linda Williams, she will adopt her Zulu name as a young woman. It is pronounced en-toh-ZAH-kee SHAHN-gay.

# Weekly Planner

WEEK OF _____

**SUNDAY**

**MONDAY**

**TUESDAY**

Gift of Lorraine Gillespie

**WEDNESDAY**

King B-Flat trumpet used by Dizzy Gillespie from the late 1970s to the early 1980s.

**THURSDAY**

**FRIDAY**

**SATURDAY**

# October

## 19

1870: **Joseph Rainey, a South Carolina barber who bought both his freedom and his family's, is elected to serve a full term in the 42nd Congress, becoming the first African American and formerly enslaved person to win a seat in the U.S. House of Representatives.** He will be sworn in on December 12 and serve with 15 other African Americans during the first decade after the Civil War. He will deliver a major speech on April 1, 1871, arguing for using federal troops to protect southern Blacks from the Ku Klux Klan. As a result, President Ulysses S. Grant will sign the Ku Klux Klan Act into law, but it will not stop the violence. Rainey will receive a letter from the KKK warning him and other Blacks to "prepare to meet your God." Rainey will serve four terms.

Scan for more information on Joseph Rainey

## 20

**Virginia Law Allows the Casual Killing of Slaves**

1669: **Colonial Virginia legislators pass the "casual killing act," which allows enslavers to inflict extreme punishment or kill enslaved people they consider obstinate without facing murder charges.** If a slave dies while resisting his master, the killing will not be presumed as premeditated malice intent against his property. By 1672, it would be perfectly legal to kill an enslaved person who resists arrest, and the owner of the dead slave would receive financial compensation for the loss of his property. In 1723, Virginia will remove all penalties for slave-killing. A slave could be killed simply for picking lousy tobacco. Slave laws passed in Virginia will establish legal standards for treating Blacks and whites differently and set chattel slavery in the colonies apart from enslavement anywhere else.

1890: **Jelly Roll Morton** (Ferdinand Joseph LaMothe) **is born** in New Orleans, LA. At 10, he will learn to play the piano and a few years later will gain experience in the city's bordellos, where he will be nicknamed Jelly Roll. He will blend musical styles —ragtime and minstrelsy and dance rhythms—making him one of the first jazz innovators. He will say he invented jazz, and while that is doubtful, his "Original Jelly Roll Blues" will be the first jazz song published.

1971: **Snoop Dogg** (Calvin Cordozar Broadus Jr.) **is born** in Long Beach, CA. Nicknamed after the cartoon character from "Peanuts," **he will become a West Coast rap icon and sell tens of millions of albums.** Eventually, he will win an American Music Award and 17 Grammy nominations. **He will run record labels, write a cookbook ("From Crook to Cook"), release an app called "Snoopify," and acquire Death Row Records.** 'nuf said.

## 21

JPRoche, Creative Commons Attribution-Share Alike 4.0 International

1917: John Birks **"Dizzy" Gillespie is born** in Cheraw, SC. He will start to play the piano at age four and teach himself to play the trombone and trumpet by age 12. Among his earliest compositions is "Pickin' the Cabbage," which he'll perform when he joins Cab Calloway's orchestra in 1939. He will go on to play with many bands, including Ella Fitzgerald's orchestra, Earl Hines's, and Billy Eckstine's. He and other musicians— including Charlie Parker, Thelonious Monk, Bud Powell, Kenny Clarke, and Oscar Pettiford—will create the radically new-sounding musical rhythms, harmonies, and chord progressions of bebop. In the 1940s, he will perform concerts with small combos and organize big bands to popularize bebop. In the late 40s, he will become an international star and symbol of this daring new style of music. In the mid-1950s, he will lead a band on a State Department tour of the Middle East and be nicknamed "the Ambassador of Jazz."

# October

## 22

**1953:** **Dr. Clarence Sumner Greene Sr. becomes the first African American neurosurgeon to be certified by the American Board of Neurological Surgery.** He will become an assistant professor of neurosurgery at Howard University's Freedmen's Hospital, where he will revolutionize neurosurgical care and perform the hospital's first aneurysm and brain tumor surgeries.

## 23

Stephanie St. Clair          Dutch Schultz

### Harlem Numbers Queen v. the Mobster

**1935:** **Mobster Dutch Schultz lay dying in a hospital after being shot in a Newark, NJ, restaurant** by crime boss Lucky Luciano's hitmen. Schultz, under investigation by Manhattan DA Thomas Dewey, has been planning to assassinate him, which could bring law enforcement down on Luciano's crime syndicate. But Schultz has other enemies besides Luciano and the DA. For years, **Schultz has been trying to take over the immensely profitable operation of Harlem numbers queen Stephanie St. Clair.** But Madam Queen, as she is known, proclaimed war, revealing the secret locations of Schultz's gambling operation. Schultz sent gangsters to kill her, but she hid in the cellar of her apartment building. "The super, a friend of mine, covered me with coal," she said. Today, with Schultz's life slipping away in Newark Hospital, Madam Queen sends him a Biblical telegram: "Don't be yellow. As ye sow, so shall ye reap. - Madam Queen of Policy." Schultz will die at 8:35 the next night, giving Harlemites a number to play: 835. The winning number will be 214, so Harlem numbers bankers, including Madam Queen, will rake in a "killing"—a parting gift loosely tied to the minute of Dutch's death.

## 24

### The Bilali Document

**During 1857:** When enslaved Bilali Muhammad, a master cultivator of rice from West Africa, dies on a Sapelo Island, GA, plantation, his handwritten 13-page manuscript is found. It is first thought to be the scribblings of an old man recalling his youth in present-day Sierra Leone. But in 1939, a study will reveal that the manuscript is a statement of Islamic beliefs and the rules for ablution, morning prayer, and the calls to prayer. It is written in Qur'anic Arabic mixed with words from the dialect Muhammad first spoke, Pulaar. Further tests will prove the manuscript parchment originated in 1700s Venice and likely found its way to an African trading post. Some American Muslims will call the manuscript the "Mother Text" of American Islamic literature, claiming it is the first Islamic text written in the U.S.

**Scan to read about the Bilali Document**

# October

## 25

Brig. Gen. Benjamin O. Davis Sr. watches a Signal Corps crew erect poles, somewhere in France. August 8, 1944

**1940: Benjamin O. Davis Sr. is promoted to brigadier general, becoming the first African American general officer in the U.S. Army and the U.S. Armed Forces.** He was one of a handful of Black officers in an era of rampant segregation. He served in the Philippine-American War and World War I but was forced to accept assignments well below the level of his leadership skills, but he slowly rose through the ranks, enduring the Army's white hierarchy. In 1930, Davis was promoted to colonel, and in 1938, he assumed command of the New York National Guard's 369th Infantry Regiment. His record of accomplishments, combined with the political tailwinds of the 1940 presidential campaign and the need to garner African American support for U.S. involvement in World War II, positioned him for a higher rank: brigadier general. He will retire in 1948. His son, Benjamin O. Davis Jr., will become the first Black general in the U.S. Air Force (see October 27).

## 26

Michael Jordan as he appeared in an ESPN advertisement published on El Gráfico magazine.

**1984: Michael Jordan makes his debut** in the regular NBA season at Chicago Stadium, scoring 16 points for the Chicago Bulls. He will become one of the greatest basketball players of all time.

A pair of game-worn Air Jordan 1s from 1985 (above) broke an auction record in 2020, selling for $560,000. Nike created this pair for Jordan to persuade him to sign a shoe deal.

## 27

General Earle Everard Partridge pinning a general's star on Benjamin O. Davis Jr.

**1954: Benjamin O. Davis Jr. is promoted to brigadier general in the U.S. Air Force, making him the service's first Black general** as he follows in his father's footsteps. In 1936, Davis Jr. became only the fourth Black to graduate from the U.S. Military Academy (West Point), the first since 1889. During his years there, he ate alone, had no roommate, and was subjected to the "silent treatment," an effort to drive him out. But his determination to succeed only won the respect of classmates. In 2015, West Point barracks will bear his name, and in 2019, the U.S. Air Force Academy will rename its airfield for him. In March 1942, Davis earned his pilot wings, became one of the first Black U.S. combat pilots, and transferred to the Army Air Corp to command a new, all-Black unit of 1,000 pilots who became known as the Tuskegee Airmen. In two years, they made military history, downing more than twice the number of aircraft they lost, destroying miles of rail lines, and sinking 40-plus ships (including an enemy destroyer) without losing a single bomber they escorted. Davis himself led 67 missions. In 1947, he joined the Air Force when it split from the Army. He pushed to end segregation and succeeded. It became the first military service to integrate.

# Weekly Planner

_____ WEEK OF _____

**SUNDAY**

**MONDAY**

**TUESDAY**

**WEDNESDAY**

**THURSDAY**

**FRIDAY**

**SATURDAY**

# October

## 28

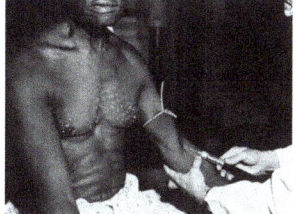

A Tuskegee Study participant in the 1930s

**1932: The Tuskegee Syphilis Study begins.** Its goal is to study the effects of untreated syphilis. In 1932, scientists believe syphilis has a pronounced impact on African Americans. Study participants are promised free medical care, but no one informs the 600 poor Black sharecroppers about the nature of the study. It will last 40 years, during which time 399 men with syphilis will not be given appropriate medical treatment, 40 patients' wives will be infected, 19 children will be born with congenital syphilis, and 100 men will die. Nearly sixty-five years from today, President Bill Clinton will apologize to study victims on behalf of the United States.

Scan to read about the lingering effects of the Tuskegee Study

**1964: James Brown & The Famous Flames will give a legendary performance at the T.A.M.I. show** (Teenage Awards Music International) in Santa Monica, CA, in 1964. (See May 3, his birthday, for a description; watch his cape act below.)

Scan to watch James Brown's Cape Act at the T.A.M.I. show

## 29

### Truth Telling
**1864: President Abraham Lincoln meets Sojourner Truth, a 67-year-old, 6-foot former slave, abolitionist, and advocate for women's rights, in the White House.** Truth will say he treated her "with the utmost kindness and cordiality," but years later, Lucy Colman, the white schoolteacher who accompanied Truth, will give a very different account of the meeting, recalling that Lincoln was polite but not warm-hearted. Before meeting Truth, Lincoln joked and was relaxed with male visitors. But Lincoln turned sour and tense when he met Truth and her two companions, including one other Black woman. Truth called him the first antislavery president, a notion he rejected. He called Truth "'Aunty' … as he would his washerwoman." Colman realized Lincoln was irritated at being loved as the Great Emancipator.

Scan to read more

Uncredited photo

Alex Haley (left) with Malcolm X

**1965: "The Autobiography of Malcolm X," by Malcolm X as told to Alex Haley, is released posthumously nine months after Malcolm X is assassinated.** Doubleday paid the authors a $30,000 advance but then canceled its publication. Grove Press publishes it instead and sells millions of copies. The book will influence generations of readers and rank as an American classic.

## 30

Judith Jamison...

**1965: Judith Jamison debuts as a dancer with the Alvin Ailey American Dance Theater** at the Harper Theater Dance Festival in Chicago in choreographer Talley Beatty's "Congo Tango Palace." She will soon become the company's star and an international figure in dance. In 1971, Ailey will choreograph the solo "Cry" for her.

How Good Was...

**1980: the Professional Basketball Writer's Association names Bill Russell the greatest player in the history of the NBA.** A Hall of Famer, he was a five-time NBA Most Valuable Player and 12-time All-Star, and he won 11 NBA championships, more than any other player.

**1991: Black Entertainment Television** (**BET**), launched in 1980, goes public, becoming the first Black-controlled company listed on the New York Stock Exchange.

**Busting through the NBA Color Barrier**

1950: **Earl "Big Cat" Lloyd,** a 6-foot 8-inch, 220-pound forward with the Washington Capitols, **becomes the first African American player in a National Basketball Association game.** He makes his NBA debut in the Capitols' season opener. After seven games with the Capitols, he will be drafted into the military and sent to Korea. When he returns in 1954, the Capitols will no longer exist. He will play as a starter for the Syracuse Nationals, averaging 10.2 points and 7.7 rebounds per game, helping to win the 1955 NBA championship. He will complete his nine-season career with the Detroit Pistons. In 1970, he will become the NBA's first full-time African American head coach. In 2003, he will be inducted into the Basketball Hall of Fame.

"Even when there was a known quota, no one talked about it. No one ever said, 'We can't have but two blacks.' Who admits they're racist? It was like a secret society, and it was understood. What really changed the landscape was the advent of the Players Association. Suddenly there was an organized manner to speak up against unfairness. I always laugh when people asked me if playing in the NBA was a goal of mine. How the hell you gonna plan a career where there's no predecessor?"

*Earl Lloyd*

# November

| SUN | MON | TUE | WED | THU | FRI | SAT |
|-----|-----|-----|-----|-----|-----|-----|
|     |     |     |     |     |     |     |
|     |     |     |     |     |     |     |
|     |     |     |     |     |     |     |
|     |     |     |     |     |     |     |
|     |     |     |     |     |     |     |

Louis Armstrong

# November

**WEEK 1**

_____
_____
_____
_____

**WEEK 2**

_____
_____
_____
_____

**WEEK 3**

_____
_____
_____
_____

**WEEK 4**

_____
_____
_____
_____

**WEEK 5**

_____
_____
_____
_____

**TRUTH IS POWERFUL
AND IT PREVAILS.
SOJOURNER TRUTH**

**MAJOR**

**MINOR**

**HABIT TRACKER**     S   M   T   W   T   F   S

_____
_____
_____
_____

**MISC**

# To-Do List

Date:

# NOTES

# Weekly Planner

_____ **WEEK OF** _____

**SUNDAY**

_____

**MONDAY**

_____

**TUESDAY**

_____

**WEDNESDAY**

_____

**THURSDAY**

_____

**FRIDAY**

_____

**SATURDAY**

_____

# November

## 1

November 1945: The **first issue of Ebony magazine is published.** The magazine will chronicle the Black American experience for generations, projecting positive images of African Americans to counter stereotypes that have persisted for centuries.

1955: **"The Sweet Flypaper of Life,"** a fiction and photography book by Roy DeCarava and Langston Hughes, **is published.** The story, narrated by Sister Mary Bradley, a fictional grandmother of 10, is set in Harlem in 1954. The book includes 140 photographs—close-ups of children, scenes of family life, portraits, shots of the neighborhood undergoing change, and of people working, speaking, laughing, protesting, coming and going, standing and staring, smiling, sitting, cuddling on the stoop—all of which Hughes "meditated" on and then wrote "what came into his head," according to DeCarava.

**"Flypaper" will be a critical success, described as "a pioneering exercise in merging image and text as well as a revealing glimpse into the everyday lives of Harlem's black community."** DeCarava, whose career will span six decades, will be considered a founder of black-and-white fine art photography.

## 2

NEW-YORK AFRICAN FREE-SCHOOL, No. 2.
Engraved from a drawing taken by P. Reason, a pupil, aged 13 years.

1787: The **African Free School, the nation's first school for African Americans, opens in Lower Manhattan.** Founded by the New York Manumission Society, whose members include Alexander Hamilton and John Jay, it began as a single-room schoolhouse with about 40 students, mostly the children of slaves.

Land deed for the African Free School, linked to Alexander Hamilton

1983: **President Ronald Reagan signs into law a bill making Martin Luther King Jr's birthday a federal holiday.** On January 20, 1986, Martin Luther King Jr. Day will be celebrated as a federal holiday for the first time. It will be observed on the third Monday in January. Dr. King's birthday is January 15.

## 3

All-Negro Hour

1929: **"The All-Negro Hour," the first African American radio show, premieres on WSBC** (World Stage Battery Company) in Chicago, **hosted by Jack L. Cooper, a former welterweight boxing champion and vaudevillian-turned-journalist.** The show will run until 1935 with Black guests—performers, actors, musicians, and comedians. Some segments will feature live broadcasts of Sunday church services. Eventually, Cooper will adopt a disc jockey format with prerecorded music.

1992: **Carol Moseley Braun is elected as Illinois's first female U.S. senator.** She becomes **the first African American woman to serve in the Senate.**

# Weekly Planner

WEEK OF

**SUNDAY**

**MONDAY**

**TUESDAY**

**WEDNESDAY**

**THURSDAY**

**FRIDAY**

**SATURDAY**

# November

## 4

Barack Obama at his victory rally at Grant Park on election day

**2008: Barack Obama is elected the 44th President** of the United States.

President Barack Obama, official portrait

## 5

**1948: Carver Federal Savings Bank** (named for George Washington Carver) receives a federal bank charter. Under the leadership of "banker-priest" M. Moran Weston II, the bank will open its first branch in Harlem in January 1949 and **become the largest and oldest continually Black-operated bank in the U.S.**

**1956: Nat King Cole hosts the debut of his variety show, "The Nat King Cole Show," on NBC.** It is the first nationally broadcast television show hosted by an African American. Many celebrities will financially support the show, but a national sponsor will not step forward, so the show will not survive; Cole will decide to end it. The final episode will air on December 17, 1957. Due to the lack of sponsors, Cole will comment: "Madison Avenue is afraid of the dark."

On April 10, 1956, seven months before the debut of his TV show, Nat King Cole was performing for a crowd of 4,000 in Birmingham when three white supremacists knocked him down. Police rushed from the sides of the stage to apprehend the attackers. Cole, who was born in Mobile, AL, then finished his performance. Scan right to hear an interview about the incident.

## 6

**1895:** Fort Valley State University, an HBCU first known as Fort Valley High and Industrial School, is founded in Fort Valley, GA.

**The Birth of Black Studies**

1968: The Black Student Union at San Francisco State College begins a five-month strike, the longest student strike in U.S. history, leading to the creation of a comprehensive Black studies program, the hiring of Black staff and faculty, the admittance of more Black students, and the establishment of the nation's first College of Ethnic Studies. The strike spread to 200-plus colleges and universities across the nation.

**1968: Louis Stokes is elected as the first Black member of the U.S. House of Representatives from Ohio.** He will serve 15 consecutive terms and become the first African American to retire, having completed 30 years in office.

# November

## 7

**1967: Carl Stokes is elected the first African American mayor of a major city, Cleveland, OH.**

**1972: Barbara Jordan, a Texas Democrat, becomes the first Black woman elected to the U.S. House of Representatives from the South.**

**1989: David Dinkins is elected the first African American mayor of New York City,** defeating three-term incumbent mayor Ed Koch. Dinkins will serve as mayor until December 31, 1993.

## 8

Scan for full text of "Color"

**1925: Countee Cullen publishes his first book of poetry, "Color."** It contains 72 poems and will become a hallmark of the Harlem Renaissance.

**1944: Adam Clayton Powell Jr. is elected to Congress representing Harlem. He will** be one of only two Black Congressmen in office until 1955. He will serve 12 terms.

**1966: Edward Brooke is elected U.S. Senator for Massachusetts— the first popularly elected Black senator in the nation's history,** ending an 86-year absence of Black senators.

**1989: Douglas Wilder is elected the 66th governor of Virginia, becoming the first African American to be elected state governor in the U.S.**

## 9

Northeast No. 4 boundary marker stone of the original District of Columbia in Washington, D.C. and Prince George's County, MD, placed in 1791-92 by Andrew Ellicott and Benjamin Banneker

**1731: Benjamin Banneker, who will become the first African American mathematician, astronomer, and almanac author, is born** in Baltimore County, MD. At age 21, he will reportedly carve a wooden clock that will strike on the hour, modeling it on a pocket watch. Largely self-taught, **Banneker will assist in the survey to establish the original boundaries of the District of Columbia. He will also make astronomical calculations to predict eclipses and planetary conjunctions for his almanac and ephemeris,** published in a six-year series of at least 28 editions in seven cities: Baltimore, Philadelphia, Wilmington, Alexandria, Petersburg, Richmond, and Trenton.

Scan

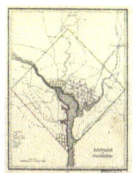

1885 map of Washington, DC

# Weekly Planner

_____**WEEK OF**_____

**SUNDAY**

**MONDAY**

**TUESDAY**

**WEDNESDAY**

**THURSDAY**

**FRIDAY**

**SATURDAY**

## 10

1891: **Granville T. Woods is issued a patent for a "third rail invention" for operating electrified railways. It conducts electric power to railway cars and will be adopted in subway systems worldwide.** The patent describes a concealed underground electrical line. In his words, it is "a cheap, simple, and efficient electric-railway system ... which entirely dispenses with overhead wires or with exposed feeders and does not require conduits or openings in the street." Woods will secure over 65 patents for electrical, communication, and mechanical devices during his lifetime. **Among his other inventions are the "dead man's brake," which stops a train if the conductor is incapacitated, and the "telegraphony," which combined the telephone and the telegraph. Alexander Graham Bell, who invented the telephone, purchased the telegraphony out of fear that Woods would become a major competitor.** Woods received no formal education beyond age 10, when he became a machine shop apprentice.

1969: **Sesame Street, set in a neighborhood that resembles Harlem, debuts to high viewership** on NET (National Educational Television), a precursor to PBS. The educational children's TV series was conceived to reaffirm children's identities, particularly Black children's.

## 11

Shane Balkowitsch

Jon Batiste

1986: **Jon Batiste is born** in Metairie, LA, into a musical family that includes Lionel Batiste of the Treme Brass Band, Milton Batiste of the Olympia Brass Band, and Russell Batiste Jr. Jon will become a singer, songwriter, multi-instrumentalist, bandleader, composer, TV personality, and creative director of the National Jazz Museum. He will win an Academy Award, Grammy, Golden Globe, and BAFTA Film Award for co-composing the score for the animated film "Soul." He will win five Grammys, including Album of the Year for his album "We Are."

That chip, that crack is where the light gets in.
*Jon Batiste*

## 12

1851 wet plate collodion process of pure silver on glass

1874: **Bert Williams is born** in Nassau, The Bahamas. He will be one of his era's leading entertainers and best-loved comedians. He will also be the first Black man to play a leading role in a film, "Darktown Jubilee" (1914).

### Montgomery Heroes You've Never Heard of

1956: Upholding a lower court decision, the U.S. Supreme Court rules racial segregation on Alabama buses unconstitutional 381 days after the start of the Montgomery Bus Boycott. History will remember a lone boycott heroine, Rosa Parks. Four others will be all but forgotten: Aurelia Browder, Mary Louis Smith, Claudette Colvin, and Susie McDonald. Fifteen-year-old Colvin was the first person arrested in March 1955 for refusing to give up her bus seat. Colvin was charged with assault and battery, disorderly conduct, and breaking the segregation law. Browder, Smith, and McDonald were arrested on similar charges in 1955. Nine months after Colvin's arrest, Rosa Parks was arrested for refusing to give up her bus seat. So organizers decided to create a parallel transportation network of carpools and taxis. With the Montgomery bus system suffering huge financial losses, the mayor decided to "get tough," fomenting violence by white supremacists. Within a month, they bombed the home of the boycott leader: Martin Luther King Jr. The Montgomery Improvement Association then adopted a legal strategy: fight bus segregation in the federal court system. Browder, Smith, Colvin, and McDonald sued the city, claiming bus segregation violated their 14th Amendment rights. After the case, Browder v. Gayle, was filed, Browder's family found dynamite sticks on their front porch. The case would become a legal milestone, ending racial segregation on public transportation in Alabama. While Rosa Parks continued to dominate the story behind the bus boycott, she was not involved in the landmark case.

### Teddy Bear Hunter

1902: Veteran bear hunter **Holt Collier, a former slave and Confederate cavalryman, leads Theodore Roosevelt's hunting party near Onward, MS,** when **Collier corners a full-grown black bear** with Collier's dog in its clutches while Roosevelt eats lunch elsewhere. Collier saves the dog by knocking the bear unconscious with his rifle butt. **He drags the bear and ties it to a willow tree.** Roosevelt appears and, seeing the injured bear, refuses to shoot it, though men in the hunting party, including the governor of Mississippi, yell, **"Shoot it, Mr. President!" News of Roosevelt's refusal to shoot will be viewed in the media as a noble act,** cartoons will depict the hunting scene, and **a shop owner will create a stuffed animal he nicknames Teddy's Bear.** The name will stick, and cuddly teddy bears will become a much-beloved, huggable toy. **Eventually, more than 100 million stuffed animals, mostly teddy bears, will be sold in the U.S. yearly.**

1866: **Cathay Williams becomes the first documented Black woman to serve in the U.S. Army.** Under the male alias William Cathay, **she enlists in the 39th U.S. Infantry Company A** in St. Louis, MO, **which will become the Buffalo Soldiers.** She will be discharged on October 14, 1868, after her gender is revealed. "I wanted to make my own living and not be dependent on relations or friends," she will explain later, adding that **her cousin and a friend knew about her ruse.** "They never 'blowed' on me."

1960: **Etta James's song "At Last," from her debut album of the same name, is released** on Argo Records, rising to the top of the R&B charts and crossing over to pop radio. It will become her signature song and will be inducted into the Grammy Hall of Fame in 1999 and the Library of Congress's National Recording Registry in 2012. According to music polls, it will rank among the top songs of all time.

# Weekly Planner

WEEK OF

**SUNDAY**

**MONDAY**

**TUESDAY**

**WEDNESDAY**

**THURSDAY**

**FRIDAY**

**SATURDAY**

# November

## 16

William Christopher Handy at age 19

1873: **W.C. Handy is born** in Florence, AL. He will be among the most influential songwriters and composers in U.S. history. He will call himself the father of the blues. Though he did not create the genre, he will be the first to publish music in it, bringing the regional Mississippi Delta blues, focusing on slide guitar and harmonica, to a large audience.

Ba-dee-ya

## 17

1911: **Omega Psi Phi Fraternity is founded** inside the Science Building of Howard University by three juniors: Edgar Amos Love, Oscar James Cooper, and Frank Coleman. It is the first fraternity founded at a historically Black college or university. On December 15, 1911, the founders will organize the Alpha chapter with 14 charter members. Love, Cooper, and Coleman will be elected the chapter's first Basileus, Keeper of Records, and Keeper of Seals, respectively.

## 18

Harriette Anderson

1907: The **Saint-Gaudens Double Eagle $20 U.S. coin is struck,** by the direction of President Theodore Roosevelt, **most likely featuring Harriette Eugenia Anderson (1873-1938), an African American model** posing in a flowing gown as Liberty. At first, only two dozen coins are struck. **The double eagle will be considered the most beautiful U.S. coin ever minted.** The 1933 edition will differ slightly from the original and will be among the most valuable U.S. coins ever struck. A sole example in private hands will sell at auction in 2002 for $7.6 million. In 2021, it will sell for $18.9 million.

1978: **Earth, Wind & Fire releases its single "September,"** written and recorded in September with the help of Motown-trained songwriter Allee Willis, who at first was bothered by the gibberish lyric band leader Maurice White was singing: *"ba-dee-ya."* But she came to love it. "I learned my greatest lesson ever in songwriting from him," Willis will confess, "which was never let the lyric get in the way of the groove."

Roy Campanella tags Billy Martin at home plate for the final out in game four of the 1953 World Series.

**1921: Roy Campanella, who will be considered one of the greatest catchers in baseball history, is born** in Philadelphia, PA. At age 15, he will play in the Negro Leagues, and at age 22 will play in the Mexican and Venezuelan leagues before moving to the minor leagues in 1946. In a game in 1946, when the team manager was ejected, Campanella assumed the manager's duties, becoming **the first African American to manage white players of a professional team.** The team overcame a three-run deficit to win the game, partly due to his lineup decisions. Campanella will make his MLB debut on April 20, 1948, playing for the Brooklyn Dodgers as a teammate of Jackie Robinson. He will be inducted into the Baseball Hall of Fame in 1969, becoming the second Black player to receive the honor after Robinson.

Roy Campanella's dark brown leather catcher's mitt.

**1884: The first print edition of the Indianapolis Freeman is published.** It will be called "A National Illustrated Colored Newspaper" or a national race paper. Its circulation: 25,000. Published on Sundays, it will cover events from small Black communities to large cities, including sports, entertainment, and other news. By 1914, it will have the largest circulation of any Black newspaper.

**Scan to view most issues**

**The Man Who Stopped Traffic**

**1923: Garrett A. Morgan receives a patent for the three-position traffic signal, which replaces the two-position "stop" and "go" signs.** The addition of the "all hold" signal will become the amber light, warning drivers to be cautious, thus preventing accidents and saving countless lives globally.

**1934: Ella Fitzgerald, age 17, makes her debut performance at the Apollo Theater's first amateur night.** She won a chance to perform when her name was pulled in a weekly drawing. She enters the show intending to dance, but from the wings, she sees a fantastic tap dance act and thinks, *there's no way I'm going to dance.* When it's her turn to perform, she pauses in the wings, and the M.C. tells her, *"Just do something!"* Wearing a raggedy dress and workman's boots, Fitzgerald, who's homeless and has never performed in public, steps on stage and sings Hoagy Carmichael's song "Judy." Years later Fitzgerald will recall the audience's reaction: "Everybody says, 'Oh, that girl can sing.'" In just months, she will become a star and perform with Chick Webb's band at the Savoy.

**"Just *do* something!"**

# November

## 22

**1950:** **Arsonists firebomb the Oak Park, IL, home of chemist Percy Julian,** who synthesized medicinal compounds from plant sources so they could be mass-produced. He also synthesized cortisone and hydrocortisone from soybeans, enabling the mass production of pain relief drugs for people with arthritis. The Julians are the first African Americans to move to all-white Oak Park, the village where Ernest Hemingway was raised. **Julian's home will be dynamited seven months later, but he will refuse to move. He will sit on the porch with a shotgun to guard his home** until the community supports him.

**JULIAN'S HOME**

**Chicagoan Of The Year's House Target Of Vandals**

## 23

Janney coupler

**1897:** Black inventor Andrew Beard receives U.S. Patent No. 594,059 for his Janney railroad car coupler, an improvement on the original 1873 coupler that automatically hooks rail cars together when they bump into each other. Beard states, "Horizontal jaws engage each other to connect the cars." Previously, coupling cars was done manually. Beard, born into slavery and freed at age 15, will sell his patent rights for $50,000 ($1.83 million in 2023). He will follow up with U.S. Patent 624,901 in 1899. His patents will revolutionize the railroad industry.

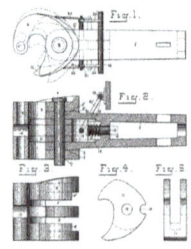

## 24

c.1868: **Scott Joplin is born** in Texarkana or Linden, TX. He will be called the King of Ragtime, writing 40-plus original compositions, including "Maple Leaf Rag," a ragtime ballet, and two operas. To him, ragtime is classical music.

Katherine Johnson at her desk at NASA Langley Research Center with a globe, or "Celestial Training Device."

**2015:** **President Barack Obama awards Katherine Johnson, mathematician and NASA "human computer," the Presidential Medal of Freedom,** saying: "Katherine G. Johnson refused to be limited by society's expectations of her gender and race while expanding the boundaries of humanity's reach." She was one of the first African American women to work as a NASA scientist.

# Weekly Planner

WEEK OF

**SUNDAY**

**MONDAY**

**TUESDAY**

**WEDNESDAY**

**THURSDAY**

**FRIDAY**

**SATURDAY**

# November

## 25

November 1863: President **Abraham Lincoln appoints Henry McNeal Turner,** age 29, **as the first African American chaplain in the U.S. Army.**

## 26

Tina Turner, 1970

1939: **Tina Turner** (Anna Mae Bullock), **future queen of rock 'n' roll, is born** in Brownsville, TN.

**Scan for Tina Turner Museum**

1969: Future painter, silhouettist, print-maker, filmmaker, and installation artist **Kara Walker is born** in Stockton, CA.

## 27

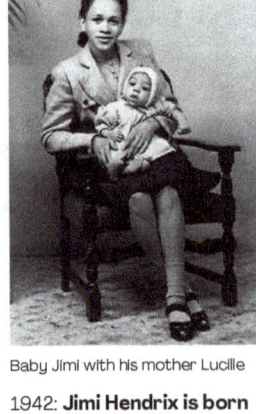

Baby Jimi with his mother Lucille

1942: **Jimi Hendrix is born** in Seattle, WA.

**Life After "Sugar Baby"**

After the Sphinx, Kara Walker is a New Kind of Public Figure

And she's figuring out a whole new approach to public art.

Kara Walker's sugar mammy-as-sphinx at the Domino Sugar Refinery. The sphinx measures 75-and-a-half feet long by 35-and-a-half feet high. With "black" features and a bleached-white body, the giant sphinx is the physical manifestation of the slave labor that put sugar into teacups and pie recipes worldwide. In the 1870s, this factory supplied over half of the sugar produced in the U.S.

## 28

© Motown Museum

Motown recording studio

**1929: Berry Gordy III is born** in Detroit, MI, the 7th of 8 children. A future record producer, songwriter, and film-and-television producer, **Gordy will found Motown Records and sign such recording artists as The Miracles, Stevie Wonder, the Jackson 5, the Supremes, the Temptations, Martha and the Vandellas, the Contours, the Four Tops, and Gladys Knight & the Pips.** Together, they will create a soundtrack for modern life.

HITSVILLE: THE MAKING OF MOTOWN (2019) [...
HITSVILLE: THE MAKING OF MOTOWN

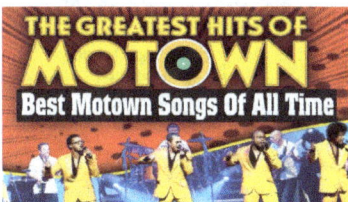
THE GREATEST HITS OF MOTOWN
Best Motown Songs Of All Time

2 hours and 24 minutes of hits

## 29

**1982: Michael Jackson's "Thriller,"** his second album produced by Quincy Jones, **is released. It will become the best-selling album in history, with sales of 70 million copies worldwide.** Jackson and Jones worked on 30 songs; 9 are included on the album, and 7 of those will be released as singles: **"The Girl Is Mine," "Billie Jean," "Beat It," "Wanna Be Startin' Somethin'," "Human Nature," "P.Y.T. (Pretty Young Thing)," and "Thriller."** The album was recorded over seven months at Westlake Recording Studios in Los Angeles. When they finished the recordings, Jackson and Jones spent weeks remixing every song. "Thriller" will set a record for the most top-10 singles from an album and win a record-setting eight Grammys.

DANCE OF THE AFRICAN DIASPORA
Pearl Primus
A dancer, choreographer, and proselytizer for African dance, Pearl Primus (1919-1994) trained at the New Dance Group and worked with Asadata Dafora.

**1919: Pearl Primus is born in Port of Spain, Trinidad and Tobago.** She will become an American dancer, choreographer, and anthropologist who promotes African dance, codifies its technical details, and presents it to U.S. audiences as a discipline worthy of research and performance. She will dance on Broadway, teach, found her own company, command the stage with five-foot-high leaps, and choreograph dances about American life, including setting Langston Hughes's poem "The Negro Speaks of Rivers" and the lyrics of Billie Holiday's mournful song "Strange Fruit" to dance, the latter portraying a woman member of the lynch mob as she leaves the lynching ground gripped by the horror which she has just seen. Primus will develop a movement language akin to those developed by the pioneers of modern American dance. She will found the Pearl Primus Dance Language Institute, conduct cultural projects worldwide for major foundations and organizations, and become known as a griot— the voice of dance cultures.

# November

## 30

Gordon Parks

**Renaissance Man**

1912: **Gordon Parks, future photojournalist, pianist, composer, author, poet, painter, film director, and cofounder of Essence Magazine, is born** in Fort Scott, KS, the youngest of 15 children. He will be the first African American to produce and direct a feature film financed by a major Hollywood studio and help create the blaxploitation film genre with his 1971 movie "Shaft."

1933: **Sam Gilliam, who will be a pioneering abstract and color field painter, is born** in Tupelo, MS.

1987: **Reginald F. Lewis becomes the first African American billionaire** after negotiating the $985 million acquisition of Beatrice International Foods. The deal, the largest offshore transaction in US history at the time, establishes **TLC Beatrice International Holdings Inc. It will be the first African American-owned enterprise to surpass the billion-dollar mark.** It will gross $1.8 billion in sales in its first year.

Hakeem Jeffries

**House Democratic Leader**

2022: **Hakeem Jeffries,** the 52-year-old six-term Democrat representing New York's 8th Congressional District in the U.S. House of Representatives, **is elected to lead House Democrats, becoming the first Black person to lead a major party in Congress.** He will assume office on January 3, 2023.

# December

| SUN | MON | TUE | WED |  |  | SAT |
|-----|-----|-----|-----|-----|-----|-----|
|  |  |  |  |  |  |  |
|  |  |  |  |  |  |  |
|  |  |  |  |  |  |  |
|  |  |  |  |  |  |  |
|  |  |  |  |  |  |  |

Rosa Parks

# December

**WEEK 1**

-------------------------------------------------------
-------------------------------------------------------
-------------------------------------------------------
-------------------------------------------------------

**WEEK 2**

-------------------------------------------------------
-------------------------------------------------------
-------------------------------------------------------
-------------------------------------------------------

**WEEK 3**

-------------------------------------------------------
-------------------------------------------------------
-------------------------------------------------------

**WEEK 4**

-------------------------------------------------------
-------------------------------------------------------
-------------------------------------------------------
-------------------------------------------------------

**WEEK 5**

-------------------------------------------------------
-------------------------------------------------------
-------------------------------------------------------

HOLD FAST TO DREAMS,
FOR IF DREAMS DIE,
LIFE IS A BROKEN-
WINGED BIRD THAT
CANNOT FLY.
LANGSTON HUGHES

**MAJOR**

**MINOR**

**HABIT TRACKER**          S   M   T   W   T   F   S

-------------------------------------------------------
-------------------------------------------------------
-------------------------------------------------------
-------------------------------------------------------

**MISC**

# To-Do List

Date:

# NOTES

# Weekly Planner

**WEEK OF**_____

**SUNDAY**

**MONDAY**

**TUESDAY**

"**Right is of no Sex—
Truth is of no Color—
God is the Father of us
all, and we are all
Brethren**"

*Motto of Frederick
Douglass's antislavery
newspaper The North Star*

**WEDNESDAY**

**THURSDAY**

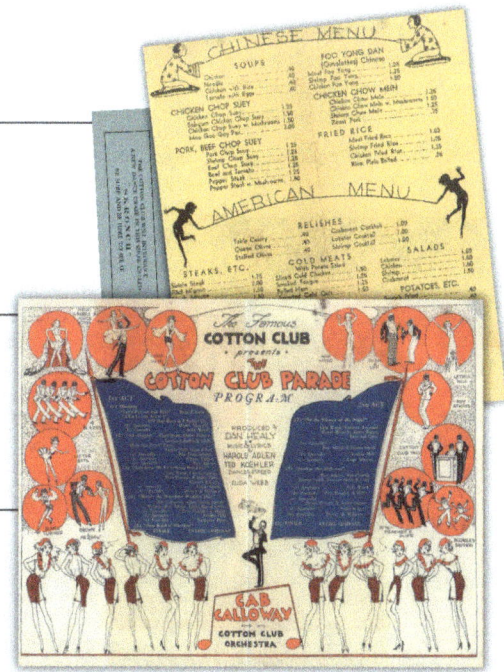

**FRIDAY**

**SATURDAY**

Cotton Club menu; Parade Program ca. April 1932

# December

## 1

1955: **Rosa Parks is arrested and jailed for refusing to give up her seat on a crowded bus to a white man in Montgomery, AL, as required by the city's racial segregation laws.** This will spark the Montgomery Bus Boycott, organized by the Montgomery Improvement Association. Needing a spokesperson to bring attention to their fight against segregation, the group will decide on an untested, little-known pastor who'd just moved to Montgomery: Martin Luther King Jr. The boycott will be one of the most successful efforts to end segregation.

1940: **Richard Pryor is born** in Peoria, IL.

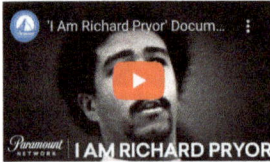

## 2

1875: The **Mississippi Plan to violently overthrow the Republican Party and reestablish white supremacy in the South is enacted.** Devised and organized by white southern Democrats, it calls for persuading 10-15% of Democrats to join the Republican Party, intimidating Blacks who had recently been granted voting rights, and suppressing the Black vote by organized violence and murder. **The plan will be successful, and South Carolina and Louisiana will adopt it.**

1983: **Michael Jackson's highly anticipated "Thriller" music video is launched.** The 13-minute 42-second video, co-written by Jackson and director John Landis, narrated by Vincent Price, and shot on 35mm film, is a horror flick gone ... wonderfully. The video will double album sales, making it the best-selling album in history (70 million sold). The video will also sell a million VHS copies, break down MTV's racial barriers, and transform music videos into a high art form, making Jackson a global pop icon while play-scaring everybody. Just about everyone will consider it the greatest music video of all time. The zombie dance sequence will be duplicated in movies and performed everywhere from the White House (Michelle and Barack Obama will dance to it with kids on Halloween) to city plazas to prisons. In Mexico City, 13,000 "zombies" will dance together, and a battalion of 1,500 zombie-fied inmates in orange will dance in a prison yard, starring in a YouTube video that will attract 59 million views.

## 3

THE NORTH STAR.
ROCHESTER, DECEMBER 3, 1847.

OUR PAPER AND ITS PROSPECTS.

We are now about to assume the management of the editorial department of a newspaper, devoted to the cause of Liberty, Humanity and Progress. The position is one which, with the purest motives, we have long desired to occupy. It has long been our anxious wish to see, in this slave-holding, slave-trading, and negro-hating land, a printing-press and paper, permanently established, under the complete control and direction of the immediate victims of slavery and oppression.

**Read Vol. 1 No. 1**

1847: **Frederick Douglass founds and edits his first antislavery newspaper, The North Star,** a weekly named for the star that guides runaway slaves North to freedom. It contains abolitionist news, editorials, articles, poetry, and advertisements. The North Star will merge in June 1851 with The Liberty Paper under the title Frederick Douglass' Paper. His final newspaper venture will take place in Washington, DC, in 1870, when he becomes editor-in-chief and co-owner of the New National Era.

**1923:** **The Cotton Club, owned by gangster Owney Madden, opens on Lenox Avenue in Harlem.** It occupies the site of former heavyweight champion Jack Johnson's Club de Luxe, a 1,000-square-foot, 400-500 seat supper club at Lenox Avenue and 142nd Street. Opened in 1920, Club de Luxe had been a hit, so Madden decided it was the ideal nightspot to peddle his "Number One" beer to white customers during the Prohibition era. Madden took over de Luxe, increased the seating capacity to 700, added plantation/jungle décor, and booked the best Black entertainers of the day, including **Fletcher Henderson, Fats Waller, Duke Ellington, Ella Fitzgerald, Adelaide Hall, Cab Calloway, Ethel Waters, Bill "Bojangles" Robinson, Earl "Snakehips" Tucker, and one-legged tap dancer Clayton "Peg Leg" Bates.** Also appearing are **chorus lines of "tall, tan, and terrific" "copper-colored gals"** (each at least 5'6" and able to dance and carry a tune), including **Lena Horne and Josephine Baker.** The club's 1925 poster will have the image of a doorman with enormous ruby-red lips and a too-wide smile, bowing and ushering a white couple into the club. Caricatures appear on menus, programs, and matchboxes.

**1927:** **Duke Ellington and his band, The Washingtonians, debut at Harlem's Cotton Club.** The 23-year-old bandleader turns out in a top hat and tails. Weekly radio broadcasts will bring Ellington national fame and attract white clientele to the club.

**1969:** **Jay-Z** (Shawn Corey Carter) **is born** in Brooklyn, NY.

Anthony Barboza

**1833:** **The American Anti-Slavery Society holds its first meeting in Philadelphia,** with 60 abolitionist leaders from 19 states meeting to work for emancipation.

Library of Congress

Declaration of the Convention printed on satin. Scan for full text.

**1935:** **Mary McLeod Bethune founds the National Council of Negro Women** in NYC. Its mission is "to advance opportunities and the quality of life for African American women, their families and communities." Delegates representing 14 organizations attend the founding meeting. More than 4 million women will be associated with the Council, which will establish its headquarters in Washington, D.C., in 1942.

# December

## 6

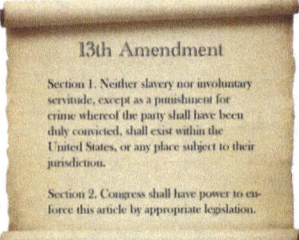

### 13th Amendment

Section 1. Neither slavery nor involuntary servitude, except as a punishment for crime whereof the party shall have been duly convicted, shall exist within the United States, or any place subject to their jurisdiction.

Section 2. Congress shall have power to enforce this article by appropriate legislation.

**1865: The 13th Amendment to the U.S. Constitution, which abolishes slavery, is ratified.**

**1838: Slaves sold by Jesuit priests to save the college that will become known as Georgetown University from financial ruin are shipped south today.** The priests sold 272 slaves from six Maryland plantations to three Louisiana sugar plantations for $115,000 (equivalent to $3.8 million in 2023). Turmoil breaks out on the ship Katherine Jackson as panic and fear set in. An older woman falls to her knees, asking what she has done to deserve this. Families are split and will be sent to different plantations. A few slaves escape. Some priests are deeply disturbed, worried about losing their souls with the sale of slaves. They know how brutal life will be on sugar plantations in the Deep South. But the ship departs, and the slaves vanish from history.

## 7

**1941: Doris "Dorie" Miller, a kitchen worker on the USS Arizona, becomes one of the first American heroes of World War II when he shoots down warplanes during the Japanese attack on Pearl Harbor.** When alarms sound, he rushes onto the deck of the USS West Virginia and carries wounded men to safety. Ordered to the bridge, he finds the captain mortally wounded, then mans a machine gun and begins firing on Japanese planes, shooting down three or four. For his heroism, he will be awarded the Navy Cross, one of the Navy's highest honors.

## 8

**1982: Nicki Minaj** (Onika Tanya Maraj) **is born** in Saint James, Port of Spain, Trinidad and Tobago. The future rap queen will release her debut album, "Pink Friday," in 2010 and eventually be called the **Queen of Rap, with more than 100 million records sold worldwide** and enough honors to fill a room: 8 American Music Awards, 12 BET Awards, 5 MTV Video Music Awards, 4 Billboard Music Awards, 3 Guinness World Records, and others. Minaj will become one of the world's most-followed musicians on social media, with more than 200 million Instagram followers. She will become a business mogul too, with her line of fragrances, lipsticks, clothing collections, housewares, wine beverages, potato chip flavor, "Bar-B-Quin' with My Honey Truffle," and "Nocho Nachos" nachos flavor, inspired by a lyric on one of her singles. She will collaborate with luxury fashion house Fendi, launch her radio show ("Queen Radio"), and create a record label imprint, "Heavy On It Records." What will her encore be? Only Nicki knows.

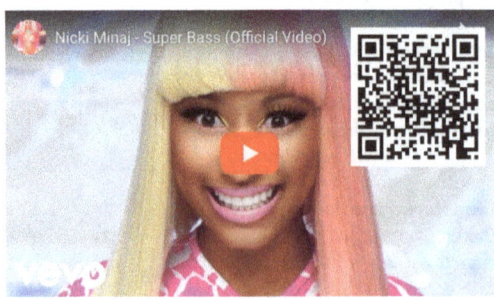

Nicki Minaj - Super Bass (Official Video)

# Weekly Planner

WEEK OF_____

**SUNDAY**

**MONDAY**

**Scan**
**Bill of sale for 272 slaves**

**Scan**
**Ship's manifest**

**TUESDAY**

**WEDNESDAY**

1838: **To save a struggling college from financial ruin, Jesuit priests in Maryland sell 272 slaves,** shipping them to Louisiana sugar plantations, where they will lead brutal lives and disappear from history. The college will survive and become known as Georgetown University. Scan above for more information.

**THURSDAY**

**FRIDAY**

**SATURDAY**

**1872: P.B.S. Pinchback, an attorney and member of the Louisiana State Senate, becomes the first African American governor of a U.S. state, Louisiana.** He had been serving as president of the Louisiana State Senate in 1871 when Lieutenant Governor Oscar Dunn died. Pinchback was appointed lieutenant governor, serving until 1872, when Governor Henry C. Warmoth was removed from office due to impeachment charges. Pinchback takes the oath of office on this day, succeeding Warmoth as governor. He will make many appointments and sanction 10 bills. After serving for 36 days, Pinchback will be elected to Congress but be denied a seat. He will later help to found Southern University and serve on its board of trustees.

**1922: Redd Foxx is born** in St. Louis, MO.

**1964: John Coltrane records his album "A Love Supreme" in a four-hour session** at Van Gelder Studio in Englewood Cliffs, NJ. Impulse! Records will release the iconic album, which will be considered Coltrane's masterpiece, in January 1965. **The album is consistently listed among the greatest albums ever recorded.**

**1748: James Armistead Lafayette, a slave who will become a double agent during the American Revolution, is born** around this date on a plantation in New Kent, VA. During the Revolutionary War, he will pretend to spy on the American army for the British while spying on the British army for the Americans. He will report conversations overheard while waiting tables at the headquarters of British General Charles Cornwallis and smuggle papers out of British headquarters. His activities will help secure an American victory at the Battle of Yorktown. Despite his contributions, he will return to slavery after the war and petition the government for emancipation. He will be freed on January 1, 1787, and granted $60 relief and a pension of $40 per year, which he will collect for the rest of his life.

**Bebop Baroness**

**1913: Kathleen Pannonica "Nica" de Koenigswarter Rothschild is born** in London to the world's wealthiest family. She will pilot her plane across the English Channel, fight for the French Resistance against the Nazis, and become a lieutenant in the Allied armies. After the war, she will divorce her husband, move to the U.S., fall in love with jazz, and become a jazz patroness. She will support, champion, and protect Thelonious Monk, Charlie Parker, and other musicians. She will help manage the careers of Horace Silver, Hank Mobley, and the Jazz Messengers. Charlie Parker will die while watching television in her Stanhope Hotel suite in 1955. Monk will retire to her Weehawken, NJ, mansion, where he will die in 1982.

**1950: Ralph J. Bunche becomes the first African American to be awarded the Nobel Peace Prize.**

Scan for Ralph Bunche's Nobel Lecture

Ralph Bunche greets Martin Luther King Jr. and Coretta Scott King on a visit to the United Nations in 1964.

**1964: Martin Luther King Jr. becomes the second African American to be awarded the Nobel Peace Prize.**

**1993: Toni Morrison becomes the first American woman to be awarded the Nobel Prize in Literature in 55 years and the first African American ever.**

Scan for Toni Morrison's Nobel Lecture (Audio)

**2009: Barack Obama becomes the third African American** (and fourth U.S. President) **to be awarded the Nobel Peace Prize.**

# December

## 11

Newspaper ad for the sale of Harriet Tubman's niece in 1849. The sale was postponed, enabling the family to coordinate a rescue plan.

December 1850: **Harriet Tubman, who had escaped slavery a year earlier, returns to Maryland to help rescue her 25-year-old niece Kessiah Bowley and Bowley's children, James Alfred, and baby Araminta, who are to be auctioned** in front of the Dorchester County Circuit Courthouse in Maryland. Slave-auction bidding starts, and Kessiah's husband, John, a free ship carpenter, outbids everyone. The auctioneer breaks for lunch. But when he returns to collect John's payment, he discovers that Kessiah and her children are missing. John has hidden them in a safe house. Later, John will transport them via boat to Baltimore, where Tubman, who is close in age to Kessiah (they are like sisters), will take charge. Tubman will spirit the family to Philadelphia and Chatham, Ontario, Canada. By 1865, there will be 25,000 Black residents in Chatham, many with stories like Kessiah's. After the Civil War, John and Kessiah will return to Dorchester County, MD, with most of their seven children. Kessiah's son James will serve as a landsman in the U.S. Navy. He will educate newly emancipated slaves in Georgetown, SC, become a lawyer, serve two terms in the South Carolina House of Representatives, found a weekly newspaper (the Georgetown Planet), and in 1873 become a trustee of the University of South Carolina.

## 12

1968: **Yale College decides to create a degree-conferring Afro-American studies major,** becoming the first major university to do so.

Scan for
Yale Course Selection (Search African American Studies - AFAM)

2018: The Library of Congress's National Film Registry adds a sweet treasure to its archive: a 29-second, restored silent film clip shot in 1898 by vaudeville-performer-turned-film-producer William Selig, titled **"Something Good-Negro Kiss."** The original clip, rediscovered by a University of Southern California film historian, is the earliest known footage of affection between a Black man and woman on film.

## 13

### Mother of the Civil Rights Movement

1903: **Ella Baker, who will become a civil rights icon, is born** in Norfolk, VA. Although a much lesser-known figure than Martin Luther King Jr., she will raise political consciousness across the nation for more than a half-century and play pivotal roles in several major organizations: the NAACP, the Southern Christian Leadership Conference, and the Student Nonviolent Coordinating Committee. Her behind-the-scenes work to mobilize people and build organizations will be indispensable to the Civil Rights Movement. She will not seek the spotlight, but she will fight male chauvinism in an era when "the preacher ego" can present an obstacle for non-males or people who aren't church leaders. The granddaughter of slaves, Baker will visit small towns to convince Blacks to unite and claim fundamental human rights after surviving centuries of enslavement, violence, and terrorization. She will create anti-lynching campaigns, voter registration drives, and job training programs, organize coalitions, campaign for school desegregation, launch protests, lay the groundwork for boycotts, recruit leaders from the rank and file, and confront mayors. Baker will earn the nickname Fundi, a Swahili word meaning a person who teaches a craft to the next generation.

1967: **Jamie Foxx** (Eric Marlon Bishop) **is born** in Terrell, TX.

# Weekly Planner

WEEK OF _____

SUNDAY

MONDAY

TUESDAY

WEDNESDAY

THURSDAY

FRIDAY

SATURDAY

# December

## 14

### The Father of Black Basketball

December 1907: **Edwin B. Henderson,** who learned the game of basketball while studying physical education at Harvard University's Dudley Sargent School of Physical Training, returns home to Washington, D.C., and is turned away from a basketball game at the Central YMCA by the athletic director. Henderson **decides then and there to bring basketball, a sport dominated by white players, to Black America.** Henderson—the nation's first certified Black physical education instructor and a direct protégé of James Naismith, who invented basketball just a decade before Henderson met him—will become the "father of Black basketball." He will raise funds to open Washington, D.C.'s first YMCA for African Americans, found the D.C.-based Basket Ball League, and get young people to love the game. He will captain the 12th Street YMCA team, which will go undefeated in the 1909-10 season and win the Colored Basketball World Championship. He will mentor Duke Ellington and coach future physician and blood bank innovator Charles Drew.

## 15

1883: **William Hinton is born** in Chicago, IL. **He will become a public health pioneer and the first Black professor at Harvard University.** Hinton will enroll in Harvard Medical School in 1909 but will refuse a scholarship reserved for Black students. He will compete instead for scholarships open to all students, win them for two years, and graduate in three. He will be denied a medical internship and residency due to racial discrimination and volunteer in the Pathology Laboratory at Massachusetts General Hospital, where he will develop his expertise in syphilis. In 1927, he will develop the Hinton Test for detecting syphilis, which the U.S. Public Health Service will begin using in 1934. Hinton will teach at Harvard for more than 30 years, but the university will not make him a full professor until the eve of his retirement in 1950.

## 16

2003: **President George W. Bush signs the National Museum of African American History and Culture Act** (H.R. 3491), authorizing the creation of a Smithsonian Institution museum dedicated to the legacy of African Americans in America.

### Time-lapse construction

### 50-second tour

### True significance

Lonnie Bunch, founding director of the National Museum of African American History and Culture, explains the need for the museum. In 2019, Bunch was appointed the 14th secretary of the Smithsonian, in charge of 19 museums, 21 libraries, the National Zoo, and an annual budget of $1.5 billion.

2010: **Marcus Samuelsson, the Ethiopian-born Swedish-American chef, opens Red Rooster,** a $2 million, 100-seat restaurant in Harlem, **named in honor of a speakeasy that catered to Harlemites, jazz legends, and bold-face names** such as Adam Clayton Powell Jr., Nat King Cole, and James Baldwin. "I hope people will feel like they're coming home," says Samuelsson, one of the nation's best-known chefs. Red Rooster draws a "gorgeous mosaic" of people from every walk of life, including Grammy Award winners, presidents, Harlemites, and Wall Street wizards.

Scan for Menus

Scan for Reservations

Billie Holiday at Café Society in 1939

**Café Society Breaks Racial Barriers**

1938: New Jersey shoe salesman **Barney Josephson opens Café Society at 2 Sheridan Square in Greenwich Village, Manhattan. It is a venue where musicians of any race can perform, and guests of any color will be treated equally.** "I wanted a club where blacks and whites worked together behind the footlights and sat together out front," Josephson says. "There wasn't, so far as I know, a place like that in New York or in the whole country." **The club will thrive for 10 years. A cavalcade of great musicians will perform here,** including Art Tatum, Lena Horne, Sarah Vaughan, Mary Lou Williams, Lester Young, and Ella Fitzgerald. **Billie Holiday will sing "Strange Fruit" publicly for the first time here, ending her sets with the song on three consecutive nights in early 1939.** When she sings it, waiters will stop serving, and the club will be darkened, except for a spotlight on her face.

1865: **South Carolina enacts post-Civil War Black Codes.** Its new laws make freed Blacks subservient to whites, stating that "all persons of color who make contracts for service or labor, shall be known as servants, and those with whom they contract, shall be known as masters." The Black Codes apply only to Black people. In South Carolina, they're prohibited from any occupation but farming or servant work unless they pay an annual tax of $10 to $100. Mississippi's new Black Codes require African Americans to have written evidence of employment each January. If they leave their jobs before the end of their work contract, they forfeit all wages and are subject to arrest for vagrancy. In both South Carolina and Mississippi, they are subject to forced plantation labor if accused of vagrancy. Other freedoms are severely restricted.

1875: **Carter G. Woodson, who will be called the Father of Black History, is born** to formerly enslaved parents in New Canton, VA. He will open the field of Black studies to scholars and make it accessible to students in schools and colleges nationwide. In February 1926, he will organize the first Negro History Week. It will be expanded to Black History Month in 1976.

## The Great Escape

1848: Setting: pre-dawn Macon, GA, a slave cabin in the shadow of a white mansion. **Ellen and William Craft prepare to flee slavery together, not as husband and wife but disguised as a sickly, wealthy white man and "his" male slave. William cuts fair-skinned Ellen's hair, and she disguises herself as a man in a gentleman's suit, cravat, and boots with inch-high, lead-weighted soles. Ellen cannot read or write, so she puts her arm in a sling to avoid being asked to sign hotel registers.** William wears a white beaver-skin hat, the perfect touch to pass as a gentleman's slave. **The pair peer out the cabin door and then step into the night, fearful of hounds at first and then slave catchers. They will slip through many close calls in their 1,000-mile journey via train and steamboat.** The couple will reunite as husband and wife in Philadelphia and travel to Boston. Their bold, high-drama story will electrify abolitionists, but bounty hunters will try to catch them. President Millard Fillmore will say the couple must return to slavery by military force if necessary. **The Crafts will flee to England,** where they will have five children before returning to the U.S. in 1868.

1860: In an attempt to preserve the institution of slavery, **South Carolina becomes the first Southern state to secede from the Union.** Legislators in a state convention in Charleston conclude: "The union now subsisting between South Carolina and other States, under the name of 'United States of America,' is hereby dissolved."

Martin Luther King Jr. and others on Montgomery's first integrated bus

1956: **The Montgomery, AL, public buses are officially integrated,** following the successful boycott that was started after Rosa Parks was arrested for refusing to give her seat to a white passenger and moving to the back of the bus. On November 13, the U.S. Supreme Court upheld a lower court ruling that bus segregation violated the due process and equal protection clauses of the 14th Amendment.

1948: **Samuel L. Jackson, who will be the highest-grossing live-action actor of all time, is born** in Washington, D.C. One of the most prolific actors of his day, he will appear in films that collectively gross over $27 billion. He will receive an Academy Honorary Award in 2022.

1964: The first Black-controlled bank, **the Freedom National Bank, opens in Harlem, with Jackie Robinson as chairman.** It will attract 22,000 depositors but close on November 9, 1990, during a recession.

1964: **Motown Records releases the 2-minute, 55-second single "My Girl" by The Temptations,** written by Smokey Robinson and Ronald White of the Miracles and recorded September 25th, November 10th & 17th in Studio A of Hitsville USA. The song, the first to feature David Ruffin on lead vocals, will climb to the top of the U.S. pop charts in January 1965 to become the Temptations' first No. 1 hit. One of Motown's most popular songs, it will be inducted into the Grammy Hall of Fame in 1998.

# Weekly Planner

**SUNDAY**

**MONDAY**

**TUESDAY**

**WEDNESDAY**

**THURSDAY**

**FRIDAY**

**SATURDAY**

Read Ellen &
William
Craft's book

## How to Act on an Integrated Bus

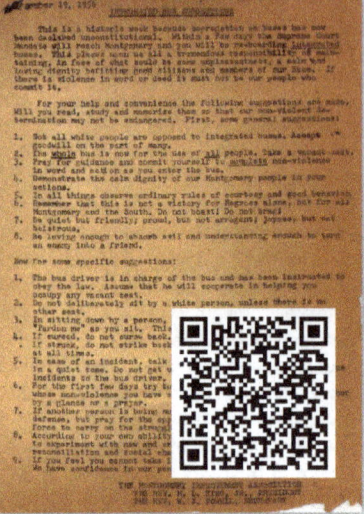

Inez Jessie Baskin Papers, Alabama Department of
Archives & History, Montgomery, AL

**The Temptations**

Clockwise from top: David Ruffin, Melvin
Franklin, Otis Williams, Eddie Kendricks and
Paul Williams

# December

## 22

1960: **Jean-Michel Basquiat is born** in Park Slope, Brooklyn, NY. He will become a highly successful artist in the 1980s. He will gain notoriety first as part of the graffiti duo SAMO (for Same Old [Expletive]) with Al Diaz. They will scrawl epigrams all over Manhattan, mainly on the Lower East Side, where street art will merge with music to create hip-hop culture. Basquiat will exhibit for the first time in June 1980 in the "Times Square Show" held in a former massage parlor. At his next exhibition, at P.S. 1 in Queens, NY, the show's director will call Basquiat "the new Rauschenberg." By the show's end, buyers will seek out Basquiat's work, and he will go from selling drawings on the street for $50 in 1980 to selling paintings so briskly that the paint is barely dry. His paintings are rife with symbols, marks, words, and logos. He will die in 1988 at 27 of a heroin overdose, leaving 917 drawings, 25 sketchbooks, 85 prints, and 171 paintings described by a writer as "one of the defining [ouvres] of the 20th century." Basquiat's 1983 work "Untitled" will sell for $110.5 million, setting an American record, a sale said to put Basquiat in the "same league" as Picasso.

## 23

1867: **Madam C.J. Walker is born** in Delta, LA, to formerly enslaved parents; her birth name Sarah Breedlove. She will become a beauty and hair product pioneer, head her own company, and be recognized as the nation's first self-made woman millionaire. As one of the wealthiest African Americans, she will spend $10,000 yearly to educate young Negro men and women in Southern colleges and send six youths to Tuskegee Institute each year. In 1918, she will build a 34-room, 20,000-square-foot estate, Villa Lewaro, in Irvington, NY, 30 miles north of NYC, along the Hudson River, at a cost of $250,000 and as an inspiration for others. Her hair-care brand will be reborn in the 21st century.

## 24

1865: The **Ku Klux Klan is founded in a law office in Pulaski, TN**. It is named for the Greek word "kyklos," which means circle. Its first Grand Wizard is former Confederate Lieutenant General Nathan Bedford Forrest. In the 1920s, it will claim more than 2 million members. (See KKK application below.)

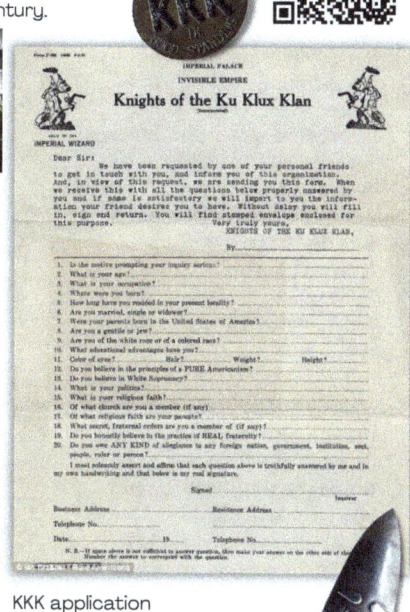

KKK application

# December

## 25

1907: **Cabell "Cab" Calloway III, who will become one of the most popular singers and band leaders of the swing era, is born** in Rochester, NY. Known as the "Hi-de-hoe" man, Cab Calloway will become a household name due to his many performances in the U.S. and abroad. He will learn to scat from scat master Louis Armstrong and lead his own orchestra at the Cotton Club in Harlem. It will feature many notable musicians, including trumpeter Dizzy Gillespie, saxophonist Ben Webster, and bassist Milt Hinton. Cab Calloway will perform twice weekly radio broadcasts, become the first African American to have his own nationally syndicated radio show and create hit records in the 1930s and 40s, the most famous being "Minnie the Moocher," the first single by an African American to sell over a million records. He will entertain troops before they are shipped overseas during World War II. He will write a gossip column and become the first African American to publish a dictionary ("Cab Calloway's Cat-ologue: A 'Hepster's' Dictionary," in 1938; see June 16).

1994-present: **Mariah Carey's hit single, "All I Want for Christmas Is You," released in October 1994, will become the best-selling holiday song by a female artist** and a Christmas phenomenon. By 2017, it will sell over 16 million copies worldwide and earn over $60 million in royalties.

## 26

**Jack Johnson, Great Black Hope**

1908: **Jack Johnson wins the world heavyweight title, beating Canadian Tommy Burns in the Sydney Stadium in Australia. By becoming the first Black heavyweight world champion, Johnson has forever changed boxing.** His career will span 33 years and five months. His last bout will occur on April 28, 1931. His boxing record will be 69 wins (33 by KOs), 11 losses (6 by KOs, 36.7%), 10 draws, and 3 no contests—a total of 93 fights in 858 rounds.

Jack Johnson In 1908

## 27

December 1853: **"Clotel," the first novel written by an African American, is published in London in 1853. Written by William Wells Brown,** the novel's full title is "Clotel; or, The President's Daughter: A Narrative of Slave Life in the United States." It is the fictional tale of Thomas Jefferson's slave-born daughters, but the novel strays little from reality. On his father's side, Brown is a descendant of Mayflower passenger Stephen Hopkins; his mother was a slave. Brown escaped slavery in 1834 at age 20 and traveled to England to avoid being reenslaved under the Fugitive Slave Act. (His brother Joe was the slave of William B. Travis, commander at the Alamo.) **William Wells Brown traveled on the lecture circuit and mastered many forms of writing, including a narrative on his escape from slavery, travel writing, and drama. In 1858, he will become the first published African American playwright, and in 1867, he will write the first history of African Americans in the Revolutionary War.**

# Weekly Planner

SUNDAY

MONDAY

TUESDAY

WEDNESDAY

THURSDAY

FRIDAY

SATURDAY

# December

## 28

In this 1863 print, a slave breeder sells his own mulatto son to a southern trader.

### Slavery Follows the Mother

December 1662: Colonial legislators in Virginia pass a legal doctrine (*partus sequitur ventrem,* translated as "the offspring follows the womb") determining the legal status of children: children whose mothers are enslaved will also be enslaved. In short, slavery is anchored in women's reproductive lives. It is inherited and thus virtually perpetual. This doctrine will provide a legal basis for racialized slavery, leaving Black women powerless to control the fate of their children. It will also undergird the Virginia economy, serving as a "maternal conduit" for the steady supply of slaves. After the American Revolution, Virginia will pass a law on October 17, 1785, maintaining inheritable slave status. Other states will follow suit: Kentucky in 1798, Mississippi in 1822, Louisiana in 1825, and Florida in 1828.

1954: **Denzel Washington,** who will become a two-time Academy Award-winning actor and star in blockbuster films, **is born** in Mount Vernon, NY, the son of a Pentecostal minister and a beauty shop owner. He will win acclaim as a star of both screen and stage and become a major box office success while proving Black actors can defy stereotypic roles and draw mainstream white audiences.

## 29

Mayor-elect Tom Bradley with supporters, May 1973

1917: **Tom Bradley, who will become the first Black mayor of Los Angeles and the longest-serving mayor in its history, is born** to sharecropper parents who live in a log cabin near Calvert, TX. The Bradleys will move to Arizona to pick cotton, then in 1924 to Los Angeles, where he will attend UCLA in 1937. In 1940 he will join the Los Angeles Police Department. While an officer, he will attend Southwestern University Law School and begin practicing law upon retirement from the force. In 1963, he will be elected to the City Council. Ten years later, he will be elected LA's 38th mayor, serving for 20 years. In 1993, **69 scholars will rank Bradley, the grandson of a slave, as one of the 10 best mayors in U.S. history.**

Bradley as a police officer

## 30

1975: **Tiger Woods is born** in Cypress, CA. He will become one of the greatest golfers of all time and among the most famous athletes in history.

1984: **LeBron James is born** in Akron, OH. He will be nicknamed King James and become the leading scorer in NBA history and the subject of debates about the all-time greatest basketball player in NBA history.

1928: **Bo Diddley** (originally named Ellas Otha Bates McDaniel) **is born** in McComb, MS. Playing his rectangular Gretsch guitar as a percussive instrument, he will be a pivotal figure in the transition from blues to rock and roll. His songs will emphasize rhythm over melody, differing from country blues guitarists who accent their plucked rhythms with single notes; every member of Diddley's bands will take a percussive approach that reinforces rhythm over melody. His signature Bo Diddley beat, a syncopated, five-accent rhythm, will become a musical cornerstone in rhythm and blues, rock and roll, pop music, and hip hop.

# December

## 31

### Watch Night - New Year's Eve 1862

1862: Enslaved and free African Americans gather, sometimes in secrecy, to celebrate the new year and hear the news that President Abraham Lincoln's Emancipation Proclamation will take effect at the stroke of midnight, legally freeing slaves in Confederate states. During this first Watch Night, people pray, worship, sing, and dance.  Future Watch Night worship services will traditionally include a "fortuitous meal" featuring Hoppin' John, a dish of black-eyed peas, rice, red peppers, and salt pork, said to bring good fortune to those who eat it.

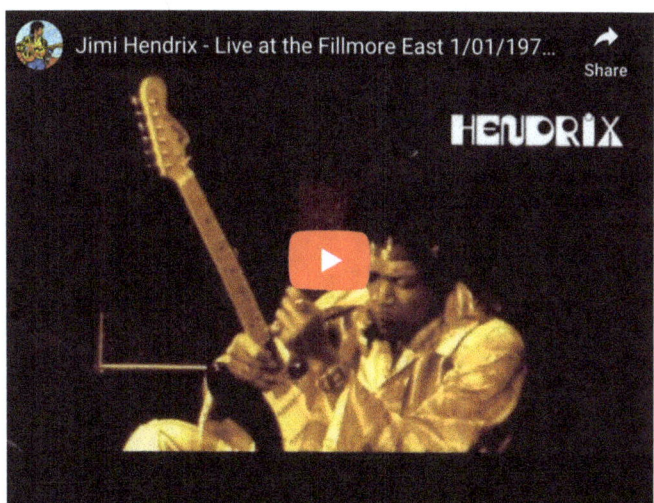

1969-1970: **Jimi Hendrix and the Band of Gypsys bring in the new year live at the Fillmore East in Manhattan.** A posthumous live album, released nearly three decades later, documents the performance. (See rare footage.)